PICK-A-PARTY COOKBOOK

By Patty Sachs

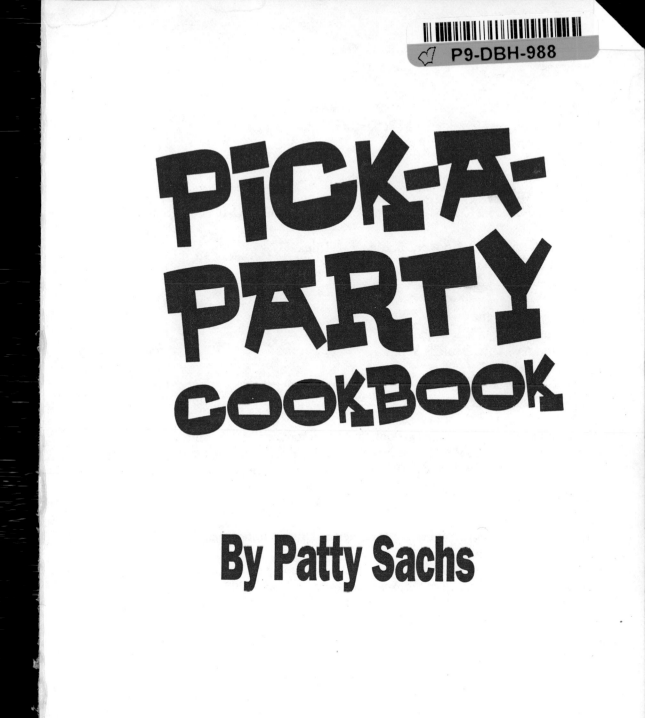

m Meadowbrook Press

Distributed by Simon & Schuster

New York

MS

Library of Congress Cataloging-in-Publication Data

Sachs, Patty.
  Pick-a-party cookbook/ by Patty Sachs.
    p. cm.
    ISBN 0-88166-310-7 (Meadowbrook Press). —ISBN 0-671-02386-1 (Simon &
Schuster)
    1. Entertaining. 2. Cookery. 3. Menus. I. Title.
  TX731.S25 1998
  642'.4—dc21   98-4415
                                                          CIP

Editor: Liya Lev Oertel
Production Manager: Joe Gagne
Production Assistant: Danielle White
Cover Art: Jack Lindstrom

© 1998 by Patty Sachs

Published by Meadowbrook Press, 5451 Smetana Drive, Minnetonka, MN 55343

BOOK TRADE DISTRIBUTION by Simon & Schuster, a division of Simon and
Schuster, Inc., 1230 Avenue of the Americas, New York, NY 10020

02 01 00 99 98   10 9 8 7 6 5 4 3 2 1

Printed in the United States of America

Dedication

To the ingredients for my most delicious and delectable menu:

Sweet Kisses from my granddaughters Jasmine, Mackenzie,
Aysia, and Sophia
Casseroles of Comfort from my children Frank, Vicki, Cathy, and Deena
Just Desserts from my siblings Art Jr., Terry Sr., Laurie, Bill, and Scott
A "Four Alarm" Birthday Cake from my darling mother, Elsie
Sparkling Toasts from my dearest friends Kelly and Gil

Acknowledgments

Thank you to the following people for giving me their generous servings
of confidence and support:

Joan Arvidson, Maxine Baird, Roni Brunner, Jackie Cameron, Shirlee
Clein, Dan Desmond, Lynda Emon, Carol Iverson, T.J., Sr., Nancy Jones,
Jacqueline Morrow, Adrienne Sioux Koopersmith, Robin Kring, Misty
Taggart, Dick Taylor, Judith Anne Vincent

For wielding the gentle editing knife and the vigorous mixing spoon that
whipped my ingredients into a culinary accomplishment, I give thanks
and kudos to Liya, my editor at Meadowbrook Press

And finally, thanks to all of those who managed to keep a straight face
when I announced that I was going to write a cookbook

TABLE OF CONTENTS

INTRODUCTION

Any celebration can be enhanced by delicious foods and refreshing beverages. Of course, you *can* offer your guests the standard party fare—veggie, fruit, and cold cut platters, party subs, and so on. However, if you make an effort to design the perfect menu and serving strategies to complement your party, those efforts will pay off in a successful and memorable experience for you and your guests.

Pick-A-Party Cookbook includes complete menus for 102 party themes, including 25 holidays. Each menu offers suggestions for snacks, beverages, buffet items, and desserts that complement the theme and each other. Selected recipes are provided to supply the basis for your party fare (the recipes included in the book are marked with an asterisk). In addition, in the back of the book you will find dozens of party favorites that you can mix and match for any theme—traditional and unusual recipes for sloppy joes, meatballs, pasta and potato salads, coleslaw, dips, gelatin shooters, punches, martinis, and more.

This book also includes a "first time ever" feature—a section for table decor and other decorative suggestions that includes a host of ideas for

- table and chair coverings
- food and beverage containers
- innovative decorative touches for buffet and dining tables
- dramatic and fun buffet table backdrops
- matching table favors and seating assignments

To make your party planning easier and more efficient, *Pick-A-Party Cookbook* also includes a list of resources, a variety of decorative ideas, as well as step-by-step how-to instructions for dozens of the creative craft projects or special touches suggested throughout the book. Whether you pluck the components for these items out of your wastebasket or discover them at a neighborhood thrift or craft store, the finished products will amuse and impress your guests.

Planning a party menu has become a lot like putting on a little theatrical production, complete with starring and supporting roles, sets and costume designs, special effects, and a sensational finale. As the curtain falls on your spectacular party and its delicious and creatively presented foods and beverages, you will hear the delightfully pleasing sound of applause—enthusiastic praise and thanks from your thoroughly satisfied guests.

Part One
HOLIDAYS

Holidays provide one of the main reasons for celebrating. The major holidays, which include Easter, Thanksgiving, Christmas, Hanukkah, Kwanzaa, and New Year's Eve, bring people together and serve to strengthen our relationships with others.

At these yearly events, we take time to meet and greet our families, friends, neighbors, schoolmates, and work mates at parties and gatherings of all sizes and descriptions. In addition, members of congregations, communities, and associations gather to share worship or fellowship, and/or celebration.

You might choose one of these popular holidays to launch your party-hosting career. If so, your task will be relatively simple, since most of the holidays already come with a manual of sorts—traditional, tried-and-true recipes and party strategies. You can stick with those, or you can blend them with your personal touches and innovations. Even the staunchest traditionalist will be pleased and amused by a new or surprising twist on holiday celebrating. Start your own traditions!

But why stop with the big holidays? Invite folks for such less-traditional holidays as St. Patrick's Day, Cinco De Mayo, Mardi Gras, Valentine's Day, and Halloween—the menus, recipes, serving suggestions, and decorative touches you will find in this book will enable you to pull together a fun and delicious party sure to delight your guests.

Finally, for those who proudly wear the title of "party animal"—those who plan a party at the drop of a pointed cardboard hat—you have not been forgotten. Your novel Leap Year's, Earth Day, or Once in a Blue Moon party could even get you on the evening news. Never again will you be at a loss for those creative and off-the-wall treats that your guests have come to expect. This section of *Pick-A-Party Cookbook* will provide you with the fresh inspiration and confidence to succeed at whatever level of holiday entertaining you may attempt.

NEW YEAR'S DAY BRUNCH

A New Year's Day brunch is a great way to kick off the year. Your guests will appreciate a chance to recover from New Year's Eve and to ponder what the upcoming 365 days may bring. An afternoon of delicious foods, refreshing beverages, and gracious good times will help your guests welcome the new year.

Party Menu

Snacks
*Black-Eyed Peas with Ham (for luck)
Chips, Pretzels, Popcorn

Beverages
Soft Drinks/Mineral Waters
Bloody Marys (with or without beer shooters)
Orange Juice Screwdrivers
Coffees/Teas

Buffet
*Super Year Starter Casserole
English Muffins with Jams and Jellies
Fresh Fruit Tray

Dessert
*Chilled Chocolate Cheerleader
Holiday Fruit Cake
Baked Fruit Crisp

Black-Eyed Peas with Ham (for luck)
Makes: 6 servings

3½ cups black-eyed peas, fresh or frozen, thawed
3 cups chicken stock or canned low-salt broth
4 ounces ham, finely chopped
1 small yellow onion, chopped
2 tablespoons balsamic or red wine vinegar
3 large garlic cloves, minced
1 bay leaf
½ teaspoon dried thyme, crumbled
¼ teaspoon dried crushed red pepper
Salt and pepper, to taste

1. In a large heavy saucepan, combine all ingredients except salt and pepper; bring to a boil.
2. Reduce heat and simmer, stirring occasionally, until peas are tender (about 45 minutes). Season to taste with salt and pepper.
3. Serve in small punch-sized cups to all guests as they enter, and explain that black-eyed peas are for luck.

Super Year Starter Casserole
Makes: 6 servings

6 large eggs
2 cups milk
1 teaspoon salt
1 teaspoon dry mustard

2 slices white bread, cubed
1 pound sausage, browned
1 cup sharp or mild cheddar cheese, grated

1. Beat eggs; add milk, salt, and mustard; mix well.
2. Grease the bottom of a 9-by-13-inch baking dish.
3. Layer bread cubes on the bottom; top with sausage and cheese.
4. Pour the egg mixture over the top.
5. Refrigerate overnight.
6. Preheat the oven to 350 degrees.
7. Bake for 45 minutes.
8. Let stand about 5 minutes before cutting.

Chilled Chocolate Cheerleader

Makes: 5 servings

2 ounces unsweetened chocolate squares   2½ cups milk
¼ cup sugar   1½ cups cola drink, chilled
1 cup hot coffee, double-strength   Whipped cream or vanilla ice cream

1. Melt chocolate squares in a double boiler over hot water.
2. Stir in sugar.
3. Slowly add hot coffee, mixing thoroughly.
4. Add milk and cook until chocolate dissolves and the mixture becomes smooth (about 10 minutes).
5. Pour into a jar or pitcher, cover, and chill until serving.
6. When ready to serve, stir in chilled cola. Serve over ice cubes in tall glasses. This drink can be served as a beverage or a dessert. If serving as a beverage, top with whipped cream. For a dessert, add a scoop of vanilla ice cream.

Food Service and Decorative Touches

- Include real or prop replicas of good luck symbols in the table decor: four-leaf clovers, rabbits' feet, horseshoes, lucky pennies.
- Lay calendar pages out on table, then cover with clear plastic. (See How-To's #19.)
- Stand large decorative wall calendars on the buffet table, or use them in centerpieces, mixed with flowers, greens, and leftover, slightly mangled New Year's Eve decor (for a humorous touch).
- For Rose Bowl parties, drape garlands of roses on the tables and/or use a rose vase arrangement as a centerpiece. Add football-theme items to your decor.
- Write each guest's name on a small note pad, and use the pads with pencils as place cards. The pad should be used for writing resolutions.
- Take instant photos of guests as they arrive, and set the photos on the table to designate seating assignments.
- Decorate small cardboard frames with Lucky Charms cereal as a favor.

CHINESE NEW YEAR

Chinese New Year begins on the first full moon after January 21 and lasts for fifteen days. You can celebrate one, several, or all of these days, if you like. Fantastic Chinese foods, prepared at home or ordered out, will bring good fortune and happiness to all.

Party Menu

Snacks
*Lobster Toast
Chinese Pot Stickers

Beverages
*Chinese Cocktail
Chinese Beer
Rice Wine
Green Tea

Buffet
Chinese Takeout Favorites
Fried Rice
Stir-Fried Vegetables

Dessert
*Chinese Citrus Almond Cookies
Mandarin Orange Sherbet
Fresh Orange Slices
Fortune Cookies

Lobster Toast
Makes: 40 toast pieces

2 6½-ounce cans lobster, drained and finely minced
½ teaspoon paprika
2 teaspoons prepared mustard
1 teaspoon Worcestershire sauce
6 drops hot sauce
6 tablespoons sherry
1 cup mayonnaise
10 slices white sandwich bread, crusts trimmed

1. Mix lobster, seasonings, sherry, and mayonnaise.
2. Cut each bread slice into 4 diamond shapes.
3. Pile the lobster mixture onto bread diamonds.
4. Broil until bubbly; serve hot.

Tip: This recipe may be prepared ahead and broiled just before serving.

Chinese Cocktail
Makes: 1 cocktail

½ ounce grenadine
1½ ounces Jamaican Rum
Dash of bitters
1 teaspoon maraschino liqueur
1 teaspoon curaçao
Ice

1. Combine all ingredients and shake well
2. Serve in a 3-ounce cocktail glass.

Chinese Citrus Almond Cookies

Makes: 4½ dozen cookies

2¾ cups flour, sifted
1 cup sugar
½ teaspoon baking soda
½ teaspoon salt

1 cup butter
1 egg, slightly beaten
1 teaspoon orange or lemon extract
⅓ cup whole almonds

1. Preheat the oven to 325 degrees.
2. In a large bowl, sift together flour, sugar, soda, and salt.
3. Cut in butter until the mixture resembles cornmeal.
4. Add egg and extract; mix well.
5. Shape the dough into 1-inch balls and place the balls 2 inches apart on an ungreased cookie sheet.
6. Place an almond on top of each ball and press down to flatten slightly.
7. Bake for 15 to 18 minutes.
8. Cool on the rack.

Food Service and Decorative Touches

- Write table numbers on small slips of paper and stuff them into fortune cookies for seating assignments. (See Resources #8.)
- Print place cards on bright red paper with gold lettering.
- Cover tables in red, black, and gold—satins, silks, brocades, and paper.
- Use standing folding screens and bamboo curtains to create a backdrop for your buffet or serving table.
- Use black lacquer trays, mirrored trays, and bamboo-handled trays to display and serve appetizers.
- Display a set of Chinese checkers as a buffet table centerpiece.
- Pour tea from ornately decorated tea pots into small cups.
- Knot bright red napkins around decorative chopsticks.
- Spray-paint takeout cartons with black or red lacquer or shiny gold, and fill with poppy flowers and Chinese greens for centerpieces. Set the arrangements on mirror tiles and surround with votive candles in red glass holders.
- Use embroidered satin runners on buffet or dinner tables.

VALENTINE'S DAY COCKTAIL PARTY

Valentine's Day is traditionally a day for couples to express their love for one another. A cocktail party is an appropriate way to celebrate, since the party's early beginning and ending will allow plenty of time for guests to move on to their more personal celebrations. The early hour also works well when Valentine's Day falls on a weekday.

Party Menu

Snacks
*Salmon Heart Sandwiches
*Cream Cheese and Taco Sauce
with Crackers
Cherry Tomatoes, Celery Hearts,
Radishes, and Red Pepper Strips
Pick A Dip

Beverages
Sodas/Mineral Waters
*Cranberry Sweetheart Punch

Dessert
*Raspberry Gelatin Shooters
Heart-Shaped Sugar Cookies (with red
icing and sprinkles)
Whole Strawberries (first dipped in sour
cream, then in brown sugar)

Salmon Heart Sandwiches
Makes: 36 squares

1 tablespoon lemon juice
1 tablespoon onion, grated
¼ teaspoon liquid smoke
Dash of pepper

8 ounces cream cheese, softened
1 16-ounce can salmon, drained and flaked
¼ teaspoon salt
18 slices very fresh white sandwich bread

1. Combine all ingredients except for bread and mix well; refrigerate.
2. Trim the crusts from the bread and cut each slice into 4 squares.
3. Spread half the squares with salmon spread.
4. From remaining squares, cut out heart shapes with a small metal cookie cutter.
5. Place the bread hearts on the bread squares and refrigerate until serving time. If making the sandwiches many hours ahead of time, cover them with a damp cloth to prevent the bread from drying. Best if served soon after preparation, so the bread doesn't get too soggy.
6. Serve the sandwiches on a doily-covered tray, plate, or platter.

Cream Cheese and Taco Sauce with Crackers

Makes: approximately 24 servings (1 cracker per serving)

8 ounces cream cheese
Mild taco sauce
Heart-shaped Lahvosh crackers

1. Shape cream cheese into a flattened mound.
2. Drizzle taco sauce over the cream cheese mound.
3. Surround with heart-shaped Lahvosh crackers.

Cranberry Sweetheart Punch

Makes: 30 punch cups

4 cups cranberry juice   *2 64-ounce bottles ginger ale, chilled*
2 cups orange juice   *Thin orange and lemon slices for garnish*
1 cup pineapple juice

1. Combine all fruit juices and pour into a large punch bowl over a fruit juice ice ring.
2. Pour in cold ginger ale. Float orange and lemon slices on top

Raspberry Gelatin Shooters

Makes: as many as you like

Raspberry Jell-O gelatin
Liquor (vodka, tequila, white rum, aquavit, peppermint schnapps), chilled

1. Prepare a large package of gelatin, replacing cold water with cold liquor
2. Pour into clear plastic cups (2-ounce sampler size).
3. Refrigerate until set.
4. Serve with a small toothpick for stirring before shooting.

Food Service and Decorative Touches

- Use anything red, red-and-white, pink, or heart-shaped: bowls, baskets, boxes, tins, plates, or vases.
- Invert bright-red straw hats, line with white tissue or cellophane, and use as decorative containers or napkin/utensil holders on the buffet table.
- Use red plastic heart-shaped cookie cutters for napkin holders.
- Use small heart-shaped plastic frames for place cards.
- Cover buffet and dining tables with white linens or sheets, then top with lace tablecloths, runners, doilies, red satin ribbon streamers, and beautiful recycled Valentine's greetings. Laminate greeting cards in groupings to place under serving containers or centerpieces.
- Cover chairs with white pillowcases and tie with red ribbons or lace. Run less-than-sparkling-white linens through your washer with a package of red fabric dye.
- Serve small amounts of salad, snack food, or dessert in plastic champagne glasses (not flutes) trimmed with lace and red bows.
- Decorate any party favors or prizes with Valentine candy messages

MARDI GRAS

Parades and party revelry, not eating, take up most of a Mardi-Gras-goer's time, but your theme party can concentrate on food and drink served in the best restaurants in New Orleans. So even without the folderol and fanfare, your Mardi Gras party can be a veritable carnival of fanciful foods.

Party Menu

Snacks
*Shrimp Remoulade
*Artichoke Heart Dip (page 64)
Crackers and Bread Rounds

Buffet
Cajun Catfish
Jambalaya
*Ambrosia Salad

Beverages
Soft Drinks/Mineral Waters
*Louisiana Bayou
*New Orleans Gin Fizz Punch
Coffees/Teas

Dessert
*Mardi Gras Cake of Many Flavors
Pralines

Shrimp Remoulade
Makes: 3 cups sauce

½ cup dill pickles, chopped
1 tablespoon mustard
2 cups mayonnaise

2 tablespoons capers, chopped
1 tablespoon parsley and tarragon, chopped

Mix all ingredients together and serve as sauce with boiled shrimp.

Louisiana Bayou
Makes: 1 serving

1 ounce Baileys Irish Cream
½ ounce crème de cacao
Ice or 2 scoops ice cream

½ ounce Kahlua
Cream or vanilla ice cream

1. Pour liqueurs over ice and top with cream to fill the glass.
2. If serving as a dessert, instead of using cream, blend 2 scoops of ice cream with the liqueurs and pour into a glass. Leave out the ice.

New Orleans Gin Fizz Punch
Makes: 16 ½-cup servings

12-ounce can orange juice concentrate, thawed
1 cup orange-flavored liqueur
2 cups cold water

4 cups club soda, chilled
Ice
Orange slices for garnish

1. In a large pitcher, combine orange juice concentrate, liqueur, and water; mix well.
2. Just before serving, slowly add club soda; stir gently to blend.
3. Serve over ice; garnish with orange slices.

8

Ambrosia Salad

Makes: 4 servings

¼ cup powdered sugar
⅛ teaspoon cinnamon
2 cups fresh orange sections (3 to 4 peeled oranges)
1 banana, peeled and sliced
½ cup flaked coconut

1. Mix together sugar and cinnamon.
2. In a serving bowl, arrange layers of orange sections, banana slices, and coconut, sprinkling each layer of fruit with some of the sugar mixture.
3. Cover and chill for several hours before serving.

Mardi Gras Cake of Many Flavors

Makes: 18 2-by-3-inch pieces

2 packages white cake mix
⅛ cup rum
Butter cream frosting (a favorite recipe or purchased in can)
⅛ cup crème de cacao
⅛ cup crème de menthe
⅛ cup raspberry liqeuer
Crushed walnuts or pecans

1. Prepare cake mix according to package directions, pour into 2 9-by-12-inch baking pans, and bake.
2. When cool, cut the cake into six or seven thin layers.
3. Sprinkle rum on first layer, then frost with butter cream frosting.
4. Repeat layers with a different liqeuer on each, frosting each layer.
5. Cover entire cake with butter cream frosting and sprinkle with nuts.

Food Service and Decorative Touches

- Use Mardi Gras colors of gold, green, and purple in decor and linens.
- Include brightly colored balloons, streamers, and confetti in table arrangements.
- Set up miniature New Orleans-style lampposts for extraordinary table decor.
- Arrange faux jewels, ornate crowns, jeweled scepters, fancy capes, masks, and any other colorful fabrics or papers to jazz up the table decor.
- Include inflatable or miniature musical instruments as part of your table decor, along with spray-painted and glittered foamcore musical symbols.
- Wrap trinket necklaces and bracelets around napkins as festive holders.
- Use half masks, trimmed with feathers, jewels, ribbons, and lace as place cards/favors.
- Place a small treasure chest filled with foil-covered chocolate coins on each table.

PRESIDENT'S DAY

Hail to the Chiefs! Throw a President's Day party resplendent with food and drink typical of a state dinner. While playing up president's names and presidential catch sayings, you can prepare a menu fit for White House guests.

Party Menu

Snacks
*White House (Castle, that is) Pâté
Crackers and Small Bread Rounds
Teddy's Big Veggie Sticks
Pick A Dip

Beverages
Soft Drinks/Mineral Waters
*Presidential Mint-Flavored Punch
Coffees/Teas
Beer/Wine

Buffet
Sandwich Bar Labeled "From Abe's Deli"
Ben-Franklin-Roosevelt Franks
Pick A Potato Salad

Dessert
*Honest George's Cherry Chocolate Bars
Jimmy C's Peanut Butter Cups
John F.'s Jelly Beans

White House (Castle, that is) Pâté

Makes: 2½ to 3 cups

15 White Castle hamburgers (no cheese)
¼ cup water
4 ounces cream cheese, softened

½ cup Spanish olives, sliced
½ cup chives, chopped

1. Preheat the oven to 325 degrees.
2. In a food processor fitted with a steel blade, blend hamburgers 3 at a time, with a small amount of water, scraping sides as you go. Finished product should look like refried beans.
3. Grease a 9-by-5-inch loaf pan with vegetable shortening (avoid butter or margarine, as these will cause the pâté to brown too much).
4. Turn the pâté mixture into the loaf pan; smooth with a spatula.
5. Bake for 45 minutes.
6. After removing from oven, immediately turn the pâté onto a serving plate; allow to cool, then wrap in plastic and refrigerate.
7. When ready to serve, frost the pâté with softened cream cheese.
8. Garnish with olive slices, chives, and small American flags.
9. Serve as a spread with bread rounds and crackers.

Tip: Have copies of the recipe on hand, as your guests will never believe what's in this delicious "pâté."

Presidential Mint-Flavored Punch

(A favorite thirst-quenching beverage of President James Monroe.)

Makes: 13 4-ounce servings

⅔ cup sugar

½ cup fresh mint leaves, lightly packed

2 cups boiling water

2 cups red grape juice, chilled

2 cups orange juice, chilled

¾ cup lime juice, chilled

Crushed ice

Fresh mint leaves for garnish

1. Combine sugar, mint, and boiling water; stir until the sugar dissolves; chill.
2. Strain, reserving liquid; discard leaves.
3. Stir together reserved liquid, grape juice, orange juice, and lime juice.
4. Serve over crushed ice. Garnish with fresh mint leaves.

Honest George's Cherry Chocolate Bars

Makes: 15 bars

Cake:

1 box devil's food cake

2 eggs, beaten

¼ teaspoon cinnamon

1 can cherry pie filling

1 teaspoon almond extract

1. Preheat the oven to 350 degrees.
2. Mix all ingredients together using a large spoon.
3. Grease and flour a 9-by-13-inch baking pan.
4. Spread the mixture into the pan and bake for 30 minutes.

Frosting:

⅓ cup milk

5 tablespoons butter or margarine

1 cup sugar

6 ounces chocolate chips

1. Bring milk, butter, and sugar to a boil; boil for 1 minute.
2. Remove from heat and add chips. Cool until the mixture is spreadable, then frost the cake.

Food Service and Decorative Touches

- Create centerpieces of presidential memorabilia in inverted campaign-style straw hats.
- Drape tables with red, white, and blue bunting.
- Use stars-and-stripes design bandannas for napkins.
- Set up a big desk with an oval room backdrop as a buffet table.
- Decorate each table to represent a president: use a small hatchet, plastic cherries, three corner hat, stove pipe hat, old law books, miniature log cabin, and White House souvenirs arranged with photos of Washington and Lincoln and other presidents. Assign guests to seats with a token or photo associated with their designated-president's table.
- Set the guest-of-honor's or host's chairs on either side of a podium, set for a press conference.

LEAP YEAR

Every fourth year, February has twenty-nine days. According to tradition, single women use the extra day to propose marriage. This Leap Year's party for singles follows a wedding theme and has an "engaging" menu to get all guests into the marryin' mood.

Party Menu

Snacks
*Punch Cup Orzo Salad
Dainty Finger Sandwiches
Nuts and Mints
Fruit and Veggie Trays
"Take the Plunge" Seafood Dip

Beverages
*Love Potion #9
*Mocha Date Frosty

Dessert
*Chocolate "Who Needs a Date?"
Dessert
Mini-Wedding Cake (bite-sized pieces)

Punch Cup Orzo Salad
Makes: 7 punch-cup servings

1 cup orzo
1 teaspoon salt
1 cup frozen baby peas, thawed
1 small red bell pepper, seeded and diced

1 tablespoon fresh dill, chopped
1 to 2 tablespoons fresh lemon juice
1 teaspoon olive oil
Salt and fresh-ground black pepper, to taste

1. Bring a large pot of water to a rolling boil.
2. Stir in orzo and salt and return to a boil. Cook, stirring occasionally to keep the orzo from sticking, for 6 to 10 minutes, or until the pasta grains are tender, but firm.
3. Drain the orzo and transfer to a serving bowl.
4. Add peas, red pepper, dill, 1 tablespoon lemon juice, and olive oil.
5. Mix well, taste, and adjust seasonings, adding more lemon juice, if desired.
6. Season with salt and pepper.
7. Serve chilled in small cups.

Love Potion #9
Makes: 2 servings

2 ounces vodka
⅔ cup lemonade mix*
⅔ cup cranberry juice

2 ounces raspberry schnapps or liqueur
⅔ cup orange juice
Cracked ice

Shake all ingredients; serve over ice.

(*To make a mix, dilute lemonade concentrate with ⅛ the required amount of water.)

Mocha Date Frosty

Makes: 2 servings

½ cup lightly packed pitted dates, minced to paste
½ cup whole milk
2 teaspoons dark corn syrup
4 ice cubes
1 pint coffee ice cream

1. Combine dates, milk, and corn syrup in a blender and blend until smooth.
2. Add ice cubes, then ice cream; blend until thick and smooth.
3. Pour into 2 chilled glasses and serve immediately.

Chocolate "Who Needs a Date?" Dessert

Makes: 6 servings

1 cup whipping cream   *1 tablespoon crème de cacao liqueur*
1 pasteurized egg   *6 ounces semisweet chocolate chips*
1 teaspoon vanilla   *Whipped topping (frozen nondairy or aerosol can)*
1 teaspoon almond extract

1. Pour whipping cream into a microwave-safe container and microwave until the cream begins to boil (2 to 3 minutes).
2. While the cream is heating, blend together egg, vanilla, and almond extract.
3. Add the hot cream and liqueur and mix well.
4. Mix in chocolate chips.
5. Fill champagne flute glasses ¾ full (plastic will do for large groups) and refrigerate for several hours.
6. Top with whipped topping and a few chips. Serve with tall soda spoons.

Food Service and Decorative Touches

- Set up the buffet table in front of an altar decorated with flowers, tulle netting, candles, and so on. After dinner, remove the table and use the altar setting for emergency wedding ceremonies.
- Set up a few chairs with an aisle leading up to the altar.
- Use plate/cup trays for easy grazing. (See Resources #9.)
- Have napkins imprinted or hand-painted to read "_____ Married _____, February 29, 1997."
- Set all tables with centerpieces, candles, and white linens—just as at a wedding reception.
- Use elegantly wrapped gift packages, trimmed with flowers, tulle, and other wedding-related decorations, as centerpieces. (See How-To's #9.)
- Tie frothy bows around champagne flute stems—those you use for champagne and those you use for dessert.
- Use Little Black Books as seating assignments/favors.
- Include books on "how to get your man/woman" as part of the table decor.

ST. PATRICK'S DAY

Each March 17, the entire "party animal" population becomes Irish. Party goers gather in private or public places to pay boisterous and loyal tribute to St. Patrick, the patron saint of Ireland. Traditionally, the color green is present in every detail—decor, apparel, and, as unappetizing as it might seem, food and beverages. So, hosts, arm yourselves with large bottles of green food dye and prepare the feast!

Party Menu

Snacks
*Bangers in Rum Sauce
*Devils on Horseback
Shamrock-Shaped Sandwiches with
Green Cream-Cheese Filling
Baked, Stuffed Potato Skins with
Toppings
Potato Chips and Green Dips

Beverages
Soft Drinks/Mineral Waters
*Shamrock Gelatin Shooters (page 219)
Green Beer
Irish Whiskey

Buffet
*Authentic Irish Stew
Corned Beef and Cabbage with Boiled
Carrots and Potatoes
Green Salads and Slaws
Irish Soda Bread

Dessert
Irish Coffee
Lime Sherbet with Green Crème de
Menthe
Shamrock-Shaped Jell-O Jigglers
Leprechaun Cake (green angel food cake)
Green Mint Ice Cream

Bangers in Rum Sauce
Makes: 6 to 8 servings

1 pound traditional sausages (bangers)
Oil for cooking

1½ to 2 ounces rum (white or dark)
2½ tablespoons dark brown sugar

1. In a skillet, cook sausages with a little oil until lightly browned. Place the sausages on paper towels to drain off the oil.
2. Slice each sausage into 3 equal parts and put all the parts into a shallow saucepan.
3. Pour rum over the cut sausages and let them sit for 2 hours. Stir after 1 hour to make sure the sausages are covered with rum on all sides.
4. Preheat the oven to 325 degrees.
5. Sprinkle sugar over rum and sausages and cook in the oven for 15 to 20 minutes or until bubbling.
6. Serve the sausage chunks with cocktail picks.

Devils on Horseback
Makes: 24

12 strips traditional Irish bacon
Hot buttered toast (optional)

24 prunes, soaked in water overnight and stoned,
or 24 fresh dates

1. Cut each bacon strip in half, widthwise.
2. Wrap a bacon slice around one prune or date; secure with cocktail picks or skewers.
3. Cook in a skillet on medium heat, turning frequently, until the bacon is crisp.
4. Drain on paper towels.
5. Serve plain or on rounds of hot buttered toast.

Authentic Irish Stew

Makes: 4 servings

2½ pounds boned lamb	*½ cup celery*
4 large potatoes	*2 to 3 cups water*
2 large onions	*1 sprig of parsley, chopped*
3 to 4 medium carrots	*Salt and pepper, to taste*

1. Cut meat into chunks.
2. Clean the potatoes, onions, carrots, and celery and cut them into thick slices.
3. Layer the meat and the vegetables in a heavy pot, beginning and ending with a layer of potatoes. The rest of the ingredients can be layered in any order.
4. Cover everything with 2 or 3 cups of water. Sprinkle with chopped parsley and season with salt and pepper.
5. Cover the pot tightly and cook for 1½ hours, or until the meat is tender and the water has thickened.
6. Serve the stew in bowls as an entrée or in small cups as an appetizer.

Food Service and Decorative Touches

- At casual galas, use green-and-white paper and plastic linens and serving utensils.
- Lavishly decorate the party room with the customary green shamrock, Irish-motif decorations, and green-and-white balloons, both helium and air-filled.
- Use shamrock plants as decorative arrangements and centerpieces.
- Incorporate heather and moss in all floral arrangements.
- Cover walls with travel posters and brochures promoting Ireland and all things Irish.
- Use books on Ireland as decorative accents.
- Cover the buffet table with colorful sheet music or album covers featuring Irish songs or artists; overlay with clear plastic. (See How-To's #19.)
- Line large wicker or woven baskets with moss and fill them with fresh potatoes, cabbage, Brussels sprouts, and onions.
- Bring out the antique lace, Irish crystal, and china for more formal dinners.
- Paint guests' names on small stones and trim them with green satin ribbons to use as place cards. Paint table numbers on rocks for seating assignments.
- Add an *O* or an *Mc* before each surname on name tags or place cards.
- Tie napkins around toy Irish pipes and set them by plates for guests to play with and then take home.
- Scrub potatoes and carve an indentation in each potato to fit a candle.

EASTER

Since this holiday is based on a religious celebration, you cannot tamper with certain traditions. However, you can still restructure your Easter event to include some fun variations on the "springtime" and "bunny" aspects. The suggested menu and recipes are sure to be a "hoppin'" big hit. You can safely put all your eggs in this party basket!

Party Menu

Snacks
Deviled Eggs
*Deviled Egg Dip (page 98)
Celery Sticks Stuffed with Pastel-Tinted
Cream Cheese
Bread Bowls/Baskets Filled with Dip

Beverages
Soft Drinks/Mineral Waters
*Eggstra Special Gelatin Shots
Champagne Punch
Specialty Coffees/Teas

Buffet
Basket Lunches to Include:
Ham Salad Sandwiches on
Whole-Grain Buns
Rainbow Pasta Salad
Fresh Fruit Cups
Ambrosia Salad
*Cheery Cheesy Sticks

Dessert
Bunny-Shaped Coconut Cake
Pastel Frosted and Decorated Cupcakes
Carrot Cake with Cream Cheese Frosting
Candies and Cookies in Baby Farm-
Animal Shapes

Eggstra Special Gelatin Shots

(Contributed by Brad Gudim, Magical Productions, Minneapolis, Minnesota. See Credits.)

Makes: 36 shots

3 6-ounce packages Jell-O (3 different colors)
Alcohol, as suggested
36 jelly beans for garnish

1. Prepare selection of gelatin mixtures using the recipes in the Gelatin Shooters section (page 218), adding alcohol as suggested.
2. Fill clean egg cartons (foam-type) ¼-full with basket grass.
3. Place half of a small plastic egg in each indentation and fill with slightly thickened gelatin mix. Set the filled cartons in the refrigerator until ready to serve.
4. Insert jelly beans onto toothpicks and stick into the eggs.

Cheery Cheesy Sticks
Makes: about 40 sticks

2 teaspoons mustard powder
¼ teaspoon cayenne pepper
½ teaspoon each of paprika,
  thyme, chili powder, and salt

1 cup flour
¼ cup margarine
2 cups aged cheddar, grated
¼ cup cold water

1. Preheat the oven to 325 degrees.
2. Mix together mustard powder, seasonings, and flour; cut in margarine.
3. Add grated cheese to the flour and mix well.
4. Add water and knead until the dough forms a ball.
5. Divide the dough into 4 parts and roll out each part to about ⅛-inch thick.
6. Cut the dough into long strips and bake them on a greased cookie sheet for about 10 minutes, or until lightly browned. Cool the strips for a short time, then break them into 3- to 4-inch lengths.
7. Refrigerate the cheese sticks overnight, uncovered.

Food Service and Decorative Touches

- Use bright and light colors for linens and all decorative items.
- Decorate baskets of all sizes and descriptions to use as food containers and as decorations.
- Cover the buffet table with Astroturf/imitation grass. Elevate some areas with boxes and bowls.
- Fill tiny baskets (they come in all colors) with decorative grass and jelly beans to use as place cards. Print the guests' names on small tags and tie the tags to the basket handles.
- Decorate colorful plastic come-apart eggs and fill them with tiny toys or candy to use as place favors. Guests' names and table numbers can be imprinted on these with special pens.
- Decorate each table in a different spring color, and assign seats with correspondingly colored eggs.
- If seating space is limited, serve lunch or brunch in individual baskets.
- Mix stuffed, ceramic, cloth, or wooden animals into decorative arrangements on buffet or dining tables.
- Decorate Leggs hosiery eggs and fill them with treats and trinkets for prizes or party favors.
- Tuck dyed and decorated hard-boiled eggs into table decorations and serving areas.
- Spray-paint baskets in bright or soft colors and fill them with fresh or silk flowers and plants for table centerpieces.
- String soft Easter candies on fishing wire and drape them around the edges of the buffet table and across chair backs.
- Tie pastel napkins around small bunches of spring flowers and set at each place.
- Hot-glue small stuffed or toy bunnies, duckies, or chickies to ponytail holders to use as napkin holders.
- Stencil or hand-paint a tulip design onto plain colored napkins for a festive and fresh look.

APRIL FOOLS' DAY

The day for tricks and treats and practical jokes is a natural theme for a party thrown for the person born on April 1 or for the friend or family "funster" who is famous for his/her questionable sense of humor. The menu blends silly selections that are surprisingly savory—no joke!

Party Menu

Snacks
Prankster's Frank Fingers (cocktail weiners in barbecue sauce)
Silly Celery (tinted orange)
Daffy Dilly Dip

Beverages
Soft Drinks/Mineral Waters
*Pickle Puss Shooter
Tutti Frutti Punch
Coffees/Teas

Buffet
*Fu"silly" Salad
Hamburger "Dogs" in Hot Dog Buns
Hot Bologna Rounds in Hamburger Buns
Gelatin in Christmas-Tree-Shaped Mold

Dessert
*Rhubarb Fool
Ding Dongs Cupcakes
HoHos
Upside-Down Cake

Pickle Puss Shooter
Makes: 1 serving

1 ounce tequila
1 ounce pickle juice

Pour tequila and pickle juice into separate shot glasses and serve. Tell your guests to drink the pickle juice first, then tequila.

Fu"silly" Salad
(A bright festive salad from Eileen Parker's *Eat Outside the Box, An Irreverent Approach to Eating Healthy While Still Maintaining Your Sanity.* See Credits.)

Makes: about 10 servings

3 eggs
2 cups fusilli noodles
½ pound side bacon (the best quality you can find)
3 to 4 radishes, finely chopped
½ cup cucumber, chopped
½ cup zucchini, chopped
½ cup onion, finely chopped

½ cup red pepper, chopped
½ cup green pepper, chopped
Black pepper, to taste
3 tablespoons safflower or sunflower oil or another light flavorful oil (not a heavy oil like olive oil because it covers the flavors) or
4 tablespoons mayonnaise and ½ teaspoon sugar

1. Boil eggs on medium heat for 8 minutes until hard; cool and chop into small pieces.
2. Cook noodles until they are just firm; rinse and cool.
3. Cook bacon until crisp, roll it in a paper towel, then break into small pieces.
4. Combine all the ingredients, except oil or mayonnaise, mix well, then cover the bowl and chill for 1 hour or more to allow the flavors to mix.

5. Just before serving, add oil or mayonnaise and toss well.
6. Serve in a dark-colored bowl, perhaps deep blue, to bring out the colors of the radishes and red pepper, and to contrast with the light colors of the pasta and eggs.

Tip: You can eliminate the red pepper and the zucchini and it won't affect the flavor. But do not remove or substitute the other ingredients—the flavor combination of these particular vegetables is what makes this salad so good.

Rhubarb Fool
Makes: 10 to 12 servings

1 cinnamon stick
3 whole cloves
Peel of 1 lemon, sliced thin
2¼ pounds rhubarb, chopped (8 cups)

1¼ cups sugar
16 ounces vanilla yogurt
½ cup whipping cream

1. Tie cinnamon, cloves, and lemon peel in a bag.
2. Cook rhubarb, sugar, and the bag of spices 6 to 8 minutes.
3. Pour off the water from the yogurt.
4. Whip the cream and fold it into the yogurt.
5. Place the cream/yogurt mixture into serving bowls. Swirl in cooked rhubarb.

Tip: Add a few drops of red food coloring if the rhubarb is not pink enough.

Food Service and Decorative Touches
- Cover all tables with Sunday funny papers or with colorful fabrics in stripe, polka-dot, or large-geometric-print patterns.
- Arrange gag items, such as dunce hats, pop-out-of-the-can snakes, googly-eye glasses, silly noses with glasses, inverted flop-hats, or big clown shoes, as part of your table decor.
- Use mismatched plates, cups, and silverware, set backwards or upside down.
- Glue some of the serving ware to the table.
- Display luscious looking fake desserts, glued to the plate. You can borrow these from a bakery or grocery store or buy them at gag gift shops.
- Serve snacks from incongruous containers, such as potato chips from a motor oil carton, popcorn from a shoe box, or veggies from a plastic-lined roller paint pan. (Be sure that all containers are clean and lined with aluminum foil or plastic wrap.)
- Arrange dishes on the buffet table on a drying rack.
- Write names backwards on place cards.
- Tie licorice candy strings in bows around napkins.
- Serve drinks in dribble glasses.
- Use Silly Putty to attach place cards to crazy straws, and stick the straws into juice boxes either at each place setting or on the table sign.

EARTH DAY

April 22, Earth Day, is dedicated to contemplating and discussing the condition of our planet and reestablishing the ways we can preserve its natural beauty and wholesomeness. The menu plan follows an ecological formula that features "recycle, reuse, and creatively conserve" cuisine.

Party Menu

Snacks
*Stuffed Mushrooms (page 137)
Fresh Vegetables Tray
Pick A Dip

Beverages
Soft Drinks/Mineral Waters
*Dandelion Wine
Fresh Ground Coffees/Herbal Teas

Buffet
*Easy Lentil and Brown Rice Soup
Hearty Multigrain Rolls
Leftovers Casserole
Pick A Salad

Dessert
*Makes-Its-Own-Crust Apple Pie

Dandelion Wine
Makes: 2 gallons

4 quarts boiling water
4 quarts dandelion blossoms
6 oranges

4 lemons
2 yeast cakes
4 pounds sugar

1. Scald dandelion blossoms in boiling water and let stand overnight.
2. The next morning, strain, add the pulp and juice of 6 oranges, juice of 4 lemons, yeast, and sugar.
3. Let ferment for 4 days, then strain and bottle.
4. Serve in small glasses at room temperature.

Easy Lentil and Brown Rice Soup
Makes: 6 servings

5 cups chicken broth
3 cups water
1½ cups lentils, sorted and rinsed
1 cup brown rice
32 ounces whole tomatoes, drained
  and chopped (reserve the juice)
3 carrots, cut into ¼-inch pieces
1 onion, chopped
1 celery stalk, chopped

3 garlic cloves, minced
½ teaspoon dry basil
½ teaspoon dry oregano
¼ teaspoon thyme
1 bay leaf
½ cup fresh parsley, minced
2 tablespoons cider vinegar (or to taste)
Salt and pepper, to taste

1. In a heavy kettle, combine broth, water, lentils, rice, tomatoes and reserved juice, carrots, onion, celery, garlic, basil, oregano, thyme, and bay leaf.
2. Bring the mixture to a boil; cover and simmer, stirring occasionally, for 45 to 55 minutes, or until lentils and rice are tender.
3. Stir in fresh parsley, vinegar, and salt and pepper to taste.
4. Discard the bay leaf.
5. Serve in earthenware mugs.

Tip: The soup will be thick, and will thicken more as it stands. If you like, thin it with chicken stock.

Makes-Its-Own-Crust Apple Pie

(To commemorate Arbor Day and Johnny Appleseed)

Makes: 8 to 10 servings

1 cup flour	*1 egg*
1 teaspoon baking powder	*⅔ cup shortening*
½ teaspoon salt	*¼ cup water*
1 tablespoon sugar	*1 can apple pie filling*
1 teaspoon cinnamon	*Whipped topping, ice cream, or chedar cheese*

1. Preheat the oven to 425 degrees.
2. Combine flour, baking powder, salt, sugar, cinnamon, egg, shortening, and water; blend well.
3. Pour the batter into a greased pie pan.
4. Pour the pie filling into the center of the batter—do not stir.
5. Bake for 45 to 50 minutes.
6. Serve with whipped topping, homemade ice cream, or cheddar cheese.

Food Service and Decorative Touches

*   Serve all foods in handcrafted earthenware containers.
*   Set small, potted seedlings at each place, as place cards.
*   Cover tables with recycled craft paper or newspaper hand-painted with a leaf pattern.
*   Cover two-inch lengths of wrapping-paper cardboard rolls or toilet-paper tubes with festive paper, handmade or recycled, and use for napkin rings.
*   Add pictures of butterflies and actual butterfly nets to the table decor.
*   Include various decorative items made of brown paper bags. (See How-To's # 16.)
*   Set colorful globes of any size on the buffet table.
*   Cover empty facial tissue boxes, shoe boxes, milk cartons, and cardboard paint buckets with discarded maps, then use the containers to serve dry snacks. Or place small plants and vases in the boxes.
*   Decorate tables with craft projects made from egg cartons, milk cartons, newspapers, magazines, string, tissue boxes, old nylons, tin cans, plastic bottles, paper rolls, and fabric.

CINCO DE MAYO

Not only do we celebrate with a Mexican Fiesta on May 5, Cinco de Mayo, but many of us enjoy traditional Mexican food, drink, music, and festivities many times a year. South of the Border is one of today's most popular party themes, since it is easy, inexpensive, and a sure-fire winner.

Party Menu

Snacks
*Guacamole Dip
Salsa
Tortilla Chips

Beverages
Soft Drinks/Mineral Waters
*Tequila Lime Punch
*Margarita Gelatin Shooters (page 218, #5)
*Mexican Hot Chocolate

Buffet
Tacos
Burritos
Enchiladas
Rice and Beans

Dessert
*Margarita Cheesecake Pie
Flour Tortilla Crisps with Sugar and Cinnamon

Guacamole Dip
Makes: about 2 cups

2 ripe avocados
1 medium onion
2 green chili peppers, finely chopped (optional)
1 tablespoon lemon juice

1 teaspoon salt
½ teaspoon coarse black pepper
1 medium tomato, chopped (optional)
½ cup mild cheddar cheese, shredded

1. Peel, pit, and mash the avocados.
2. Add onion, chili peppers, lemon juice, salt, and pepper; mix until creamy.
3. Fold in tomato, cover with cheese, and refrigerate until serving.

Tequila Lime Punch
Makes: 15 to 20 servings

2 cups cold water
1½ cups white tequila
6-ounce can frozen pineapple-orange juice concentrate, thawed
½ cup lime juice

2 tablespoons sugar
2 28-ounce bottles 7-Up or Sprite, chilled
1 lime, sliced
1 orange, sliced
Ice ring

1. In a large punch bowl, combine water, tequila, concentrate, lime juice, and sugar.
2. Slowly pour carbonated beverage down the side of the bowl; stir punch gently with an up-and-down motion.
3. Float lime and orange slices on top of the punch. Serve over an ice ring.

Mexican Hot Chocolate
Makes: 9 8-ounce servings

2¾ cups nonfat dry milk powder
½ cup unsweetened cocoa powder

½ cup powdered sugar substitute (not aspartame)
1 teaspoon ground cinnamon

1. Combine dry milk powder, cocoa powder, sugar substitute, and cinnamon. Mix well. (You can store the mix, covered, in a cool, dry place for up to 8 weeks.)
2. For each serving, place ⅓ cup of the cocoa mix in a mug.
3. Fill the mug with boiling water; stir to mix.

Margarita Cheesecake Pie
Makes: 10 to 12 servings

Crust
Ready-made graham cracker crust

Filling
3 8-ounce packages reduced-fat
* cream cheese, room temperature*
1¼ cups light sour cream
¾ cup + 2 tablespoons sugar

2½ tablespoons triple sec or other orange liqueur
2½ tablespoons tequila
2½ tablespoons fresh lime juice
4 large eggs

Topping
¾ cup light sour cream
1 tablespoon fresh lime juice
1 tablespoon sugar

Very thin lime slices, cut in half
Very thin lime peel strips

1. Using an electric mixer, beat cream cheese in a large bowl until fluffy.
2. Beat in sour cream, then sugar, triple sec, tequila, lime juice, and eggs.
3. Pour filling into the crust. Bake until the outside 2 inches are set and the center moves only slightly when pan is shaken (about 50 minutes).
4. Remove from the oven. Turn off the oven.
5. To make the topping, whisk sour cream, lime juice, and sugar in a small bowl; blend well. Spread the topping evenly over the cheesecake.
6. Return the cheesecake to the hot oven. Let stand 45 minutes. (Cheesecake will look very soft, but will firm when chilled.)
7. Refrigerate the cake until well chilled, up to 1 day.
8. Decorate the cheesecake with lime half-slices and peel.

Food Service and Decorative Touches
- Use brilliantly colored paper flowers on all tables and serving areas. Wrap the flowers around napkins, for colorful napkin holders. (See How-To's # 13.)
- Add balloons and streamers for a festive fiesta touch.
- Create centerpieces out of small cacti, dried chili peppers in bunches or garlands, and desert flowers.
- Arrange souvenir-type carnival booths for snacks and beverages.
- Set up "make-your-own" grazing stations. This works well with chips and salsa and with tacos, burritos, and enchiladas.
- Display beautiful cookbooks, along with such Mexican props as corn grinders, dried peppers, and ornate sombreros, on top of brightly colored serape clothes.

MOTHER'S DAY

How about giving a tea for Mom? This tribute to Mom will include dainty food and drink served in a casual, yet slightly formal, setting. The whole family will get into the spirit of daintily raising their pinkies as they praise "Mom, Our Favorite Celebra-Tea."

Party Menu

Snacks
*Crumpets
*Stuffed Cantaloupe

Beverages
Soft Drinks/Mineral Waters
*Tea Party Punch (page 221)
Variety of Hot Teas
Iced Tea Drinks

Buffet
*Very Proper Cucumber Sandwiches
Assorted Finger Sandwiches
Pick A Salad

Dessert
*Elegant Tea Cakes
Fruit Tarts

Crumpets
Makes: 12 crumpets

1 cup scalded milk
½ cup butter
½ teaspoon salt

1 softened yeast cake in ¼ cup lukewarm water
2 cups flour

1. Add butter and salt to scalded milk and stir to melt the butter; cool to lukewarm.
2. Add yeast and flour; beat well. Cover. Let rise until fluffy.
3. Fill buttered crumpet rings (see tip below) ½ full, place on a hot griddle, and cook slowly until brown on 1 side. Turn and brown on other side.
4. Serve hot with butter and jam.

Tip: If you don't have crumpet rings around the house, improvise: Remove the tops and bottoms of a 6½-ounce tin can (such as tuna) with a smooth-edged can opener. Wash thoroughly and use as a crumpet ring; follow baking directions above.

Stuffed Cantaloupe
Makes: about 1 cup cheese mixture and about 20 melon balls

1 medium cantaloupe
White or rosé wine (or white grape juice)
½ pound ricotta or farmer's cheese

¼ pound blue cheese, crumbled
¼ cup sour cream or heavy sweet cream
Salt and freshly ground black pepper, to taste

1. Slice off the top of the cantaloupe; scoop out the fruit with a melon-ball cutter.
2. Marinate the melon balls in wine or grape juice until time to serve. Use just enough liquid to lightly coat the balls.
3. Blend together cheeses and cream; season with salt and pepper, to taste.
4. Pile the cheese mixture lightly into the cantaloupe shell. If the mixture does not fill the shell, cut a jagged edge to form a "basket edge."
5. To eat, spear melon balls with toothpicks and dip them into the cheese mixture.

Very Proper Cucumber Sandwiches

Makes: 30 sandwiches

1 large English cucumber, peeled
   and sliced paper thin
½ teaspoon salt
2 tablespoons white vinegar
1 cup unsalted butter, softened

¼ cup fresh tarragon, minced
¼ cup fresh chervil, minced
30 thin slices whole-wheat bread
Watercress leaves (optional)

1. Put cucumber slices in a large bowl. Sprinkle with salt and vinegar and toss to mix well; let stand 1 hour. Drain well in a colander.
2. Combine butter, tarragon, and chervil.
3. Trim crusts off bread slices, and spread herb butter over 1 side of each slice.
4. Cover half the buttered slices with cucumbers.
5. Close sandwiches, cut each in half, and arrange them on a platter garnished with watercress leaves. For a decorative touch, dip 1 end of a sandwich into mayonnaise, then into minced fresh parsley.

Elegant Tea Cakes

Makes: 10 dozen

½ cup butter
1 cup granulated sugar
1 egg, well beaten
1 tablespoon cream

1 teaspoon vanilla
2 cups flour
½ teaspoon baking powder
Jam, any flavor

1. In a bowl, cream butter with sugar until light and fluffy.
2. Add beaten egg, cream, and vanilla.
3. In a separate bowl, sift flour with baking powder; add creamed mixture and blend well. Roll dough into a log and wrap in aluminum foil.
4. Refrigerate overnight, or, to prepare the same day, put into the freezer for 2 hours.
5. Preheat the oven to 350 degrees.
6. Cut the chilled dough into very thin slices and place on a greased cookie sheet.
7. Bake 5 to 8 minutes.
8. Serve with a dab of jam.

Food Service and Decorative Touches

- Tuck small bunches of silk or fresh flowers into tea pots, or make dainty miniature arrangements in tea cups to use for individual table favors or place cards.
- Cover tables with lace or crochet tablecloths; use ribbons and streamers for runners.
- Set tea-bag sachets at each place.
- Use a fancy silver tea service on the buffet table.
- Set delicately framed photos of Mom on the buffet and dining tables to be admired and adored.
- Hang antique embroidered cloths or large doilies over chair backs.
- Line all trays and serving platters with fancy paper doilies.
- Tie lovely satin ribbons around napkins and tuck in a single flower.
- Serve sandwiches and sweets on a rolling tea cart.
- Use antique tea tins as attractive and unique containers and decor accents.
- Use small china creamers as individual tea pots for children at the party.

MEMORIAL/VETERANS DAY

Memorial Day, the last Monday in May, is typically celebrated with family and friends in a backyard/outdoor casual atmosphere, with barbecue grills stoked up to the max. Along with the all-time picnic favorites, hosts now add their own touches to establish new traditions for this day of remembrance.

Party Menu

Snacks
*Holiday Beer Bits
Veggies
Pick A Dip
Dry Snacks

Beverages
Soft Drinks/Mineral Waters
*Watermelon Slushies
Beer

Buffet
Grilled Burgers and Hot Dogs
Pick A Potato Salad
Pick A Slaw

Dessert
*Unforgettable Banana Ice-Cream
Dessert
Homemade Ice Cream

Holiday Beer Bits

Makes: 4 to 6 servings per 1 pound of bits

1 cup flour
1 teaspoon baking powder
½ teaspoon salt
1 egg, beaten

½ cup beer
1 pound bits of your choice (See options below.)
2 cups vegetable oil
Sesame oil (optional)

1. Sift flour, baking powder, and salt into a bowl.
2. Beat in egg and beer.
3. Dip bits in batter, coating them well.
4. Preheat vegetable oil. Add a few drops of sesame oil for flavor.
5. Bring the oil to 370 degrees.
6. Fry the bits in oil until browned.
7. Drain on paper towels and serve warm. If you like, serve these bits "forkupine" style. (See How-To's #39.)

Bits Options:
Cooked chicken or turkey breasts, cut into bite sizes
Peeled raw sweet potatoes, cut into manageable bites
Fresh mushroom caps
Cauliflower or broccoli heads, small chunks
Raw shrimp, shelled and deveined
Zucchini chunks

Watermelon Slushies

Makes: 2 servings

½ cup watermelon
½ cup crushed ice
Mint leaves and/or flower petals for garnish

1. Seed and coarsely chop the watermelon; save juices.
2. Blend pieces and juice in a blender with crushed ice until "slushed."
3. Pour into 2 tall glasses.
4. Garnish with mint leaves and/or flower petals (How-To's #32); serve with soda spoons.

Unforgettable Banana Ice-Cream Dessert

Makes: 8 servings

1 quart vanilla ice cream, softened
2 large ripe bananas, peeled and mashed
10 chocolate sandwich cookies,
  finely chopped
¼ cup chocolate syrup
Additional chocolate syrup for topping
Additional banana slices for topping
Maraschino cherries

1. Put ice cream into a large bowl; fold in bananas and cookies.
2. Pour into an 8-inch square pan.
3. Drizzle with chocolate syrup.
4. Run a knife through the ice cream to make swirls.
5. Cover and freeze until firm.
6. To serve, scoop ice cream into sundae glasses. Top with additional chocolate syrup, banana slices, and maraschino cherries.

Food Service and Decorative Touches

- Decorate with a patriotic red, white, and blue theme or a marine green or khaki color scheme, or choose your own colors.
- Set up the buffet or serving tables as you would for a picnic: paper or plastic tablecloths and plates, sturdy paper or cloth napkins, and sturdy metal or plastic utensils.
- Make napkins to match your color scheme. Use pinking shears to cut fabrics of appropriate prints and colors into squares.
- Fill baskets, buckets, vases, and pots with fresh flowers and plants.
- If your event is set at a pool area, float plastic floral wreaths in the pool: Cover Styrofoam circles with garage-sale flowers and greens. You can purchase waterproof ribbons in a craft store.
- Set out snapshot albums and framed photos of those special people who will be remembered by your guests, for all to enjoy, discuss, and ponder.

FATHER'S DAY

Since 1966, families have paid tribute to fathers, grandfathers, and, nowadays, great-grandfathers on the third Sunday in June. At these summertime galas, whole families gather to put Dad up on his pedestal, real or imagined, and shower him with gifts and loving attention. With this party menu, the hero not only soaks up all the attention, but also—along with his loyal followers—enjoys a menu of "super" stuff for a super guy.

Party Menu

Snacks
*"What a Roll" Model
Chips, Pretzels, Popcorn
Veggies
Pick A Dip

Beverages
Soft Drinks/Mineral Waters
*Man in Blue Slushy Punch
Dad's Favorite Brew
Coffees/Teas

Buffet
*Hero Sandwich Wedges
Poppa's Pasta Salad
Gelatin Salad in a Star-Shaped Mold

Dessert
*"Pop"corn Cake
Frozen Fruit "Pops"
Dad's Root Beer Floats

"What a Roll" Model
Makes: 16 servings

12 ounces cream cheese, softened
24 stuffed olives, chopped
2 teaspoons prepared horseradish
4 tablespoons cream
Salt and pepper, to taste
2 pounds rectangular ham slices

1. Combine cream cheese, olives, horseradish, cream, and seasonings; mix well.
2. Spread the filling mixture on ham slices.
3. Roll each slice, short end to short end, and fasten with a cocktail toothpick.
4. Refrigerate until just before serving.
5. Cut rolls into 1-inch pieces and place on a serving tray. Serve with crispy crackers.

Man in Blue Slushy Punch
Makes: 30 5-ounce servings

2 cups sugar
2 cups hot water
1½ 3-ounce packages blueberry Jell-O
4½ cups hot water
46 ounces pineapple juice
1½ 6-ounce cans frozen lemon-lime juice
  (or a combination thereof)
1 quart 7-Up

1. Dissolve sugar in 2 cups hot water.
2. Dissolve Jell-O in 4½ cups hot water.
3. Add the sugar water to the Jell-O water, then add juice and frozen concentrate.
4. Freeze overnight (a 5-gallon jug or barrel works well for this).
5. Thaw partially; add 7-Up and use a potato masher to break into slush consistency.
6. Serve the punch in medium-sized Superman paper cups.

Hero Sandwich Wedges

Makes: 8 servings

Round loaves of bread
Olive oil, herbed or with garlic
Mayonnaise (only if refrigeration
  is available)

Mustard
Favorite cold cuts and sliced cheeses
Shredded lettuce
Tomatoes, thinly sliced

1. Cut each loaf in half horizontally.
2. Scoop out the bread from each loaf half, leaving half an inch to an inch of bread on the sides and bottom.
3. Brush the insides of the loaves with oil, and then mayonnaise and/or mustard.
4. Layer meat, cheese, and veggies into the loaf halves.
5. Join the halves together to make a complete loaf; secure with toothpicks.
6. Cut each loaf into 8 wedges.

"Pop"corn Cake

Makes: 10 servings

¼ pound butter
1 pound minimarshmallows

1 pound peanuts or mixed nuts (salted)
Fresh-popped popcorn to fill a large angel food cake pan
1 pound M & M candy (plain)

1. Melt butter.
2. Add marshmallows to warm butter and mix until all are melted.
3. Pour the marshmallow mixture into a large pan and mix in nuts, popcorn (be sure to remove all unpopped kernels), and M & M's; mix well to coat all pieces.
4. Press everything into an angel food cake pan; let cool.
5. Turn out onto a cake plate. Keep at room temperature.

Tip: Microwave popcorn is not recommended for this recipe, because most prepackaged popcorns have added seasonings.

Food Service and Decorative Touches

- Use colorful paper and plastic products that pay tribute to kids' heroes, such as Superman, Batman, and Spiderman.
- Create place mats or table decor with covers from adventure comic books.
- Cut a Sunday hero comic section into strips for napkin rings.
- Fashion a minitorso from approximately 8½-by-11 inches of cardboard; dress it in a baby T-shirt, and cover the front with handmade or store-bought medals and awards ribbons. Create your own medals, such as "Honorary Pizza Chef," "Super Basement Workshop Guy," or "Star Carpool Driver." Use this prop as a centerpiece.
- Serve Dad a beverage in a Hero's Trophy Cup.
- Drape a "super cape" over Dad's chair.
- Fill trophy cups with snacks, veggie strips, bread sticks, or tall candies, such as licorice.
- Label a container "Beef Jerky," then cross out "Jerky" and replace it with "Hero."
- For guests' seating assignments, write names and table numbers on award ribbons and affix to a large Hero Poster blowup of Dad.
- Pile snacks in toy Batmobiles, Superman gift bags, and baskets trimmed with ribbons or medal awards.

FOURTH OF JULY

Happy Birthday, Dear America! You're all invited to the party—in your backyard, at the park, or lakeside. Traditional family outing favorites abound, but don't be shy about throwing in a few birthday surprises for your guests, too.

Party Menu

Snacks
*Firecracker Drummettes
*Patriotic Veggie Platter
Blue Tortilla Chips (in a red basket)
Cottage Cheese Dip

Beverages
Soft Drinks/Mineral Waters
*Melon Apple Pie Cocktail
Fresh Lemonade with Red and Blue
Ice Cubes
Beer/Wine Coolers

Buffet
Burger and Brat Bar (Grilled meats with all the trimmings)
Baked Beans
Pick A Potato Salad
Pick A Slaw

Dessert
*Patriotic Party Pops
*Red, White, and Blue Berry Bowl
Watermelon

Firecracker Drummettes
Makes: 8 servings

1 pound chicken drummettes
2 teaspoons salt
Black pepper, to taste
1 teaspoon honey or sugar
Pinch 5 Spice powder

1 tablespoon soy sauce
2 egg whites
2 ounces rice flour
Vegetable oil for deep-frying

1. Season drummettes with salt, pepper, honey or sugar, 5 Spice powder, and soy sauce.
2. Beat the egg white with a fork.
3. Dip the chicken in the egg white, then coat with the rice flour.
4. Deep-fry until golden brown.

Patriotic Veggie Platter
Makes: about 2½ cups dip

8 ounces cream cheese
1 small container sour cream
¼ cup pimento pieces
¼ cup onion, finely chopped
Cauliflower florets

Jicama sticks
Radishes
Cherry tomatoes
Red bell peppers

1. Combine cream cheese, sour cream, pimento pieces, and chopped onion. Mix well, scoop into a decorative bowl, and place in the middle of a large blue platter.
2. Cut vegetables into bite-sized pieces.
3. Arrange the vegetables around the dip for a good ol' USA offering.

30

Melon Apple Pie Cocktail

Makes: 1 serving

1 ounce vodka
1 ounce melon liqueur
Ice

Apple juice
Apple slices and melon chunks for garnish

1. Pour vodka and melon liqueur over ice into a low-ball glass; fill with apple juice.
2. Garnish with apple slices and melon chunks.

Patriotic Party Pops

Makes: 8 servings

1½ cups cherry (or other red)
   fruit juice drink
1½ cups yogurt, sweetened with honey

1½ cups blue drink
12 Popsicle sticks

1. Place 12 3-ounce plastic or paper cups in a baking pan.
2. Spoon 2 tablespoons cherry drink into each cup. Freeze until firm (3 to 4 hours).
3. Add 2 tablespoons of yogurt on top of the red layer and freeze.
4. Top with 2 tablespoons blue drink and freeze until firm, but not solid.
5. Insert Popsicle sticks firmly into the blue layer. Freeze until solid.
6. Dip each cup into warm water for a few seconds to release the pops.

Red, White, and Blue Berry Bowl

Makes: about 12 servings

4 cups boiling water
Red fruit gelatin, any flavor
Blueberry flavor gelatin
2 cups cold water

8 ounces nondairy whipped topping, thawed
4 cups pound cake, cubed
2 cups sliced strawberries

1. Thoroughly dissolve each flavor gelatin (in separate bowls) in 2 cups boiling water, per package directions. Stir 1 cup cold water into each bowl.
2. Pour into separate 13-by-9-inch pans; refrigerate until firm.
3. Cut gelatin into ½-inch cubes. Layer blue gelatin cubes, whipped topping, cake, strawberries, whipped topping, and red gelatin in a large, clear serving bowl.
4. Garnish with remaining whipped topping.
5. Refrigerate at least 1 hour or until ready to serve. Serve in large wine goblets.

Food Service and Decorative Touches

- Cover tables with red, white, and blue checked or striped tablecloths.
- Decorate with ready-made or handcrafted accessories—pinwheels, balloons, streamers, banners, and paper hats—anything with a stars-and-stripes design.
- Set the table with red, white, and blue table and serving ware.
- Create small firecrackers to use as place cards or favors—use bright red, shiny paper. (See How-To's #7.)
- Use red, white, and blue spray paint to dress up baskets, tins, buckets, and boxes. These recycled treasures will serve you for many holidays and themes.
- Use white luminaria bags, decorated with red and blue stars, to light your buffet and dining tables and the entrance to your party
- Reuse Christmas or Valentine's decorations by adding white and blue touches.

BASTILLE DAY

Viva La Party! Join the French as they rally 'round their flag with music, dancing, and general merrymaking. Known for epicurean elegance and excellence, French cuisine should please the most discerning palate. Bon appetit!

Party Menu

Snacks
*Brie En Croute
Hors d'Oeuvres (all kinds)
Pâté Plate
Bread Rounds and Crackers

Beverages
Soft Drinks/Perrier Waters
*Josephine Java Juice
French Wines
French Roast Coffees/Teas

Buffet
French Onion Soup
*Beef Bourguignon
Salade Nicoise on Petit Plates
French Bread and Baguettes

Dessert
Fruit and Cheese
*Berry, Berry Patriotic Ice-Cream Float
French Pastries
Petit Fours

Brie En Croute
Makes: 16 servings

1 brie round
1 pastry dough

1 egg
2 teaspoons milk

1. Preheat the oven to 350 degrees.
2. Completely enclose brie in pastry dough and place on a baking sheet, seam side down.
3. Beat the egg and mix well with milk. Brush the brie with the egg mixture.
4. Shape the pastry scraps into leaves, flowers, and so on; decorate the brie.
5. Bake for about 30 minutes or until the pastry is golden brown.
6. Slice the brie into thin slices and serve with bread rounds and crackers

Josephine Java Juice
Makes: 1 serving

1½ ounces Napoleon brandy
6 ounces black coffee
Whipped cream

Fresh mint leaves
Grated orange peel or candied oranges

1. Place brandy in a preheated mug or large wine glass.
2. Add coffee and top with whipped cream.
3. Garnish with mint and grated orange peel or candied orange.

Beef Bourguignon

Makes: 6 to 8 servings

3 pounds lean beef sirloin, chuck or round
2½ cups burgundy wine
⅛ teaspoon garlic powder
⅛ teaspoon thyme
½ bay leaf
¼ cup oil
3 tablespoons flour

1 1⅛-ounce can dehydrated onion soup mix
1½ cups water
5 small carrots, cut in 1-inch chunks
1 8-ounce can small onions, drained
1 4-ounce can mushrooms, drained, or 1 dozen
    fresh mushrooms, sautéed in butter

1. Cut beef in 1½-inch cubes.
2. Combine 2 cups burgundy, garlic powder, thyme, and bay leaf; pour over beef and allow to stand 2 hours or longer in the refrigerator.
3. Drain, saving the marinade. Dry beef cubes on paper towels.
4. Preheat the oven to 300 degrees.
5. Heat oil in a heavy skillet, add beef, and brown slowly on all sides.
6. Remove beef to a casserole dish.
7. Sift flour into oil remaining in the skillet, then add marinade, onion soup mix, and water; cook and stir until mixture boils thoroughly. Pour the marinade over the beef, cover, and bake for 2 hours, or until the beef is very tender.
8. Meanwhile, boil carrots in a small amount of salted water for 5 to 10 minutes.
9. Add carrots, onions, mushrooms, and remaining ½ cup burgundy to the beef.
10. Bake 15 minutes longer, or until vegetables are thoroughly heated
11. Serve as an entrée or in mugs for a buffet treat.

Berry, Berry Patriotic Ice-Cream Float

Makes: 1 serving

Raspberry soda
1 scoop vanilla ice cream or frozen yogurt

½ cup fresh blueberries
1 fresh strawberry or raspberry

1. Fill a tall glass ¾ full with raspberry soda; top with a large scoop of vanilla ice cream.
2. Garnish with fresh fruit, French flag, and/or a decorative stirrer.
3. Serve with a tall straw and a long spoon.

Food Service and Decorative Touches

- Use crisp white or red-and-white checked tablecloths; accent with red and blue.
- Use small, elegant gold frames as one-per-table menu holders, individual place cards, or seating assignments.
- Use French cookbooks, starchy chef's hats, and cooking utensils as decorative touches on the buffet table.
- Hang colorful chest ribbons with medals over chair backs.
- Use fresh fruit, vegetables, herbs, and spices as table decor.
- Provide French berets and neckerchiefs for servers. For a more formal party, provide bow ties and aprons for males and frilly hats and aprons for females.
- Tie each napkin around a French baguette roll.
- Use drippy candles in wine bottles for a country look or votive candles in sparkling cut-glass holders for formal decor.
- For casual affairs, use paper French Chef hats as name tags or place cards

LABOR DAY

Labor Day is celebrated on the first Monday in September, with parades, picnics, and family get-togethers. Today's hosts often organize a potluck event, with all guests bringing a favorite dish to round out the menu. Whether you plan your event with a theme or stick to the traditional scheme, try to cut down on the labor and allow plenty of time and energy for the fun.

Party Menu

Snacks
*Trucker's Taters
Veggies
Pick A Dip

Buffet
Hard at Work, Soup, Salad, and
Sandwich Bar
Individual Bags of Chips

Beverages
Fun Labels: Water Cooler Catch-up,
Switchman's Sodas, and Take a Coffee
Break
*Factory Whistle Shooters: "One toot and
you're out for the day!" (page 219)
*Slushy Payroll Punch

Dessert
*Lazy Apple-Nutty à la Mode
PayDay Candy Bars
Lunch Pail Snacks: Twinkies, Oreo
Cookies, and so on
Fresh Fruit

Trucker's Taters
Makes: 8 taters

1 medium baking potato
1 tablespoon flour
½ teaspoon seasoned salt

Dash of pepper
Margarine spray

1. Preheat the oven to 375 degrees.
2. Cut potato into 8 wedges.
3. Put flour, salt, and pepper in a paper bag, add potato wedges, and shake well.
4. Place the wedges on a baking sheet.
5. Spray with margarine.
6. Bake for 35 to 40 minutes.

Tip: Double, triple, or quadruple the ingredients as needed.

Slushy Payroll Punch
Makes: about 1 gallon

¾ cup sugar
7 cups water
1 12-ounce can frozen lemonade concentrate, thawed and undiluted
1 12-ounce can frozen orange juice concentrate, thawed and undiluted
1 6-ounce can frozen pineapple juice concentrate, thawed and undiluted
1 to 1½ cups coconut liqueur
5 to 6 cups lemon-lime carbonated beverage, chilled

1. Combine sugar and water in a saucepan; bring to a boil, stirring until sugar dissolves. Cool.
2. Add concentrates and liqueur, stirring well.
3. Pour everything into a large freezer-safe container; freeze until slushy.
4. For each serving, mix about 1 cup slush mixture with ½ cup lemon-lime beverage, stirring until slushy.
5. Serve in thermos top cups, if possible.

Lazy Apple-Nutty à la Mode

Makes: 8 servings

Topping:
¾ cup all-purpose flour
¾ cup light brown sugar, packed
½ teaspoon ground cinnamon
1 stick (½ cup) cold butter or margarine (not spread), cut into small pieces
½ cup walnuts, chopped
Whipped cream or ice cream for garnish

Filling:

3 tablespoons granulated sugar	3½ pounds Granny Smith apples (6 to 7 large), peeled,
3 tablespoons fresh lemon juice	cored, and cut in ½-inch-thick wedges (10 cups)

1. Preheat the oven to 400 degrees. Have a 13-by-9-inch baking dish ready.
2. Put topping ingredients, except garnish, into a medium bowl. Rub together with your fingers or stir with a fork until the mixture resembles coarse crumbs.
3. Put filling ingredients into a baking dish, stir to mix well, and spread evenly.
4. Sprinkle with topping.
5. Bake 35 to 40 minutes until fruit is tender and topping is crisp and lightly browned.
6. Top with whipped cream or a scoop of ice cream.

Food Service and Decorative Touches

- Serve food in old-fashioned lunch pails, kid's lunch boxes, cafeteria trays, and regular, clean pails. Add thermos jugs for decor, or fill them with beverages.
- Set up saw horses and planks for serving stations.
- Serve sandwiches in brown lunch bags.
- Print seating assignments or place cards on the backs of time cards.
- Display carpenter, plumber, auto mechanic, architect, or other tradesmen tools, such as paintbrushes, spatulas, wrenches, and so on.
- Decorate tables and room with work-related hats: hard hats, medical caps and masks, sports head gear, and hats worn by police officers, firefighters, and railroad engineers.
- Make flowers from want ads and occupation-related paper, such as legal pads, blueprint paper, computer paper, and wallpaper, to use in centerpieces or as napkin holders. (See How-To's #13.)

COLUMBUS DAY

No other day calls out more loudly for an Italian feast than October 12, the day commemorating the 1492 discovery of the New World by Christopher Columbus. Throw a festive party for America's first visitor by laying out a molto bene selection of Italian favorites, with a few new discoveries to boot.

Party Menu

Snacks
*Grilled Antipasto Sandwiches
Veggie Tray with Dip
Parmesan Cheese Toast

Beverages
Soft Drinks/Mineral Waters
*Café Vino
Italian Beer
Coffees/Teas

Buffet
Italian Pasta Bar (variety of pasta with choice of sauce)
*Italian Meatballs
Green Salad with Italian Dressing
Italian Breads and Rolls

Dessert
*La Dolce Vita Gelato
Italian Sugar Cookies

Grilled Antipasto Sandwiches
Makes: 12 sandwiches

8 slices sandwich pepperoni
8 slices capacola ham
8 slices cooked salami
4 slices provolone cheese

Lettuce pieces and tomato slices
Chopped pepperoncini (optional)
Soft-crusted sandwich roll (12-inch or more), sliced in half

1. Lightly grill meat slices and layer them on the bottom half of the sandwich roll.
2. Add provolone cheese to the griddle until it melts slightly. Place on top of the meat.
3. Add lettuce, tomato, and pepperoncini.
4. Cover the roll with the top half.
5. Cut the sandwich into 12 1-inch sections.
6. Use 12 toothpicks to hold sandwiches together.

Café Vino
Makes: 1 serving

1 cup cold strong coffee
2 tablespoons sugar
Dash of cinnamon

2 ounces tawny port or muscatel wine
½ teaspoon orange peel, grated

1. Whip all ingredients in a blender at high speed until foamy
2. Pour into chilled wine glasses.

Italian Meatballs

Makes: 30 meatballs

1 pound lean ground meat	*½ cup onion, chopped*
1 cup fresh bread crumbs	*½ cup green bell pepper, chopped*
6 ounces Italian sausage or	*1 egg, beaten*
spicy bulk sausage	*1 small can Italian tomato sauce*

1. In a large bowl, combine all ingredients; mix well.
2. Shape the mixture into 1-inch balls and oven-fry. (See page 229 for oven-frying directions.)

La Dolce Vita Gelato

Makes: 4 servings

1 cup water	*4 kiwi, peeled*
½ cup sugar	*5 tablespoons lemon juice*
½ cup light corn syrup	*¼ teaspoon lemon peel, grated*

1. In a saucepan, combine water, sugar, and corn syrup; cook and stir for 2 minutes until sugar dissolves.
2. Purée kiwi in a food processor or blender to make ¾ cup purée.
3. Add lemon juice, peel, and the sugar mixture.
4. Pour into a shallow pan and freeze for 1 hour or until the mixture is firm, but not solid.
5. Spoon the mixture into a chilled bowl and beat with an electric mixer until light and fluffy.
6. Return the mixture to the freezer for approximately 2 hours or until firm enough to scoop into individual dessert dishes.
7. Serve with Italian cookies.

Food Service and Decorative Touches

- Cover tables with "ocean" blue fabric or plastic tablecloths.
- Make place mats out of paper maps.
- Use toy ships or models as part of table decorations.
- Integrate old history text books from a thrift store into the decor.
- Glue small novelty compasses onto ponytail holders to make napkin holders.
- Search through magazines and old books for pages relating to Columbus and his explorations. Frame or mat the pages and use them in your decor.
- Write captions for the food, such as "Explore the Entrée," "Discover the Dessert," "$14.92, All You Can Eat," "Chris's Coffee Cart," and so on, and stand them near food items.
- Add a royal touch to the buffet table with a treasure chest overflowing with jewels, furs, velvets, and tapestries. Label these riches "Isabella's Investment."
- Include small globes, compasses, and telescopes in your table centerpieces.

HALLOWEEN

For a few decades, spookies and ghosties of all ages have been coming out to celebrate Halloween. Parties are planned for adults only, whole families, organization members, and just for kids. Common highlights of all gatherings are delicious and "devilishious" foods and beverages, all served in creative ways to keep guests goblin' and guzzlin'.

Party Menu

Snacks
*Roasted Pumpkin Seeds
*Pizza Pinkies
Apples for Bobbing
Fresh Vegetable Sticks
Dips Served in Small Pumpkins

Beverages
Soft Drinks/Mineral Waters
*Plasma Punch
Wine/Beer

Buffet
Franks & Steins (of beer)
Ghoul-ash
Chillin' Chili
Cole Slaw-ter

Dessert
*Beetle Bugs
*Frozen Jack-o'-Lanterns
*Wiggly Woogly Worms
Kookie Cookie Shapes

Roasted Pumpkin Seeds
Makes: 2 cups

2 tablespoons dried rosemary
2 cups fresh pumpkin seeds
2 tablespoons olive oil
Salt, to taste

1. Preheat the oven to 350 degrees.
2. Grind rosemary in a spice or coffee grinder.
3. Combine ground rosemary with remaining ingredients in a bowl; mix well and spread the coated pumpkin seeds on a baking sheet.
4. Bake 10 to 12 minutes, or until the seeds are crisp and brown.

Pizza Pinkies
Makes: 8 servings

1 red bell pepper
12 sticks (1-ounce each) mozzarella cheese
8 small (5-inch) baked pizza crusts
1 cup pizza sauce

1. Preheat the oven to 450 degrees.
2. Core, clean, and cut pepper into ½-inch-wide strips—for fingernails.
3. Cut cheese sticks in half crosswise. On the rounded edge, cut a ½-inch notch for a fingernail.
4. Lay crusts on 3 12-by-15-inch baking sheets.
5. Spread 2 tablespoons of pizza sauce on each crust.
6. Lay three cheese fingers on each crust, leaving space between each finger; fit a red-pepper nail onto each finger.
7. Bake until cheese begins to melt, about 8 minutes.

Plasma Punch

Makes: 60 4-ounce servings

40 ounces frozen strawberries, slightly thawed
1 12-ounce can frozen cranberry juice concentrate, thawed
1 12-ounce can frozen raspberry juice concentrate, thawed
1 quart strawberry frozen yogurt
2 pints raspberry sorbet
2 liters cold sparkling mineral water
2 liters cold ginger ale

1. In a blender or food processor, smoothly purée half the slightly thawed strawberries with cranberry concentrate. Pour the purée into a large punch bowl or serving container.
2. Repeat with remaining berries and raspberry concentrate; mix well.
3. Scoop yogurt and sorbet into the punch bowl. (If you like, scoop the yogurt and sorbet ahead of time and freeze the scoops on a cookie sheet.)
4. Add mineral water and ginger ale. Serve.

Beetle Bugs

Makes: about 24 bars

1 cup semisweet chocolate chips
1 cup butterscotch chips
2 cups chow mein noodles
½ cup peanuts
2 cups miniature marshmallows
Miniature chocolate candies

1. Cook chocolate and butterscotch chips in a medium microwave-safe bowl on high for 2 to 3 minutes, or until the mixture is smooth.
2. Add noodles and peanuts, mix lightly.
3. Add marshmallows, stirring until completely melted.
4. Drop the mixture by teaspoonfuls onto a tray lined with wax paper
5. Poke additional noodles into the sides to form legs.
6. Make eyes with chocolate candies.
7. Store the bugs at room temperature until ready to serve

Frozen Jack-o'-Lanterns

Makes: 12 servings

12 large oranges
½ gallon dark chocolate ice cream
12 cinnamon sticks

1. Cut off tops of oranges; put aside to use in Step 4. Gently scoop out the center of each orange from top to bottom, leaving a thick shell.
2. Cut or draw jack-o'-lantern faces on each orange.
3. Pack chocolate ice cream into the shells.
4. Cut a hole large enough to insert a cinnamon stick in each orange top.
5. Set tops back on the ice-cream-filled oranges, and insert a cinnamon stick through each hole.
6. Place the oranges in the freezer for at least 3 hours.

Wiggly Woogly Worms

Makes: 100 worms

1 6-ounce package raspberry or
  grape gelatin
3 envelopes unflavored gelatin
3 cups boiling water

100 flexible plastic straws
1 tall 4-cup container (milk or juice carton)
¾ cup whipping cream
12 to 15 drops green food coloring

1. In a bowl, combine raspberry and unflavored gelatins with boiling water and stir until the gelatin dissolves. Chill about 20 minutes.
2. Straighten the straws and place them into a tall container.
3. Blend whipping cream and food coloring with the gelatin mixture.
4. Pour the gelatin/cream mixture into the tall container, making sure to fill all the straws.
5. Chill until firm (8 hours to 2 days).
6. Pull the filled straws from the container (if using a carton, peel away the sides) and separate them. Run hot tap water over 3 to 4 straws at a time for about 2 seconds.
7. Squeeze the gelatin from the straws onto wax-paper-lined cookie sheets. Cover and chill until ready to serve (1 hour to 2 days). The worms will hold their shape at room temperature for 2 hours.
8. Serve the worms on a bed of crushed chocolate cookies (or see Food Service, below, for other serving suggestions).

Food Service and Decorative Touches

- Serve dips and sauces in small pumpkins, and hot soups, drinks, or chili in larger pumpkins.
- Drape Wiggly Woogly Worms in, out, and over a plastic skull sitting on top of crushed chocolate cookie "dirt."
- Follow traditional black and orange decor, or improvise with your favorite colors.
- Dye sheets and pillowcases black or gray for muddy, murky, morbid table covers.
- Create centerpieces by scrunching brown paper bags and filling them with dead flowers and leaves.
- Serve punch in a black cast-iron kettle with fake cobwebs draped on the handle.
- Poke candles into apples for table lights. (See How-To's #24.)
- Fill small burlap bags with penny candy and set a bag at each place.
- Tie raffia or dried vines around napkins.
- Create centerpieces to salute monsters, witches, and ghosts: Frankenstein, Dracula, Wolfman, Casper, Wicked Witch of the West. Assign seating with monster-appropriate buttons, masks, or goodie bags.

THANKSGIVING

I've learned the hard way that changing or omitting traditional Thanksgiving foods can cause dinner guests to riot. Family and friends show up expecting their favorite foods, fixed their favorite way. Any and all potluck entries must follow tradition. This section includes ideas and suggestions for slight, safe-to-serve twists on the traditional fare. If you are serving your first Thanksgiving feast, why not start your own traditions with a meal that expresses your creativity and personality? (The following recipes are from a fantastic Web site created by Wendy Zientek. See Resources.)

Party Menu

Snacks
*Wen's Snack Mix
Cheese Ball with Crackers
Vegetable Platter

Beverages
Soft Drinks/Mineral Waters
Wines/Beers
*Hot Cranberry Tea Punch (page 223)
Coffees/Teas

Dinner
Turkey (naturally)
*Sweet Potato, Pear, and Sausage Stuffing
Mashed Sweet and White Potatoes
Cranberry Sauce
Assorted Vegetables
Gelatin Salads
Muffins, Breads

Dessert
*Cran-Apple Sweet Potato Crisp
*Baby Pumpkin Sundaes

Wen's Snack Mix

(This recipe is a bit different than most snack mixes. It is very tasty and combines a few of my favorite things. The cranberries are optional, since they are a bit of an acquired taste.)

Makes: about 12 cups

8 cups popped popcorn
2 cups mixed nuts, roasted
¼ cup butter, melted

¼ cup Parmesan cheese, freshly grated
½ teaspoon garlic powder
1 cup dried cranberries

1. Preheat the oven to 325 degrees.
2. In a large bowl, mix popcorn and nuts.
3. In a small bowl, mix butter, Parmesan cheese, and garlic powder.
4. Toss the butter with the popcorn; spread the mixture in a large baking pan.
5. Bake for 10 minutes, stir, and bake for 5 minutes more.
6. Stir in the cranberries and spread on wax paper to cool; or serve hot.

Sweet Potato, Pear, and Sausage Stuffing

(The benefit to this stuffing is that it can be made ahead and refrigerated. Make sure the stuffing is at room temperature before stuffing the turkey or baking alone.)

Makes: enough stuffing for a large turkey, plus a little extra

1 tablespoon olive oil
2 pounds turkey sausage
1 onion, chopped
4 stalks celery and leaves, chopped
4 cups day-old bread, cubed
6 large sweet potatoes, peeled,
  cooked, and mashed

1 cup mushrooms, chopped
4 large pears, coarsely chopped
Salt and black pepper, to taste
1 teaspoon nutmeg
1 teaspoon thyme

1. Heat olive oil in a medium frying pan, add sausage, and sauté until the sausage is browned.
2. Remove the sausage and add chopped onion and celery to the pan; sauté until the onion is soft.
3. In a large bowl, combine all the ingredients; mix well.
4. Stuff the turkey and bake according to label instructions. Put the remaining stuffing into a greased casserole and bake alongside the turkey for 1 hour.

Cran-Apple Sweet Potato Crisp

(Wow, what a mouthful! This was a daring experiment that came out exceedingly well. Although unusual, this dish is full of your favorite Thanksgiving flavors. Serve as a side dish or a dessert.)

Makes: 12 servings

4 sweet potatoes, peeled
  and thinly sliced
3 medium, tart baking apples,
  peeled and thinly sliced
½ cup brown sugar

1 cup cranberries, chopped
1 teaspoon cinnamon
1 teaspoon nutmeg, freshly grated
¼ cup butter, softened
1 cup uncooked oats

1. Preheat the oven to 350 degrees.
2. Layer sweet potatoes and apples in a medium casserole, alternating layers. Lightly sprinkle each layer with brown sugar.
3. When you have used half the sweet potatoes and apples, make a layer of cranberries and liberally sprinkle with brown sugar. (Be sure to leave a little sugar to use in Step 5.)
4. Continue to layer the sweet potatoes and apples until you use them all.
5. In a small bowl, combine leftover brown sugar, cinnamon, nutmeg, butter, and oats. Stir the mixture with your fingers until it resembles coarse crumbs.
6. Press the crumb mixture over the layered sweet potatoes and apples.
7. Bake for 40 to 45 minutes or until the potatoes and apples are tender.

Baby Pumpkin Sundaes

(This recipe was sent by Maxine Baird, *Balloons N FunTimes Newspaper*. See Credits.)

Makes: 6 to 8 servings

1½ quarts reduced-fat vanilla ice cream
  or frozen yogurt, softened
1 16-ounce can pumpkin
1 tablespoon pumpkin pie spice
¾ cup caramel topping

6 to 8 miniature pumpkins, hollowed
2 tablespoons rum (optional)
6 to 8 large pieces peanut brittle
½ cup peanut brittle, crushed

1. Mix ice cream or frozen yogurt, pumpkin, pumpkin pie spice, and 4 to 6 tablespoons caramel topping, to taste.
2. Spoon equal portions of ice cream mixture into hollowed miniature pumpkins.
3. Mix ½ cup caramel topping with rum; spoon over ice cream.
4. Cover the filled pumpkins and freeze until firm (at least 2 hours or overnight).
5. Remove the sundaes from the freezer 15 to 20 minutes before serving.
6. Garnish each pumpkin sundae with a large piece of peanut brittle, and sprinkle crushed peanut brittle on top.

Food Service and Decorative Touches

- Decorate your table and room with the natural and inexpensive look of fresh fruits, vegetables, herbs, plants, and flowers from the market or your yard.
- Hollow out miniature pumpkins and squashes to make serving bowls and containers for cranberry sauces, relishes, dips, individual soups or desserts, even small fresh flower arrangements. To make the container sit flat, cut a piece off the bottom, making sure not to cut all the way through. (You can also attach the pumpkin containers to the table with florist's gum. However, in this case, they would be difficult to pass around the table.)
- Tie bunches of herbs and wild fresh flowers together with string to make a garland. Drape the garland along the table, wall, or mantel.
- Tie sprigs of autumn wheat or herbs to the napkins with straw or paper ribbons.
- Collect, rinse, and pat dry an assortment of colorful autumn leaves. Place them between tissue paper, pile heavy books on top, and leave them in a warm room for a week. This will ensure that the leaves dry flat. Once dried, scatter the leaves on your buffet table before setting down the serving dishes.
- Use very large pressed leaves (see previous bullet) as liners on serving plates or under stemmed glasses.
- Press cranberries or wild flowers into an ice mold for wine coolers.
- Fill a traditional cornucopia (basket weave, ceramic, or glass) with gourds, fruit, vegetables, and berries to use as a table centerpiece.
- Trim festive ribbons with berries or flowers, tie them around fresh bread loaves, and place the loaves on the buffet or dining tables.
- Place fresh fruits, gourds, vegetables, and berry branches on a table runner down the center of a long banquet table.
- Use cookies cut in Thanksgiving shapes as place cards. (See How-To's #6.)
- Glue small Thanksgiving favors to ponytail holders and use as napkin rings.
- Place a "Magic Slate" at each place for a "What I am thankful for" reading. (See How-To's #5.)

HANUKKAH

Over 2,000 years ago, the Jews reclaimed their Temple from the Greeks. When they attempted to light the sacred flame, they discovered that only a day's-worth of holy oil remained. They lit the oil anyway, and, miraculously, the oil burned for eight days—the amount of time needed to procure more oil. Hanukkah—the Festival of Lights—is celebrated for eight days, to commemorate the Jewish victory, the rededication of the Temple, and the miracle of light. Candles are lit during each of the eight days, and most of the food served during Hanukkah is cooked, appropriately, in oil. When gathering your guests for a Hanukkah party, blend expected old favorites with some delightful new taste treats.

Party Menu

Snacks
*Sweet and Sour Corned Beef Rounds
Pickled Herring

Beverages
Soft Drinks/Mineral Waters
Seltzer Water
Hebrew Grape Wine
Coffee/Teas

Buffet
*Lotta Latkes
Baked Brisket with Vegetables
Sweet and Sour Cucumber Salad

Dessert
*Sufganiyot (Doughnuts)
*Cheese-Filled Sufganiyot
*Chocolate Mousse
Macaroons

Sweet and Sour Corned Beef Rounds
Makes: as much as you want

Corned beef   Mustard
Cocktail bread rounds   Orange marmalade

1. Cook corned beef as directed; slice into thin slices.
2. Pile corned beef slices on cocktail rounds.
3. Mix mustard and orange marmalade and drizzle the sauce over the corned beef.

Lotta Latkes
Makes: about 15 latkes (4 to 5 servings)

4 large potatoes, peeled   ¼ teaspoon ground white pepper
1 medium onion   2 tablespoons flour
1 large egg, beaten   ½ cup vegetable oil for frying
1 teaspoon salt

1. Grate potatoes and onion, either by hand or in a food processor.
2. Place the grated potatoes and onion in a colander and press out as much liquid as you can.
3. In a large mixing bowl, combine grated potatoes and onion with the beaten egg, salt, pepper, and flour.

4. Heat vegetable oil in a deep, heavy skillet.
5. For each latke, drop 2 tablespoons of batter into the hot oil.
6. Flatten the latke with a spatula and fry over medium heat about 4 to 5 minutes on each side, until golden brown and crisp.
7. Remove the cooked latkes with a spatula and lay out on paper towels to drain.
8. Serve hot with traditional toppings of apple sauce and sour cream, or try any or all of the topping listed below.

Variations: To vary the standard latke recipe, add chopped spinach, grated zucchini, carrots, pumpkin, and/or sweet potato to the batter.

Toppings: Apple/Cranberry Sauce
Apple-Pear Sauce
Dill Sour Cream
Herb Yogurt

Tip: You can make latkes ahead of time and either refrigerate them or freeze them individually on a cookie sheet. When needed, thaw the frozen latkes briefly and reheat them in a 450-degree oven.

Sufganiyot (Doughnuts)

Makes: 24 to 30 doughnuts

2 pounds sifted flour (maybe a little more)	½ cup oil
½ teaspoon salt	Approximately 2 cups warm water
4 tablespoons sugar	2 eggs, beaten
50 grams fresh yeast	Vegetable oil for frying
10 grams vanilla sugar	Jam for filling, any flavor
	Powdered sugar for garnish

1. Mix 2 cups flour in a bowl with salt, sugar, yeast, and vanilla sugar.
2. Add oil and water and mix until the mixture is smooth.
3. Add beaten eggs; mix again.
4. Add remaining flour, mixing until the dough is smooth and stretchy. Let rise until double in volume.
5. Knead the dough, then roll it out with a rolling pin; divide into 4 sections.
6. Roll out each section 1-inch thick and cut out circles with a cup; let rise for 1 hour.
7. Deep-fry in vegetable oil until golden brown. Drain on paper towels.
8. Inject jam, and dust lightly with powdered sugar. (Use a bakery filling "shooter" to fill the sufganiyot, or improvise with a turkey baster or a paper pastry bag.)

Cheese-Filled Sufganiyot

Make doughnuts according to the sufganiyot recipe above. Fill with one of the following mixtures:

Sweet Filling

1 cup drained cottage or farmer's cheese	2 tablespoons sugar
1 pasteurized egg	1 teaspoon vanilla

Mix all the ingredients together and inject into the doughnuts

Savory Filling

1 cup drained cottage or farmer's cheese

1 pasteurized egg

2 tablespoons salt

Dash of pepper, oregano, and parsley flakes

Mix all the ingredients together and inject into the doughnuts.

Chocolate Mousse

Makes: 7 to 8 4-ounce servings

4 ounces chocolate (milk, semisweet, or sweet)

4 eggs, separated

1 cup margarine

Whipped topping

1. Melt chocolate in a microwave.
2. Add egg yolks and margarine.
3. Place the mixture in a double boiler and cook over rapidly boiling water, stirring until mixture thickens. Set aside to cool.
4. Beat egg whites until stiff. Fold into cooled chocolate mixture.
5. Pile the mousse into small serving dishes and refrigerate.
6. Top with whipped cream immediately before serving.

Food Service and Decorative Touches

- Decorate the tables with menorahs (nine-candle candleholders) and dreidels (a spinning toy traditionally played during Hanukkah).
- Use blue, white, and silver linens, accessories, and serving ware.
- Prominently display the Star of David in all Hanukkah decorations. Plastic and paper products are readily available with this design.
- Wrap gifts in Hanukkah gift-wrap and use groups of eight as decorative table centerpieces.
- Light the table with small oil lamps.
- Tie gold cords around napkins and glue a toy or gold chocolate coin to the knot

CHRISTMAS OPEN HOUSE

The holiday season is filled with opportunities to gather family, friends, and associates. Whereas family dinners tend to include the same traditional food and beverage favorites year after year, open houses or other social events are more flexible. Most often, the refreshments are a cooperative effort, each guest contributing his or her specialty. Books, magazines, newspapers, television programs, and, now, the Internet offer thousands of recipes and serving ideas, so the menu and recipes below are simply meant to act as spark plugs to get your menu-planning motors chugging along the holiday highway.

Party Menu

Snacks
*Praline Pecan Crunch
*Easy Veggie Pizza Squares
*I'm Dreaming of White Pizza Squares
Baked Brie and Crackers (page 32)
Stuffed Mushrooms (page 137)
Chips and Dips

Beverages
Soft Drinks/Mineral Waters
*Clarence Oddbody's Heavenly Hot Wine
Eggnog/Tom and Jerrys
Cocktails/Wines/Punches
Coffees/Teas

Dessert
*Holiday Spirits Eggnog Cheesecake
*Easy Fruity Tarts
Traditional Cookies and Bars
Nut Bread
Fruit Cake
Candies and Nuts
Fresh Fruit

Praline Pecan Crunch
Makes: 10 cups

8 cups Quaker Oats Squares cereal
2 cups pecan pieces
½ cup light corn syrup
½ cup brown sugar, firmly packed
¼ cup margarine (½ stick)
1 teaspoon vanilla
½ teaspoon baking soda

1. Preheat the oven to 250 degrees.
2. Combine cereal and pecans in a 13-by-9-inch pan; set aside.
3. Combine corn syrup, brown sugar, and margarine in a microwave-safe bowl. Microwave on high 1½ minutes; stir.
4. Microwave on high ½ to 1½ minutes more, or until the mixture boils.
5. Add vanilla and baking soda, mix well, and pour over the cereal mixture.
6. Stir until the cereal is evenly coated.
7. Bake 1 hour, stirring every 20 minutes. Spread on a baking sheet to cool; break into pieces.

Easy Veggie Pizza Squares

Makes: 48 to 60 pieces

2 8-ounce cans Pillsbury Crescent Dinner Roll dough
8 ounces cream cheese, softened
1 teaspoon dried dill weed
⅛ teaspoon garlic powder
Sliced and chopped green and red veggies (tomatoes, broccoli, green/red bell peppers, scallions,
   red onions, pimento bits, and so on)

1. Preheat the oven to 375 degrees.
2. Press dinner roll dough into an ungreased 15-by-10-by-1-inch baking pan to form
   a crust.
3. Bake for 13 to 17 minutes or until golden brown. Cool completely.
4. Combine softened cream cheese, dill weed, and garlic powder; spread over the
   cooled crust.
5. Cover the pan and refrigerate for 1 hour.
6. Top the cream cheese spread with chopped fresh vegetables.
7. Cut the pizza into small squares; serve cold.

I'm Dreaming of White Pizza Squares

(From Cathy Sachs, Minneapolis, Minnesota.)

Makes: 48 2-inch pieces

4 cups assorted toppings: chicken chunks,
   small shrimp, chopped onions and green
   peppers, sliced mushrooms, bulk Italian sausage
Garlic oil for frying
1 stick butter or margarine
Garlic cloves, crushed, to taste
½ cup cream

1 cup grated Parmesan cheese
Salt and pepper, to taste
2 teaspoons corn starch
¼ cup water
2 Pillsbury frozen pie crusts
5 pounds mozzarella cheese, shredded

1. Sauté all the toppings in garlic oil.
2. Melt butter in a saucepan and add crushed garlic to taste; add cream and
   Parmesan cheese. Season to taste with salt and pepper.
3. In a cup, mix cornstarch with water until diluted.
4. Slowly add the cornstarch mixture to the cream and cheese mixture; cook for a
   few minutes, stirring constantly, until the sauce is thick enough to hold together
   on the crust.
5. Preheat the oven to 350 degrees.
6. Press out the pie crust dough on large pizza or cookie sheets; pinch edges upward
   to hold the sauce.
7. Spread enough sauce to cover the crusts. Then add a ½-inch layer of shredded
   mozzarella cheese and sprinkle with sautéed toppings.
8. Cover the toppings with the remaining sauce and shredded mozzarella cheese.
9. Bake the pizzas for about 45 to 60 minutes or until the cheese on top is brown.
10. Cut the pizzas into 2-inch squares to serve as appetizers, or cut them into larger
    pieces to serve as entrées with salad.

Clarence Oddbody's Heavenly Hot Wine

(From *It's a Wonderful Life Cookbook*. See Credits.)

Makes: 8 to 10 servings

5 cups burgundy wine
10 whole cloves
5 cups fresh apple cider
1 pinch allspice

½ cup dark brown sugar
3 cinnamon sticks
Orange slices for garnish

1. In a large saucepan, combine all ingredients except orange slices.
2. Heat to desired temperature, stirring occasionally.
3. Remove the cinnamon sticks and pour wine into mugs.
4. Garnish with orange slices.

Holiday Spirits Eggnog Cheesecake

Makes: 10 servings

1 cup graham cracker crumbs
¼ cup sugar
¼ teaspoon ground nutmeg
¼ cup margarine, melted
1 envelope unflavored gelatin

¼ cup cold water
8 ounces cream cheese, softened
¼ cup sugar
1 cup eggnog
1 cup whipping cream, whipped

1. Combine crumbs, sugar, nutmeg, and margarine; press into the bottom of a 9-inch springform pan.
2. In a saucepan, soften gelatin in water; stir over low heat until dissolved.
3. Combine cream cheese and sugar and beat on medium speed with an electric mixer until well blended.
4. Gradually add the gelatin mixture and the eggnog to the cream cheese mixture, mixing until blended.
5. Chill until slightly thickened; fold in whipped cream.
6. Pour the filling over the crust; chill until firm.

Easy Fruity Tarts

Makes: as many as you like

Prebaked tartlet shells
Lemon curd

Fresh strawberries, sliced
Mint leaves for garnish

1. Fill prebaked tartlet shells with lemon curd.
2. Top with sliced strawberries.
3. Garnish with mint leaves 1 hour before serving.

Holiday Party Serving Tips

- Set bottles of alcohol on your beverage table. Guests can "spike" their hot or cold drinks.
- Plan one bottle of champagne per three people at champagne/coffee/dessert parties.
- Gelatin shooters are very popular. Prepare Jell-O in any flavor, and replace the required cold water with vodka, tequila, or rum. Pour into small plastic cups, such as those used to dispense pills. Add festive toothpicks to Jell-O cups so guests can stir and slurp! (See Gelatin Shooters, page 218.)

Food Service and Decorative Touches

- Poke peppermint sticks through lemon slices and float them in the punch bowl.
- Freeze green limeade in ice trays, with a red maraschino cherry in the middle of each ice cube.
- Tie a string of battery-operated twinkle lights around an elegantly wrapped package and make a bow on top. Set the package on a mirror tile for a dramatic centerpiece. (See How-To's #9.)
- Float candles in bowls half-filled with water. (See How-To's #22.)
- Recycle various light bulbs by spray-painting them gold, silver, white, or any favorite color. Apply a thin layer of glue, and dust with glitter. Tuck the bulbs into evergreens for a festive arrangement.
- Make table and chair covers from white sheets and pillowcases, respectively. Tie corners with gold or silver braid or tassels.
- Make exquisite table centerpieces by spraying grapevine with white paint and dusting it with glitter. Tie and trim the arrangements with white tulle. The snow-white sparkle effect is incredible. Lay these arrangements on mirror tiles down the middle of a long banquet table.
- Group mismatched thrift-store stem glasses as votive- or taper-candle holders. Tie decorative ribbons around stems.
- Light the way to your party with frozen luminaria lights. (See How-To's #21.)

Holiday Themes

Add a theme to your holiday festivities. Your home or work open house, employee party, client appreciation, neighborhood get-together, fundraiser, or school function will sparkle when you plan it around a twist or a theme. Consider one of the following theme ideas to put a sparkle into your celebration:

Caribbean Christmas	Hollywood Holiday
Christmas Carnival	International Holiday
Christmas Cruise	Tour of Lights
Handicrafter's Holiday	Toyland Tea Party
Hawaiian Holiday	Viva La Holiday
Holiday Hoedown	Winter Wonderland

KWANZAA

Dr. Maulana Kareng created this African-American seven-day holiday in the United States in 1966. Kwanzaa, celebrated from December 26 to January 1, allows Americans of African ancestry to reflect upon and discuss their heritage, their good fortune over the past year, and their prospects for the coming year. The word *Kwanzaa* is Swahili, meaning "first fruits of the harvest." Based upon seven principles, the holiday encourages the creation and continuation of family traditions. The menu for a Kwanzaa party consists of authentic African dishes, as well as modern favorites, blending history with present day.

Party Menu

Snacks
*African Tomato-Avocado-Buttermilk
Soup
*Sweet Potato Chips

Beverages
Soft Drinks/Mineral Waters
Fruit Juices
Herb Teas

Buffet
*First Fruits of the Harvest Bowl
*Nigerian Groundnut Stew
*African Spinach and Green Pepper
Baked Sweet Potatoes
Hot Corn Bread

Dessert
*Benne Cakes

African Tomato-Avocado-Buttermilk Soup
Makes: 6 to 8 5-ounce servings

3 pounds tomatoes, peeled and seeded
2 tablespoons tomato paste
1 cup buttermilk
1 tablespoon olive oil
1 avocado, mashed to a purée
Juice of 1 lemon

2 tablespoons fresh parsley, finely minced
Salt and pepper, to taste
Hot pepper sauce, to taste
1 cucumber, peeled, seeded, and diced,
    for garnish
Sour cream for garnish

1. Purée tomatoes in a food processor or food mill, then press through a sieve to remove seeds.
2. In a large mixing bowl, beat the puréed tomatoes, tomato paste, buttermilk, and oil.
3. Toss mashed avocado with 1 tablespoon lemon juice to prevent the avocado from browning.
4. Add the avocado, remaining lemon juice, and parsley to the tomato mixture; stir to mix well.
5. Add salt, pepper, and hot pepper sauce to taste.
6. Refrigerate for several hours before serving.
7. Ladle the chilled soup into individual bowls; put out cucumber, sour cream, and hot pepper sauce for garnish.

Sweet Potato Chips

Makes: 4 to 6 servings

2 medium sweet potatoes
2 tablespoons olive oil
Salt, pepper, and paprika, to taste

1. Preheat the oven to 450 degrees.
2. Peel and thinly slice sweet potatoes.
3. Toss with olive oil.
4. Place the sweet potatoes on a cookie sheet in a thin layer.
5. Sprinkle with salt, pepper, and paprika to taste.
6. Bake about 20 minutes or until crispy.

First Fruits of the Harvest Bowl

(The following two recipes are from the family collection shared by Michelle of Oregon, via the Internet.)

Makes: as much as you like

Blood oranges   *Kiwi*
Chopped cranberries   *Black sesame seeds*
Star fruit   *Brown sugar*

1. Peel, cut, and toss the fresh fruit pieces together; spoon into fruit cups
2. Sprinkle the fruit with sesame seeds and brown sugar.

Nigerian Groundnut Stew

Makes: 8 servings

2 pounds boneless stewing lamb   *3 chili peppers, seeded*
3 large onions, sliced   *1 cup peanut butter*
Salt   *2 cups lamb soup stock*
3½ cups water   *4 cups cooked rice*
3 large tomatoes, quartered   *Hard-boiled eggs, shelled (1 per serving)*

1. In a large saucepan, combine lamb, onions, and salt with 3 cups water; bring to a boil, cover, and simmer for 1 hour or until tender. Let cool.
2. In another saucepan, combine tomatoes, chili peppers, and ½ cup water; bring to a boil, cover, and simmer for 8 to 10 minutes.
3. While the tomato mixture is simmering, shred the cooked, cooled lamb into a large saucepan; set aside.
4. Press the tomato mixture through a sieve. (You can also use a food processor, but the sieve yields a better result.)
5. Mix peanut butter, tomato mixture, and soup stock; add to the shredded meat.
6. Simmer 30 to 45 minutes, stirring occasionally.
7. To serve, fill bowls ½-full with cooked rice, nestle a peeled hard-boiled egg in the middle of each bowl, and ladle stew on top.

African Spinach and Green Pepper

Makes: about 6 servings

1 medium onion, chopped
1 medium green pepper, chopped
1 tablespoon oil
1 medium tomato, chopped

1 pound fresh spinach, stems removed
¾ teaspoon salt
⅛ teaspoon pepper
¼ cup peanut butter

1. In a 3-quart saucepan, cook chopped onion and green pepper in oil until the onion is tender, about 5 minutes.
2. Add chopped tomato and spinach. Cover and simmer until the spinach is tender, about 5 minutes.
3. Stir in salt, pepper, and peanut butter. Heat just until hot; serve.

Benne Cakes

Makes: about 32 cakes

1 cup brown sugar, packed
¼ cup butter or margarine, softened
1 egg, beaten
½ teaspoon vanilla extract
1 teaspoon freshly squeezed lemon juice

½ cup all-purpose flour
½ teaspoon baking powder
¼ teaspoon salt
1 cup toasted sesame seeds

1. Preheat the oven to 325 degrees.
2. Cream brown sugar and butter.
3. Stir in egg, vanilla extract, and lemon juice.
4. Add flour, baking powder, salt, and sesame seeds.
5. Drop the batter by rounded teaspoons onto a lightly oiled cookie sheet, 2 inches apart.
6. Bake for 15 minutes or until the edges are lightly browned.

Food Service and Decorative Touches

- Use linens, serving ware, and accessories in red, black, and green—traditional colors of Kwanzaa.
- Set out lights and candles. The *kinara,* a candleholder containing seven candles, is lighted on each of the seven nights of Kwanzaa. The kinara has three red candles on the left, a black candle in the middle, and three green candles on the right.
- Gather and arrange Kwanzaa symbols as follows:
    1. Spread the *mkeka* (straw mat).
    2. Place the kinara (candleholder) in the center of the mkeka.
    3. Place the *muhindi* (ears of corn) on either side of the mkeka. Use one ear of corn for each child in the family, or use one ear if there are no children.
    4. Creatively place the *zawadi* (gifts), *kikombe cha umoja* (unity cup), *tambiko* (water and soil), and a basket of mazao fruit on the mkeka.
    5. Place *mishumaa saba* (seven candles) in the kinara.
- Hang up a *bendera ya taifa* (flag of the Black Nation) facing the East.

NEW YEAR'S EVE

New Year's Eve is the biggest party night of the year. Every festivity, whether in a private home or a huge ballroom, will include the final countdown to midnight, hugs and kisses shared to the sounds of "Auld Lang Syne," raucous noisemakers, and shouted well wishes. According to tradition, as you meet the New Year, so will the rest of the year go. So, eat well, drink tasty beverages, and celebrate, celebrate, celebrate!

Party Menu

Snacks
Potluck, to include:
*Auld Lang Syne Cheesy Fruit and Nut Spread
Mini Meatballs
Mini Wienies in Barbecue Sauce
Mini Quiches
Snack Chex Mix
Spinach Dip in Sour Dough Bread
Cheese and Cracker Trays
Vegetables and Dips

Beverages
Soft Drinks/Mineral Waters
Punch (with and without alcohol)
*Bawdy Body Shots for Lovers (page 220)
Champagne (at midnight)
Coffees/Teas (for the road)

Midnight Breakfast Buffet
*Sausage and Egg Casserole (page 164)
*Over-the-Top Dairy Potato Bake
Fresh Fruit Trays
Sweet Rolls and Muffins

Dessert
*Start Your Diet Tomorrow Bars
Frozen Yogurt Sundaes

Auld Lang Syne Cheesy Fruit and Nut Spread
(From *It's a Wonderful Life Cookbook*. See Credits.)

Makes: 1½ cups

3 to 4 tablespoons honey
1 tablespoon apple schnapps or apple brandy
8 ounces cream cheese, softened
½ cup dried apple chunks, finely chopped
¼ cup toasted almonds, finely chopped
¼ cup sliced almonds
Whole-grain crackers, sliced apples or pears, and celery

1. Thoroughly blend honey, schnapps or brandy, and cream cheese
2. Stir in apples and chopped almonds.
3. Scatter the sliced almonds on top of the mixture, cover, and chill for 3 to 4 hours
4. Serve with whole-grain crackers, sliced apples or pears, and celery.

ONCE IN A BLUE MOON

Every 29.5 months, two full moons occur in the same calendar month. The second one is called "A Blue Moon." So once in a blue moon you have a perfectly lovely reason to gather for an evening of appetizers, drinks, and dessert while listening to the blues and a enjoying a little moon gazing. This party idea and menu was created, "out of the blue," by Kelly Ryan, Party Pro of Palm Desert, California.

Party Menu

Snacks
*Chicken Cordon Bleu Bites
*Brie and Blue Torte
Blue Tortilla Chips
Pick A Dip

Beverages
Soft Drinks/Mineral Waters
*Blue Moon Cocktail
*Blueberry Gelatin Shooters (page 210, #2)
Blue Nun Wine
Coffees/Teas

Dessert
Blueberry Cheesecake
Fresh Blueberries Topped with Sour
Cream and Brown Sugar

Chicken Cordon Bleu Bites

Makes: 16 pieces

4 whole chicken breasts, skinless
  and boneless
8 thin slices smoked ham
8 thin slices Swiss cheese
4 tablespoons flour
1 teaspoon salt

½ teaspoon pepper
½ teaspoon allspice
2 eggs, slightly beaten
1 cup dry bread crumbs
6 tablespoons oil
4 tablespoons water

1. Cut each breast in half.
2. Pound to ¼-inch thickness.
3. Place 1 slice of ham and 1 slice of cheese on each piece of chicken. Roll up carefully, beginning at the narrow end; secure with wooden picks.
4. Mix flour, salt, pepper, and allspice; coat each roll with the flour mixture
5. Dip rolls in beaten eggs, then roll them in bread crumbs.
6. In a skillet, heat oil, add the rolls, and cook until the rolls are brown.
7. Add water and heat to boiling. Reduce heat, cover, and simmer 45 minutes.
8. Remove the skillet from heat, cover, and let sit for 2 to 3 minutes to crisp.
9. Cut each roll into 4 pieces; spear with fancy toothpicks to serve.

Brie and Blue Torte

Makes: 8 to 10 servings

1 piece brie cheese (about ½ pound), creamy but not runny
½ pound soft blue cheese, such as cambozola or gorgonzola
Apple and pear wedges, sprinkled with lemon juice to slow browning
Thin baguette slices or water crackers

1. Cut brie in half horizontally. Place bottom half of the brie, cut side up, on a small platter.
2. Mash blue cheese with a fork to soften.
3. Spread the softened blue cheese evenly onto the cut side of the brie, making it level and flush with the brie sides.
4. Fit remaining piece of brie, cut side down, onto the blue cheese.
5. Serve at room temperature.
6. Slice through the cheeses and serve on apple or pear wedges and baguette slices or crackers.

Tip: To make this dish ahead, chill cheese in an airtight container for up to 4 days

Blue Moon Cocktail

(From *Smart Drinks: Alcohol-Free Natural Beverages*, by Bob Schweiers. See Credits.)

Makes: 1 serving

1 tablespoon alcohol-free Curaçao Blue   *3½ ounces milk*
1 scoop vanilla ice cream   *1 mint sprig for garnish*
1 tablespoon heavy cream

1. Put curaçao, ice cream, cream, and milk into a food processor; blend well.
2. Pour the shake into a champagne glass and garnish with mint.

Food Service and Decorative Touches

- Use table linens, serving ware, and accessories in blue, gold, and silver.
- Bottle homemade (or store-bought) blue cheese dressing in miniature blue glass bottles. Hang name tags around the bottle necks for place cards and favors.
- Hang a round, blue paper lantern for a blue moon.
- Wrap blue star garlands around blue tapers or fat candles.
- Illuminate the room with white luminaria bags with star and moon cutouts.
- Replace all light bulbs with blue ones!
- For casual events, use paper and plastic serving ware with moon and stars theme

Part Two
PARTY THEMES

A party planned with a theme has a built-in success factor—the common ground shared by the menu, decorations, and activities. Having a theme for your party is like having a road map. This map will govern the direction you take, the stops you make, and the sites you see on your party-planning trip. Your destination? A successful event, of course.

Many of the *Pick-A-Party Cookbook* themes will lead you to other parts of the country, and even of the world. In each, you and your guests can enjoy foods and beverages typical of that locale—all served in an appropriately designed setting.

Certain themes have proven popular for all kinds of parties, both personal and business. The themes topping the list include Casino, Cruise Ship, Magic, and Surfin' USA. The Popular Themes section in the table of contents lists the seventeen most popular themes.

"Yesterday is history, tomorrow is a mystery." This lovely saying is apt for the Yesterday and Tomorrow theme section. Drifting back to yesteryear seems to be extremely popular for those celebrating milestone occasions, and the idea of venturing into the future intrigues and appeals to many party goers. Time can fly in either direction with *Pick-A-Party Cookbook's* era themes.

Nothing compliments a guest of honor more than a party planned around his or her special interests, talents, or hobbies. Including sports activities, twenty-five such themes and their accompanying foods, beverages, and table decor are featured in the book.

And as a tribute to *inactivity, Pick-A-Party Cookbook* offers plans for couch potato events, such as watching the Academy Awards, Kentucky Derby, Final Four, and the Super Bowl.

ATLANTA/DEEP SOUTH

Transport your party guests back in time to Tara, the deep-south plantation home of Scarlett O'Hara. Create a splendid menu of Southern cuisine with victuals that are unusual enough to be intriguing, and yet familiar enough to be friendly.

Party Menu

Snacks	Buffet
*Southern Heat Pecans	Fried Chicken
	*Garlic Cheese Grits Casserole
Beverages	Biscuits and Gravy
Soft Drinks/Mineral Waters	Fruit Compote
*Mint Juleps (page 206)	
*Scarlett O'Hara Cocktail	**Dessert**
Southern Comfort Whiskey	*Butter Pecan Ice-Cream Pie
Iced Coffees/Iced Teas	Pralines

Southern Heat Pecans

Makes: about 2 tablespoons per serving

Salted pecans
Chili powder
Butter, melted

1. Preheat the oven to 400 degrees.
2. Sprinkle salted pecans with chili powder.
3. Drizzle the pecans with a little melted butter and place in the oven for about 2 minutes to heat.
4. Serve while pecans are still hot.

Scarlett O'Hara Cocktail

Makes: 1 serving

1 ounce bourbon   *1 part sweet sour mix**
1 ounce Triple Sec   *1 part cranberry juice*
Crushed ice

1. Combine all ingredients; shake well.
2. Strain to remove ice; serve in martini glasses.

(*To make a mix, dilute concentrate with ⅛ the required amount of water.)

Garlic Cheese Grits Casserole

Makes: 6 servings

1 cup sharp cheddar cheese, grated   *⅛ teaspoon garlic powder*
2 eggs, beaten   *⅛ teaspoon Tabasco sauce*
6 tablespoons butter, softened   *2 cups cooked grits*
1 teaspoon salt

1. Preheat the oven to 350 degrees.
2. Combine cheese, eggs, butter, salt, garlic powder, and Tabasco sauce; mix well.
3. Add cooked grits, mix well, and pour into a 1½-quart casserole.
4. Bake for 1 hour.

Butter Pecan Ice-Cream Pie

Makes: 16 servings

1 package Lorna Doone cookies
½ cup butter or margarine, softened
1 quart butter pecan ice cream, softened
2 small packages vanilla instant pudding

2 cups milk, cold
13 ounces nondairy topping
4 Heath Bars, crushed

Crust:
1. Crush cookies and mix with softened butter or margarine.
2. Pat into 9-by-13-inch pan and bake at 325 degrees for 12 to 15 minutes.

Filling:
1. In a large bowl, at medium speed, combine ice cream and dry pudding.
2. Add milk and beat 2 to 3 minutes, blending thoroughly.
3. Pour the mixture into the cooled crust.
4. Frost with nondairy topping.
5. Sprinkle with crushed Heath Bars and refrigerate. Do not freeze.

Food Service and Decorative Touches
- Cover buffet and dining tables with white or pastel linens with sheer overlays gathered at the corners with ribbon streamers and flower bunches.
- Arrange magnolia blossoms, peach leaves, weeping willow branches, and cotton blossoms in white wicker baskets trimmed with leaf-green ribbons.
- Place a white lattice folding screen behind the buffet table. Hang a large *Gone with the Wind* poster draped with material to replicate the famous green-with-yellow-trim drapes made famous by Carol Burnett in her comedy episode as Scarlett O'Hara. (See How-To's # 17.)
- Use southern-belle style hats, fancy fans, lace gloves, and parasols as props.
- Feature framed black-and-white still photos from *Gone with the Wind* on the buffet table and, if possible, as centerpiece components on dining tables.
- Combine military memorabilia with the flower and ribbon table decor.
- Fold a pastel napkin into a flower shape, lay on top of paper doily, and trim with flower greens.
- Display copies of *Gone with the Wind* and other Southern-themed books.
- Light the tables with hurricane lamps or battery-operated candles with small ornate shades.
- Make miniature fancy fans to use as place cards. (See How-To's #8.)

HAWAII/LUAU

The number-one theme of all time, a luau represents a tropical getaway in the midst of any kind of weather. Luaus are popular for events as formal as wedding receptions or as casual as backyard barbecues. The beautiful shapes and vivid colors will provide the setting for a festive island celebration feast.

Party Menu

Luau Banquet
*Kalua Pig (How-To's #36)
*Lau Lau
*Lomi Lomi Salmon
*Chicken Long Rice
Teriyaki Chicken
Poi
Sweet Potatoes Coated with Pineapple
Preserves and Butter
Corn on the Cob

Beverages
Juices
*Hawaiian Sunset Punch (page 224)
*Jungle Juice
Kona Koffees

Dessert
*Haupia
Cheesecake with Kiwi and Pineapple
Coconut Cake and Cookies
*Festive Luau Pineapple (How-To's #35)

Lau Lau
Makes: 6 servings

1 pound luau (taro leaves) or fresh spinach
1¼ pounds pork, cut in 6 pieces
1 tablespoon rock salt
¾ pound salmon, cut in 6 pieces
12 ti leaves or aluminum foil
1 cup water

1. Wash taro leaves thoroughly. Remove stem and fibrous part of veins by pulling gently with the tip of a knife from the stem to the edge of the leaves.
2. Place pork in a bowl, add salt, and mix to combine.
3. On a flat surface, stack 5 luau leaves, the largest on the bottom.
4. Place a piece of pork on the top leaf, fat side up. Then place a piece of salmon on top of the pork. Fold leaves over pork and fish to form a bundle (puolo).
5. Prepare each ti leaf by cutting partially through the stiff rib and stripping it off. Place the puolo bundles on the end of a ti leaf and wrap tightly. Wrap another ti leaf around the bundle in the opposite direction, thereby forming a flat package.
6. Tie bundles with string or with the fibrous part of the ti leaves; place them in a steamer. Bring the water to a boil, then lower the heat, and steam lau laus 5 to 6 hours. Remove string before serving.

Lomi Lomi Salmon
Makes: about 5 servings

¼ pound smoked salmon
½ onion, thinly sliced
2 green onions, chopped
2 tomatoes, cubed
6 ice cubes

1. In a large bowl, shred salmon with fingers, add onions and tomatoes; mash slightly.
2. Put ice cubes on top and refrigerate until well chilled. Serve in small side dishes.

Chicken Long Rice

Makes: about 5 servings

3 tablespoons oil
3 pounds chicken breasts, cubed
2 cloves garlic, minced
6 cups chicken broth
1 teaspoon minced fresh ginger

1½ tablespoons salt
2 1¾-ounce bundles long rice
 (cellophane noodles or bean thread)
1 6-ounce can whole mushrooms, drained
2 tablespoons green onions, thinly sliced

1. Heat oil in a large skillet; sauté chicken and garlic until browned.
2. Add chicken broth, ginger, and salt; simmer 1 hour or until chicken is tender.
3. Soak long rice in warm water for 30 minutes; cut into 2-inch pieces.
4. Add long rice and mushrooms to chicken; simmer 15 more minutes. Sprinkle with green onions just before serving.

Jungle Juice

Makes: 35 glasses

5 ripe bananas, mashed
Juice from 5 lemons
7 cups water

Juice from 5 oranges
5 cups sugar
7-Up, Sprite, ginger ale, or other carbonated clear beverage

1. Combine all ingredients except carbonated beverage; mix well. Freeze until slushy.
2. Fill a large glass ⅛ full (or more) with the slushy mixture and add 7-Up, Sprite, ginger ale, or other carbonated clear beverage.

Haupia

Makes: 16 2-inch squares

1 12-ounce can coconut milk
4 to 6 tablespoons sugar

4 to 6 tablespoons cornstarch
¾ cup water

1. Pour coconut milk into a saucepan.
2. In a separate bowl, combine sugar and cornstarch; stir in water and blend well.
3. Stir the sugar mixture into the coconut milk; cook and stir over low heat until thickened.
4. Pour the mixture into an 8-inch square pan and chill until firm.
5. Cut into 2-inch squares.

Food Service and Decorative Touches

- Cover your table with bamboo or grass mats and bright floral-printed fabrics, or use big leaves as place mats. Lay Hawaiian netting over tablecloths.
- Arrange fresh or artificial fruit in baskets or bowls.
- Serve drinks in hollowed-out fresh pineapples. (See How-To's #41.)
- Arrange island flowers and greens in green moss-covered Styrofoam bases.
- Use tissue-paper flowers as place cards, favors, and napkin rings. (See How-To's #13.)
- Decorate with miniature palm trees, tiki lamps, coconuts, fruits and vegetables, flower leis, and flower blossom candle holders. (See How-To's #23.)
- Include travel brochures, travel books, and magazines in your table decor.
- Float candles in bowls and glasses for mood lighting. (See How-To's #22.)
- Use tropical souvenir postcards as place cards or seating assignment cards.
- Serve snacks in lined beachcomber straw hats.

NEW YORK, NEW YORK

The city of New York is famous for its incredible variety of food and beverage choices. Not only can one find delectables in hundreds of restaurants, but many of the best eats are found right out in the open, from vendors' carts. Your foray into the food fare of New York City will offer endless options.

Party Menu

Snacks
*Artichoke "Heart of It" Dip with
Pita Chips
Oysters Rockefeller
Warm Pretzels

Beverages
*Two Cents Plain Soda
*Egg Cream
Long Island Iced Tea
Manhattans
Coffees/Teas

Buffet
Manhattan Clam Chowder
New York Steak Stroganoff
*Waldorf Salad
—or, for a more casual occasion—
Deli Favorites
Coney Island Hot Dogs
Pickles

Dessert
*Flatiron Fudge Spread on Crackers
New York Cheesecake

Artichoke "Heart of It Dip" with Pita Chips

Makes: 4 cups (for a crowd)

2 small jars (13 ounces) marinated
  artichoke hearts
8 ounces cream cheese
12 ounces mozzarella, shredded
1 cup mayonnaise

1 cup Parmesan cheese, grated
1 onion, finely chopped
2 cloves garlic, finely chopped
2 packages pita bread
Melted butter

1. Preheat the oven to 350 degrees.
2. Drain artichoke hearts, tear apart, and combine with all other ingredients, except pita bread and melted butter; mash until smooth.
3. Bake the mixture in an uncovered casserole dish for about 30 minutes. The mixture will bubble.
4. While the dip is baking, cut the pita bread into small triangles, brush with melted butter, and bake on a cookie sheet about 5 minutes, until crisp.
5. Serve the dip hot accompanied by the pita chips.

Two Cents Plain Soda

Makes: 1 serving

½ cup pineapple syrup
½ cup milk

1 scoop chocolate ice cream
Splash of seltzer water

1. Mix syrup and milk in a tall glass.
2. Add ice cream, then seltzer water.

Good Ol' Corn Pone
Makes: 6 to 8 wedges

2 cups cornmeal
½ teaspoon baking soda
1 egg, beaten
½ cup molasses
1 teaspoon salt
1 tablespoon bacon drippings

1. Add enough warm water to the cornmeal to make a thin dough. Put the dough in a warm place (the oven) and let it sit and rise overnight.
2. Preheat the oven to 400 degrees.
3. Add the rest of the ingredients to the dough, mix well, and bake in a skillet until golden brown on top. Slice and eat.

Rhubarb Crunch
Makes: 8 to 10 servings

1 cup flour
¾ cup raw oatmeal
1 cup brown sugar
½ cup butter, melted
1 teaspoon cinnamon
4 cups rhubarb, diced
1 cup sugar
1 cup water
2 tablespoons cornstarch
1 teaspoon vanilla

1. Preheat the oven to 350 degrees.
2. Mix the first 5 ingredients together; press half into a 8-by-10-inch pan.
3. Place rhubarb over the crumb mixture.
4. Cook sugar, water, cornstarch, and vanilla until the mixture is thick and clear, stirring constantly. Pour over rhubarb; top with remaining crumb mixture.
5. Bake for 1 hour. Cut into squares to serve.

Food Service and Decorative Touches
- Set food out on rustic tables, chairs, benches, stools, shelves, and wooden crates.
- Tie muslin napkins around dried corn cobs.
- Cover tables with magazine covers, old posters, and newspapers, then overlay with clear plastic. (See How-To's #19.)
- Spread an old-fashioned oilcloth table cover on the buffet table.
- Write place cards or seating assignments on small brown paper bags.
- Create a front porch atmosphere with rocking chairs and benches.
- Fill an old washing machine with ice and cans of beer or pop.
- Arrange appetizers on a thoroughly cleaned washboard.
- Serve snacks in tin cans, crockery bowls (chipped if possible), wooden buckets, and cast-iron cookery.
- Use cardboard scraps to make signage for the buffet table, and be sure to misspell and write names of food items backwards.
- Fill canning jars with dried or wild flowers and weeds for table centerpieces.
- Hang an old clothesline with hole-filled garments, bloomers, and long johns on the wall behind the buffet table.
- Serve beverages from big jugs (wine jugs painted brown) and small fruit jars.
- Use corn cob pipes, plaid flannels, bib overalls, colorful bandannas, Li'l Abner boots, cotton aprons, and burlap bags in your table decor.

SOUTHWEST

The Southwestern desert areas have become popular as vacation and part-time living destinations, and Southwestern decor and food have become trendy and fashionable everywhere. For a party theme filled with soft colors and flavorful food, go Southwest, young reader.

Party Menu

Snacks
*Santa Fe Bean Dip
Blue Corn Tortilla Chips
Jalapeño Jelly Drizzled on Cream Cheese
Triscuit Crackers

Beverages
*Hot Chili Mama
Cactus Juice
Sangria Punch
Beer and Wine
Coffee

Buffet
*Southwest Quiche
Citrus Grilled Chicken
Red Beans and Rice
*Southwestern Slaw (page 231)
*Southwestern Pasta Salad (page 237)
Tortillas

Dessert
*Fruit Salsa Sundaes
Chocolate Cake Squares

Santa Fe Bean Dip
Makes: 2 cups dip

1 can condensed black bean soup
1 can tomato sauce
½ cup cheddar cheese
1 teaspoon chili powder
2 tablespoons cheddar cheese

1. Heat bean soup, tomato sauce, ½ cup cheese, and chili powder over medium heat, until steaming.
2. Pour the dip into a festive bowl and sprinkle it with 2 tablespoons cheddar cheese.
3. Set the dip on a platter and surround it with blue corn chips.

Hot Chili Mama
Makes: 1 serving

1 ounce tequila
Dash of Worcestershire sauce
Ice
⅔ cup V₈ Picante juice
Salt and pepper, to taste
⅓ cup clamato juice
Squeeze of lime

1. Combine all ingredients and shake well.
2. Serve over ice.

Southwest Quiche

Makes: 6 to 8 servings

16 ounces cream cheese, softened
2 cups sharp cheddar cheese, shredded
2 cups sour cream, divided
1½ packages taco seasoning

3 eggs, room temperature
4 ounces green chilies, chopped
⅔ cup salsa
Shredded cheese for garnish

1. Preheat the oven to 350 degrees.
2. In a large bowl, combine cheeses; beat until fluffy.
3. Add 1 cup sour cream and taco seasoning. Beat in eggs, one at a time. Fold in chilies.
4. Pour into a 9-inch springform pan and bake 35 to 40 minutes or until center is firm.
5. Remove the pan from oven and cool for 10 minutes.
6. Spoon 1 cup sour cream over the top; bake 5 minutes longer.
7. Cool completely on a wire rack. Cover and refrigerate several hours or overnight.
8. Place the quiche on a serving plate. Garnish with salsa and shredded cheese.

Fruit Salsa Sundaes

Makes: 4 servings

4 6-inch flour tortillas
1½ cups peaches, peeled and diced
1½ cups strawberries, diced
1 tablespoon crystallized ginger,
  finely chopped

2 tablespoons sugar
½ teaspoon grated lime peel
4 scoops vanilla ice cream
Mint sprigs for garnish (optional)

1. Preheat the oven to 350 degrees.
2. Soften tortillas according to package directions. Press each one into an ungreased 10-ounce custard cup and bake 10 to 15 minutes or until crisp. Set aside to cool.
3. Combine peaches, strawberries, ginger, sugar, and lime peel; mix gently.
4. Remove tortillas from custard cups and place each tortilla shell on a dessert plate; fill with 1 scoop of vanilla ice cream.
5. Spoon equal portions of fruit salsa over the ice cream. Garnish with mint sprigs.

Food Service and Decorative Touches

- Use the distinct and popular Southwestern colors—soft tones of mauve, teal green, lavender, and creamy white—in all table and serving decor.
- Incorporate the symbols of the coyote, cactus, and road runner in all decor.
- Use a wreath of dried peppers for a dramatic focal point on a buffet table.
- Adorn name tags and place cards with tiny peppers, stickers, and artwork.
- Cover tables with rough pastel-colored linens in solids, plaids, stripes, or floral prints.
- Use serving containers and utensils of terra cotta clay or ceramic.
- Create a clever vase from a small (woman's or child's) cowboy boot that has been painted and decorated in Southwestern colors.
- Use the real or artificial flowers and "brownery" commonly found in the desert for table centerpieces.
- Turn pastel bandannas into napkins or place mats. Tie a bandanna napkin around the stem of a wine glass at each place setting.
- Spread serapes in pastel shades on buffet tables.
- Display cookbooks, fruits, vegetables, breads, and other foodstuffs on the table.

WEST

Yahoo, let's near it for number two! The second most popular party theme, that is. Familiar and easy-to-do, the Western theme ranks second, after Hawaiian, in the overall choice for a fun and festive party scheme. Since the props, settings, and decor are readily available, and the menu offers all-time favorites, your cowpokes will be in for a rootin' tootin' good time.

Party Menu

Snacks
*Longhorn Quick Chili Dip
Tortilla Chips, Vegetable Sticks,
Bread Sticks
Buffalo Wings

Beverages
Soft Drinks/Mineral Waters
*Texas Ice Pick Punch
*Buckaroo Beer
Sarsaparillas
Red-Eye Whiskey

Buffet
Barbecue Beef Sandwiches
Ranch-Cut Potatoes
Baked Beans
Corn on the Cob
Biscuits
Pick A Slaw
*Brunch Option: Ranch Egg Cheesy Bake

Dessert
Deep Dish Apple Pie
Fresh Fruit
Oatmeal Cookies

Longhorn Quick Chili Dip
Makes: about 3¾ cups of dip

1 cup cottage cheese
15 ounces (1 can) chili with beans
1 tablespoon hot sauce

1 tablespoon lemon juice
1½ teaspoons ground cumin
¾ cup sharp cheddar cheese, shredded

1. Cream cottage cheese using a blender, food processor, or electric mixer.
2. Add chili; mix well.
3. Add hot sauce, lemon juice, and cumin.
4. Pour into a bowl and mix in cheddar cheese, reserving a little for garnish
5. Cover and chill.
6. Serve with tortilla chips, vegetable sticks, and/or bread sticks.

Texas Ice Pick Punch
Makes: 1 serving

1 ounce tequila
Ice

2 parts lemonade mix*
1 part ice tea

1. Combine all ingredients and shake well.
2. Serve over ice.

(*To make a mix, dilute lemonade concentrate with ⅓ the required amount of water.)

Buckaroo Beer
Makes: 1 serving

1 ounce rum
Ice
Root beer

1. Pour rum into a low glass over ice.
2. Fill the glass with root beer.

Brunch Option: Ranch Egg Cheesy Bake
Makes: 8 to 10 servings

16 slices side bacon, chopped
4 cups frozen hash browns
3 cups colby cheddar cheese, shredded
12 eggs, beaten

2 cups milk
1 cup green onions, thinly sliced
Chives or scallions for garnish

1. Cook bacon in a large frying pan until crisp.
2. Drain, reserving 3 tablespoons of drippings.
3. Sauté potatoes in drippings until browned, about 10 minutes.
4. Preheat the oven to 350 degrees.
5. Spread potatoes in a shallow baking dish (approximately 13-by-9-inch)
6. Sprinkle with cheese, then bacon.
7. Beat together eggs, milk, and onions; pour on top of potatoes.
8. Bake for 20 to 25 minutes until set.
9. Garnish with snipped chives or scallions.

Food Service and Decorative Touches
- Use brown craft paper, burlap, denim, or red-and-white-checked tablecloths.
- Invert cowboy hats and trim with straw flowers and bandannas for centerpieces, or use the hats as serving containers for trail mix, beef jerky, and corn chips.
- Use bandannas as place mats, napkins, and chair-back covers.
- Tie a rope around bandanna napkins, or use silver sheriff's stars as napkin rings.
- Serve foods in enamelware, crocks, cast-iron pans, baskets, and buckets.
- Paint real or plastic horseshoes gold, and personalize them with the guest-of-honor's name and date of event; use the horseshoes as place cards or party favors
- Create a buckboard buffet of a smooth plank or door placed across two carpenter's horses.
- Tie twine, rope, straw, raffia ribbons, or cloth bandannas around baskets, bowls, crocks, or flowerpots.
- Spread sheets of western music, western comic covers, magazine pictures, or western movie promotional pieces on the tables, then cover with clear plastic.
- Cover medium-sized facial tissue boxes with straw. (See How-To's #12.)
- Spray-paint old cowboy boots and trim with silver braid and fringe to make clever and attractive vases and holders for napkins and utensils.
- Make centerpieces using cacti, tumbleweeds, and straw flowers.
- Make leather-look place mats from brown paper grocery bags. (See How-To's #16.)
- Light the tables with kerosene lamps or paper bag luminaria.
- Hang strings of party lights in western shapes behind and around the buffet table.

CARIBBEAN

The luxurious and beautiful views of the Caribbean islands will set the scene for parties destined to succeed. The vivid, brilliant colors so typical of these locales provide beautiful tropical decor to match the savory spices and exotic flavors found in a menu of island hopping fare.

Party Menu

Snacks
*"Jamaican Me Crazy" Jerk Marinade Sauce (with cooked chicken or beef strips)
Fresh Vegetable Sticks
Pick A Dip

Beverages
Soft Drinks/Mineral Waters
*Guavaberry Good Colada
Jamaican Coffees/Teas

Buffet
*Caribbean Chicken Casserole
*Island Pasta Salad (page 238)
Fresh Mango Salad
Breads, Rolls

Dessert
*Simpson Bay Spice Cookies
Fresh Fruit with Chocolate Sauce

"Jamaican Me Crazy" Jerk Marinade Sauce
Makes: 1 cup sauce

1 onion, minced
1 teaspoon salt
½ teaspoon nutmeg
1 teaspoon black pepper
1 tablespoon white vinegar

½ cup scallions, chopped
2 teaspoons sugar
½ teaspoon cinnamon
3 tablespoons soy sauce

2 teaspoons thyme, fresh
1 teaspoon allspice
1 hot pepper, finely ground
1 tablespoon vegetable oil

Combine all ingredients in a food processor until finely chopped. Use for meat or chicken. (Sauce can be refrigerated for up to 1 month.)

Guavaberry Good Colada
Makes: 2 servings

4 ounces pineapple juice
4 ounces St. Maarten guavaberry rum
4 ounces cream of coconut
2 tablespoons fresh lime juice

2 tablespoons grated coconut for garnish
2 maraschino cherries for garnish
2 slices fresh pineapple for garnish

1. Blend together first 4 ingredients for 60 seconds.
2. Pour into 2 chilled long-stemmed glasses.
3. Garnish with grated coconut, cherries, and fresh pineapple

Caribbean Chicken Casserole

Makes: 6 servings

1 package macaroni and cheese dinner
1 cup cooked chicken, cubed
½ cup ripe olives, chopped
⅓ cup sour cream

1 clove garlic, crushed
2 tablespoons parsley, chopped
½ cup slivered almonds, toasted

1. Prepare macaroni and cheese according to package directions.
2. Preheat the oven to 350 degrees.
3. Combine the cooked macaroni and cheese with the remaining ingredients except almonds; mix well. Place everything into a casserole and bake for 30 minutes.
4. Sprinkle almonds on top before serving.

Simpson Bay Spice Cookies

(Called Speckulass in Dutch, these crisp sugar cookies, filled with island spices, were brought to St. Maarten by early Dutch settlers. See Credits.)

Makes: 3 dozen

3 cups flour
½ teaspoon baking powder
½ teaspoon grated nutmeg
½ teaspoon ground cloves

2 teaspoons ground cinnamon
¾ cup butter, softened
¾ cup light brown sugar
2 teaspoons lemon rind, finely grated

2 eggs
½ cup cashews, chopped
Colored sugar crystals

1. Sift together flour, baking powder, nutmeg, cloves, and cinnamon.
2. Cream butter with sugar separately; add lemon rind and eggs; blend well.
3. Combine dry ingredients alternately with creamed mixture, stirring well after each addition. Add cashews; mix well. Refrigerate dough for 4 to 6 hours.
4. Preheat the oven to 400 degrees.
5. Roll chilled dough to ⅛-inch thickness and cut with a round cookie cutter.
6. Place the cookies on greased baking sheets and sprinkle with colored sugar crystals. Bake for 8 minutes.
7. Turn the oven down to 350 degrees and continue baking 25 minutes, until the tops of the cookies brown. Cool; store in an airtight container.

Food Service and Decorative Touches

- Make table covers and napkins with floral and geometric-printed fabrics. Or, cover tables with plain brown craft paper decorated with a collage of large floral, fish, or plant magazine cutouts. Cover with clear plastic. (See How-To's #19.)
- Make tissue-paper flowers for a brilliant display. (See How-To's #13.)
- Design centerpiece arrangements with artificial island flowers and greenery, tree branches and leaves, pods, and fresh and dried fruits.
- Fill fishbowls half full with water and add live, small tropical fish for exciting and unique table decor. (*Caution:* Do not color water with food coloring.)
- Serve beverages in coconuts, pineapples, wooden cups, and novelty glasses.
- Set up a bar or food service station on a table skirted with grass or palm leaves under a thatched canopy.
- Use sea shells in your table centerpieces, or use as place cards or napkin rings.
- Display musical instruments, such as bongo drums, wooden pipes, and maracas.

ENGLAND

Travel across the ocean for a theme party that pays tribute to the fine folks of England. Combine foods and beverages representative of a jolly good English menu commonly served to blokes in a countryside pub or at a country estate.

Party Menu

Snacks
*Rum Tum Tiddy
Fish 'n' Chips

Beverages
*Pimm's Cup
English Ale and Wines
Variety of Teas

Buffet
*Ye Old English Beef Pie
"Bangers" (sausages)
Cucumber Salad
Popovers, Breads

Dessert
*English Trifle
Tea Cakes

Rum Tum Tiddy
Makes: 6 servings

1 tablespoon butter or margarine
¼ cup onion, finely chopped
¼ cup green pepper, chopped
1 can condensed tomato soup
¾ cup milk

3 cups cheddar cheese, shredded
½ teaspoon Worcestershire sauce
1 egg, slightly beaten
¼ cup dry sherry
Toast or crackers

1. Melt butter in a saucepan over low to moderate heat.
2. Add onion and green pepper and cook until tender; remove from heat.
3. Mix in tomato soup, milk, cheese, and Worcestershire sauce.
4. Cook, stirring constantly, until cheese is melted; remove from heat.
5. In a separate bowl, blend ½ cup of cheese sauce into a beaten egg.
6. Pour egg mixture back into the cheese sauce in the saucepan and heat over moderately low heat. Stir in sherry, and spoon over toast or crackers.

Pimm's Cup
Makes: 8 to 10 servings

½ pint (6 ounces) strawberries, hulled and cut into quarters
1 lemon, sliced into ⅛-inch rounds
1 lime, sliced into ⅛-inch rounds
1 orange (blood orange, if possible), sliced into 1-inch wedges
3 cups Pimm's liquor (or amount to suit your taste)
48 ounces 7-Up or ginger ale
2 cucumbers, quartered, then cut into 4-inch spears

1. In a large pitcher, combine strawberries, lemons, limes, and oranges.
2. Add Pimm's, and mash down lightly with a large spoon.
3. Fill half each glass with ice, add ⅓ cup Pimm's mixture, and fill with 7-Up; stir.
4. Place a cucumber spear in each glass; serve.

Ye Old English Beef Pie

Makes: 8 to 12 servings

2 16-ounce cans peas
1 10¾-ounce can beef gravy or
  1¼ cup prepared gravy
½ tablespoon red wine (optional)
½ tablespoon hot sauce
4 cups cooked roast beef, cubed

8 medium potatoes, cooked, peeled, and sliced
2 16-ounce cans small white onions, drained
1 teaspoon salt
½ teaspoon thyme
1 package pastry mix, prepared, or
  ½ pie pastry recipe

1. Preheat the oven to 425 degrees.
2. Drain peas, reserving ½ cup liquid.
3. In a saucepan, combine pea liquid, gravy, wine, and hot sauce. Bring to a boil.
4. Combine peas, roast beef, potatoes, and onions in 2 2-quart casseroles; sprinkle with seasonings, then pour in the hot gravy mixture.
5. Cover casseroles with rolled pastry, cut slits in top, and bake for 25 to 30 minutes.

English Trifle

Makes: 8 servings

Custard (recipe follows)
Small sponge cake or pound cake
Raspberry jam
½ cup sherry

1 package frozen raspberries, thawed
2 cups whipping cream
1 tablespoon icing sugar
Toasted almonds

1. Make and chill the custard (see below).
2. Cut cake into 1-by-4-inch strips. Spread jam on one side of each strip.
3. Place half of cake, jam side up, in deep, clear glass serving bowl.
4. Sprinkle with half of sherry, then cover with half of raspberries and half of custard.
5. Whip the cream and sweeten with icing sugar; spread half over custard.
6. Repeat layers. Garnish the top with toasted almonds. Chill several hours.

Custard:

2 cups light cream
¼ cup sugar

4 egg yolks, well-beaten
1 teaspoon vanilla

1. Heat light cream with sugar almost to boiling.
2. Briskly stir beaten egg yolks into the heated cream.
3. Cook mixture without boiling, stirring almost constantly, until custard is smooth and slightly thickened. (When cooked, the custard will coat a metal spoon.)
4. Stir in vanilla, then pour into a bowl, cover, and chill.

Food Service and Decorative Touches

- Use the colors of the British flag (the Union Jack): red, white, and blue.
- Illuminate tables with battery-operated candles topped with paper tiffany shades.
- Lay out maps of the British Isles on tabletops and cover with clear plastic.
- Display a variety of Beatles' photos, magazine pages, and record album covers.
- Create centerpiece arrangements using flags, travel brochures, passports, picture postcards, menus, and any product packaging representing Britain.
- Set a royal table with photos, souvenirs, and books related to the monarchy.
- Use faux English crackers—traditional party favors—as place cards, seating assignment items, or party favors for guest of all ages. (See How-To's #7.)

GERMANY/OKTOBERFEST

In the robust and spirited atmosphere of the German Gasthaus, with its lively sounds and notable aromas, plan the perfect party menu to feature food and libation selections to please your favorite Herrs and Frauleins. For a private party, corporate function, or official Oktoberfest celebration, you will find that this menu is loaded with real "Oomph Pa Pa"!

Party Menu

Snacks
*Braunschweiger Spread with Crusty Rolls
Bavarian Pretzels
Sauerkraut Balls

Buffet
*Eggs in Green Sauce over Potatoes
German Bratwurst with Kraut
*German Potato Salad (page 233)
Potato Dumplings

Beverages
*Rhine Wine Cup
Apple Juice/Seltzer Spritzers
German Beers and Wines

Dessert
*Black Forest Trifle Dessert
Apple Strudel

Braunschweiger Spread
Makes: 3 cups

1 pound braunschweiger
1 cup sour cream
1 package onion soup mix
1 teaspoon Worcestershire sauce

1. Mash braunschweiger with a fork.
2. Add remaining ingredients and blend well.
3. Refrigerate overnight so ingredients blend thoroughly.
4. Serve with crusty rolls. (If you like, cut or tear the rolls into bite-sized pieces.)

Rhine Wine Cup
Makes: 2 servings

Ice cubes
½ ounce triple sec
2 ounces brandy
4 teaspoons powdered sugar
6 ounces carbonated water
½ ounce curaçao
1 pint Rhine wine
Fruit, cucumber rind, and mint for garnish

1. Fill a large glass pitcher with ice cubes.
2. Add all ingredients except garnish.
3. Stir well and pour into 5-ounce claret glasses.
4. Garnish with a variety of fruits, cucumber rind, and mint

Eggs in Green Sauce over Potatoes

Makes: 4 servings

1 cup sour cream, or ½ cup sour cream and ½ cup plain yogurt
Juice of 1 medium lemon
9 large eggs, hard-boiled
½ teaspoon salt
¼ teaspoon black pepper
½ teaspoon sugar
1½ cups fresh herbs (chives, scallions, and parsley)
Potatoes, boiled

1. Blend sour cream and lemon juice.
2. Finely chop 1 hard-boiled egg and stir into sour cream mixture.
3. Season with salt, pepper, and sugar.
4. Thoroughly rinse herbs, pat dry, and chop. Blend with the sauce.
5. Slice rest of the hard-cooked eggs in quarters and arrange in the sauce
6. Serve with boiled potatoes for a refreshing and tasty meal.

Black Forest Trifle Dessert

Makes: 12 to 18 servings

1 package devil's food cake mix
1 cup rum
2 21-ounce cans cherry pie filling

2 packages chocolate custard pudding mix, prepared
1 large package frozen nondairy topping
½ cup sliced almonds, toasted

1. Prepare and bake cake mix according to package directions; cut into ½-inch slices.
2. Line the bottom of 2 2-quart bowls or trifle dishes with half the cake slices; sprinkle each bowl of cake with ½ cup rum.
3. Spoon half a can of cherry pie filling over each cake; top with half the chocolate pudding.
4. Repeat procedure with remaining cake, rum, pie filling, and pudding.
5. Cover and chill.
6. Spread thawed whipped cream topping over the custard and garnish with almonds.

Food Service and Decorative Touches

- Display German flags in various sizes as part of your table decor.
- Use the colors of the German flag—black, red, and gold—in all your decorations.
- Arrange maps, travel books, magazines, pamphlets, and postcards as decorative accents on serving tables.
- Arrange bouquets of fresh or straw flowers in German beer mugs or steins.
- Place beer bottles with decorative German labels amongst table decor, or use the bottles to hold tapered candles.
- Cover tables with lace cloths, tapestry fabrics, and embroidered shawls.
- Remove the tops and bottoms of German beer cans and use them as napkin rings.
- Trim place cards with flag stickers or ribbons in the German flag colors.

GREECE

From Alpha to Omega, a Greek theme party is a combination of fun and colorful activities, music, decor, and especially food. Delicious and flavorful, the authentic Greek meal features the basics of fish, salad, bread, fruit, and wine. Your Greek gourmet offerings can include those and more.

Party Menu

Snacks
*Tsatsiki Dip with Pita Chips
Dolma (Stuffed Grape Leaves)
Greek Olives

Beverages
Soft Drinks/Mineral Waters
Ouzo
Retsina Wine
Coffees/Teas

Buffet
*Greek Stew
Shish Kebabs of Onion, Lamb and Zucchini
*Greek Potato Salad (page 232)

Dessert
*Phyllo Fruit and Cheese Tarts
Baklava

Tsatsiki Dip with Pita Chips
Makes: 16 servings of 2 pita chips per serving

½ cup olive oil
¼ cup fresh dill
¼ teaspoon coarse black pepper
¼ teaspoon coarse salt
4 cloves garlic, coarsely chopped

1 scallion (white only), thinly sliced on diagonal
1 seedless cucumber, peeled and chopped
1 quart nonfat plain yogurt, strained and drained
4 7-inch pita rounds

1. Combine all ingredients except pita bread; mix well and chill for 1 hour
2. While the dip is chilling, preheat the oven to 350 degrees.
3. Cut each pita round into 8 wedges.
4. Arrange the pita wedges on 2 baking sheets and bake 5 minutes. (If you like crisper chips, bake 5 minutes longer.)
5. Serve the dip in a bowl surrounded by the pita chips.

Greek Stew
Makes: 6 servings

3 pounds stew meat, chopped
5 tablespoons butter
Salt and pepper, to taste
1 onion, chopped

1 6-ounce can tomato paste
2 tablespoons red wine vinegar
1 clove garlic, diced
1½ cups water, divided

1 bay leaf
2 pounds small white onions
½ pound mushrooms, sliced
¾ pound jack cheese, grated

1. Brown meat in butter in a heavy kettle.
2. Season lightly with salt and pepper.
3. Add chopped onion and sauté until the onion is clear.
4. Mix in tomato paste, vinegar, garlic, and ¾ cup water. Add 1 bay leaf
5. Cover and simmer 1 hour, adding additional water as needed.

6. Add white onions and mushrooms.
7. Cover and simmer 1 more hour, or until the meat and onions are tender
8. Add cheese, cover, and cook 5 minutes, or until the cheese melts
9. Serve in mugs as a thick soup, or over rice as a main dish.

Phyllo Fruit and Cheese Tarts

Makes: 24 tarts

1 box (1 pound) phyllo pastry
1 pound unsalted butter, melted and slightly cooled
2 cups fruit filling of choice
1 cup cream cheese, softened

1. Brush a flattened 18-by-24-inch phyllo pastry leaf with melted butter.
2. Put another leaf on top and butter it.
3. Preheat the oven to 450 degrees.
4. Cut the pastry into four 24-inch-long strips.
5. In a medium bowl, combine fruit filling with cream cheese; mix well.
6. For each strip, put a spoonful of the fruit mixture at the top, and then flag-fold the strip into a triangle with the filling inside. Once the triangle completely covers the filling, about half way, cut it from the strip and pinch the edges closed.
7. Put another spoonful of filling at the top of the now-shorter strip and repeat Step 5. Continue until all the triangles are filled. Arrange the triangles on a baking sheet.
8. Slash the tops of the triangles carefully to prevent the dough from bubbling; do not cut through to the filling.
9. Bake for about 20 to 25 minutes, or until golden-brown.

Food Service and Decorative Touches

- Use the colors of the Greek flag—blue and white—in your decor.
- Drape fishnetting over tablecloths.
- Use blankets, shawls, and rough white linen cloths as table covers.
- Include olive branches, tulips, laurel leaves, oleander, hibiscus, and jasmine in your floral arrangements.
- Incorporate travel brochures, books, and flags into your table decor.
- Use a sign reading "Taverna" (tavern) as a backdrop for your serving area.
- Use neon in your decor, since neon is a Greek invention.
- Wrap sprays of green leaves around napkins for natural, decorative napkin rings.
- Use empty Greek beer or wine bottles as candle holders.
- Stand miniature Greek columns and small Greek sculptures on serving tables amongst the food items.

ITALY

Mama Mia—that's Italian! Your party guests will be gesturing enthusiastically when they see and taste the array of refreshments you have offered. Because pizza and pasta are favorite staples for so many people, Italian food is extremely successful at any party, regardless of its theme.

Party Menu

Snacks
Antipasto Platter
*Pizzatini Squares
*Lemon Orzo Salad (page 12)

Beverages
Soft Drinks/Mineral Waters
*Margaritas, Italian Style
Italian Wine
Cappuccino

Buffet
Pasta Bar
Sauces: Alfredo, Marinara, Pesto
Fresh Salad Bar
Garlic Bread

Dessert
*Cannoli Cones
*Gelato La Dolce Vita (page 37)
Biscotti

Pizzatini Squares
Makes: 40 pieces

½ pound bulk sausage	1 4-ounce can chopped mushrooms
½ pound ground beef	1 tablespoon onion flakes
1 8-ounce can tomato sauce	½ cup mozzarella cheese, finely shredded
Salt and garlic, to taste	10 slices white bread, crusts removed

1. Preheat the oven to 425 degrees.
2. Combine all ingredients except cheese and bread; mix well and spread on bread slices.
3. Sprinkle with cheese.
4. Bake for 15 minutes.
5. Cut into quarters and serve immediately.

Margaritas, Italian Style
Makes: 1 serving

1 ounce tequila	Ice
1 ounce amaretto	Margarita mix*

1. Shake tequila and amaretto with ice.
2. Pour into a glass and fill with margarita mix.

(*To make a mix, dilute margarita concentrate with ⅓ the required amount of water.)

Cannoli Cones

Makes: 10 servings

15 ounces part-skim ricotta cheese	*½ teaspoon vanilla extract*
⅔ cup confectioners' sugar	*2 tablespoons miniature chocolate chips*
½ teaspoon grated orange peel	*10 sugar ice-cream cones*

1. In a large bowl, combine ricotta cheese, sugar, orange peel, and vanilla; beat until smooth with an electric mixer set on low.
2. Stir in chocolate chips.
3. Cover and refrigerate 30 minutes.
4. To serve, spoon the cheese mixture directly into ice-cream cones, or fill a decorating bag without tip and pipe the mixture into cones.

Food Service and Decorative Touches

- Use the colors of the Italian flag—green, white, and red—in your decor.
- To create a country Italian decor, cover tables with red-and-white checked cloths. For a more formal atmosphere, use crisp white linens.
- Set out candles in Chianti wine bottles. Burn them down a bit to look more "lived in."
- Use Italian cookbooks, food packaging, food items, flags, maps, travel brochures, and postcards for decorative touches.
- Line baskets with red-and-white checked cloths, then fill with breads and rolls
- Tie ribbons in the country's colors around bread sticks to use as place cards, seating assignments, or party favors.
- Wrap artificial grape bunches with leaves around napkins.
- Use bottles of olive oil and varieties of pasta in fancy jars in the table decor.
- Hand-paint the Italian flag colors on wine glasses for personalized place cards or take-home favors.
- Stack pizza delivery boxes as bases for food items on your buffet table.
- Line a large basket with lettuce leaves and arrange fresh vegetables in it
- Use men's white dress shirts as chair covers. (See How-To's #26.)

 JAPAN

One of the most beautiful, yet simple, foreign themes, both in decor and food service, is Japanese. Most likely, many of your guests already have a favorite food or two from a Japanese eat-in or take-out restaurant. From teriyaki to sake to sukiyaki, the fare on your meal table (whatever height) will be met with great enthusiasm.

Party Menu

Snacks
*Yakitori Chic-kebabs
Rumaki Shrimp

Beverages
*Plum Wine Punch
Japanese Beer
Sake
Green Tea

Buffet
*Teriyaki Sandwiches
Sukiyaki
Tempura Vegetables
White and Brown Rice
Oriental Spinach Salad

Dessert
*Japanese Fruit Pie
Lemon Sherbet

Yakitori Chic-kebabs
Makes: 24

3 whole skinless boneless chicken breasts
2 tablespoons soy sauce
2 tablespoons dry sherry
½ tablespoon sugar
1 tablespoon garlic, finely chopped
1 tablespoon ginger, finely chopped

1. Soak 24 12-inch bamboo skewers in water overnight.
2. Cut chicken into 1½-inch cubes and put the cubes into a bowl.
3. In a separate bowl combine remaining ingredients; pour over chicken and toss well. Marinade for 1 to 2 hours at room temperature, or refrigerate overnight
4. Preheat broiler or grill.
5. Thread 2 to 3 pieces of chicken on each skewer and reserve marinade.
6. Broil or grill chicken 3 to 4 inches away from heat, 2 minutes per side, brushing with marinade. Stick skewers into a moss-covered Styrofoam base on a Japanese platter.

Plum Wine Punch
Makes: as much as you like

3 parts plum wine
2 parts club soda
1 part apricot juice
White raisins for garnish

1. Combine all ingredients; shake well.
2. Pour over ice.
3. Garnish with raisins on umbrella toothpicks.

Teriyaki Sandwiches

Makes: 8 servings

2 to 2½ pounds boneless beef chuck steak
¼ cup soy sauce
1 tablespoon brown sugar
1 teaspoon ground ginger
1 clove garlic, minced

2 tablespoons cold water
4 teaspoons cornstarch
8 individual French loaves, split,
    buttered, and toasted

1. Trim excess fat from the steak; cut into thin, bite-sized slices.
2. Combine soy sauce, sugar, ginger, and garlic in a 3½- to 4-quart slow cooker.
3. Stir in meat, cover, and cook on low heat for 7 to 9 hours, or on high heat 3 to 4 hours. Remove meat with a slotted spoon and set aside.
4. Pour remaining juices into a measuring cup; skim off fat.
5. Measure 1½ cups juices, adding water if needed, and place in a saucepan.
6. Combine 2 tablespoons cold water with cornstarch; add to the saucepan.
7. Cook and stir until the sauce is thick and bubbly. Cook and stir 2 minutes more.
8. Stir in the cooked meat and heat. Serve on buttered and toasted French loaves.

Japanese Fruit Pie

Makes: 6 to 8 servings

½ stick butter, softened
1 cup sugar
2 eggs
1 teaspoon vanilla
1 teaspoon vinegar
½ cup coconut, grated or shredded

½ cup pecans
½ cup white raisins
½ cup mandarin orange bits
1 unbaked 8-inch pie shell
Whipped cream and crushed pecans for garnish

1. Preheat the oven to 350 degrees.
2. Cream butter; add sugar and eggs. Stir in remaining filling ingredients.
3. Put the mixture into a pie shell and bake for 35 minutes. Chill.
4. Before serving, top with whipped cream and a sprinkle of crushed pecans.

Food Service and Decorative Touches

- Use the colors of the Japanese flag—red and white—in your decor.
- If using a long, low table and pillows for seating, cover the table with a plain or patterned sheet and place a bamboo runner down the center, lengthwise.
- Create simple flowers in black lacquer containers—not more than three flowers.
- Create decorative miniature folding fans and screens to use as accents on both buffet and dining tables. (See How-To's #8, 18.) Beautiful paper fans of foil paper serve as delightful place cards or seating assignment items.
- Make origami paper creations, which will make stunning flowers when attached to the ends of chop sticks and can be used in arrangements, as place cards, or as party favors.
- Gather interestingly shaped bottles or boxes and spray with black lacquer paint to make vases, food containers, or simple decorative pieces.

SWITZERLAND

If you like this theme, just yodel! You can create a special party that seems to take place in a Swiss chalet, without leaving your home. This is a very sociable theme, since it features a cook-it-yourself fondue plan that encourages guests to interact while they prepare their food. The good news is that you can make the fondue potluck, so you won't have to dip into your Swiss bank account.

Party Menu

Snacks
*Swiss Cheese Puffs
Cheese Fondue
Bread Chunks

Beverages
White Alpine Wine Punch
*Swiss Hot Chocolate Toddy

Buffet
Fondue Pots with Oil
Beef, Shrimp, Vegetable Pieces
Sauces and Dips
Salad

Dessert
*Swiss Cheesecake
Chocolate Fondue
Fresh Fruit to Dip

Swiss Cheese Puffs
Makes: 24 2-inch squares

8 slices white bread
8 ounces Swiss cheese, sliced
8 ounces ham, shredded
¼ cup butter, melted
3 eggs

1 teaspoon salt
½ teaspoon black pepper
¾ teaspoon dry mustard
2 cups milk
Sour cream and black olives for garnish

1. Trim the crusts and cut the bread into 1-inch squares.
2. Cut cheese into bite-sized pieces.
3. In a greased 8-by-12-inch casserole, alternate layers of bread, ham, and cheese
4. Pour melted butter over top.
5. Beat eggs well; stir in salt, pepper, mustard, and milk.
6. Combine thoroughly and pour over the casserole. Cover and refrigerate.
7. One hour before serving, bake at 350 degrees, 30 minutes covered, then 30 minutes uncovered, until the top is golden and puffy.
8. Cut into 2-inch squares and garnish with a dab of sour cream topped with a sliced black olive. Serve warm.

Swiss Hot Chocolate Toddy
Makes: 4 servings

¼ cup semisweet chocolate pieces
¼ cup granulated sugar
2 cups milk

1 cup half and half or light cream
Whipped cream
Ground cinnamon
Buttered toast, cut into strips

1. In a saucepan, combine chocolate, sugar, and ½ cup of milk.
2. Cook over medium heat, stirring continuously, until the mixture comes to a boil.
3. Stir in the remaining milk and the light cream. Heat, but do not boil.
4. Remove from heat and pour into mugs. Top with whipped cream and a sprinkle of cinnamon.
5. Serve with hot buttered toast.

Swiss Cheesecake
Makes: 10 servings

Crust
1 shortbread cookie crust

Cheesecake
2 cups cottage cheese
1 cup Swiss cheese, grated
6 tablespoons butter, softened
3 tablespoons unbleached flour
3 tablespoons cornstarch

½ cup granulated sugar
6 large egg yolks
9 large egg whites
White chocolate curls for garnish

1. Preheat the oven to 350 degrees.
2. Press cottage cheese through a sieve.
3. In a large mixing bowl, beat together cottage cheese, Swiss cheese, butter, flour, cornstarch, and sugar, blending well.
4. Add egg yolks, 1 at a time, mixing well at low speed after each addition.
5. In another large bowl, beat egg whites until they form stiff peaks; fold them gently into the cheese mixture.
6. Pour the mixture into the prepared crust; bake for 45 minutes. The cake will rise above the top of the pan, then settle down again.
7. Cool in the oven with the door propped open; then chill.
8. Garnish with white chocolate curls.

Food Service and Decorative Touches
- Use the colors of the Swiss flag—red and white—in your decor.
- Cover tables with white linen or paper cloths and sprinkle snowflakes around the centerpieces. Or cut huge paper snowflakes to use as decorative touches on the tables.
- Attach a small piece of Swiss chocolate to name tags, place cards, or seating cards.
- Decorate the room and tables with frosted branches intertwined with battery-operated lights.
- Light the table with votive candles placed in a variety of stem glasses; tie beautiful bows around the stems.
- Create a collage of travel brochures, posters, and magazine covers to use as a tablecloth on the buffet table; cover with clear plastic. (See How-To's #19.)
- Use greeting cards depicting winter scenes as part of the table decor.
- Stand a small cuckoo clock on your buffet table, or, if available, include small clocks with your table centerpieces.

INTERNATIONAL FOOD FEST

Your guests will revel in a feast of foods from around the world. One plan is to have guests bring food that represents their ethnic backgrounds. Alternately, you can design and serve the menu of your choice, including popular favorites along with lesser-known treats.

Party Menu

Snacks
*Scotch Eggs
*Creamed Swedish Meatballs (page 230)
Vienna Sausages
*Russian Dill Dip
Cocktail Rye Bread and Vegetables

Beverages
*Mimi Cocktail (French Riviera)
Aquavit Shooters (page 218)
Singapore Slings
International Coffees/Teas

Buffet
Hungarian Goulash
*Chinese Chicken Pasta Salad (page 237)
French Bread

Dessert
*Won Ton Grape Tarts
Swiss Chocolate Delicacies

Scotch Eggs
Makes: 4 servings

8 eggs, hard-boiled and shelled
2 pounds sausage meat
Lettuce

1. Wrap each egg evenly with ¼ pound of sausage meat.
2. Fry at moderate temperature until brown on all sides.
3. Drain the eggs on paper towels and chill in the refrigerator.
4. When ready to serve, line a platter with lettuce and arrange the eggs, cut in half lengthwise, among the lettuce.

Russian Dill Dip
Makes: 1½ cups of dip

½ cups cream cheese, softened
¾ cup sour cream
3 ounces red or black caviar
1 teaspoon lemon juice

1 teaspoon dried dill, crushed
2 teaspoons purple onion, diced
1 large egg, hard-boiled, finely chopped
1 tablespoon fresh dill, chopped

1. Beat cream cheese to a smooth consistency.
2. Blend in sour cream and add the remaining ingredients, except the egg and fresh dill, blending well. Cover and chill.
3. Just before serving, garnish with finely chopped egg and fresh dill.

Mimi Cocktail (French Riviera)

Makes: 1 serving

2 parts gin
1 part apricot-flavored brandy
1 part cognac
1 egg white

Cracked ice
Dash of lemon juice
Dash of grenadine
Lemon and powdered sugar for garnish

1. Pour gin, brandy, cognac, and egg white into a shaker with cracked ice
2. Add a dash of lemon juice and a dash of grenadine. Shake vigorously.
3. Serve in a cocktail glass rimmed with lemon and powdered sugar.

Won Ton Grape Tarts

Makes: 4 servings

4 tablespoons unsalted butter
8 3-inch square won ton wrappers
½ cup sugar
2 teaspoons freshly squeezed lemon juice

6 ounces grapes, such as champagne
  or green, sliced in half
½ cup sour cream
Brown sugar

1. In a large skillet, melt butter over medium-low heat.
2. Add 4 won ton wrappers and fry, turning often, until just crisp (about 3 minutes).
3. Remove won tons from the skillet and transfer to a platter.
4. Repeat with remaining 4 won tons.
5. Sprinkle the skillet with the sugar, add 4 of the partially cooked won tons, and cook until sugar begins to caramelize.
6. Add lemon juice and cook the won tons, turning often, until crisp and generously coated with caramel (2 to 3 minutes).
7. Remove the won tons to a platter, and repeat process with remaining 4 won tons.
8. Mix grapes with sour cream until lightly coated.
9. Place 2 won tons on a small doily-lined plate, top with a tablespoon of grapes, and lightly sprinkle with brown sugar.

Food Service and Decorative Touches

- Include the flags from a variety of countries in your decor.
- Arrange cookbooks, foreign travel books and brochures, magazine covers, and photos as part of the table decor.
- Decorate tables with displays of breads, fresh produce, and pasta.
- Set up "'round the world" food stations representing different areas of the world.
- Create a sidewalk café atmosphere for guest dining, if possible.
- Decorate each table to represent a specific country.
- Tie ribbons in flag colors around napkins.

CASINO/GAMBLING

The casino/gambling theme is the most popular theme of the day. All kinds of "for fun" gambling seems to add excitement and, at the same time, recreational relaxation for guests. The food and drink, whether served sit-down, buffet, or grazing-style, must be of the right combination to hit the "perfect party" jackpot.

Party Menu

Snacks
*Poker-tater Chips
Veggie Chips (sliced in flat rounds)
*Clams Casino Dip

Beverages
Soft Drinks/Mineral Waters
*Nevada Cocktail
Coffees/Teas

Buffet
Hit the Jackpot-Luck Dinner:
*Wheel of Fortune Pasta Salad (page 238)
Dice-Shaped Meatballs
*Hot Shot Slaw (page 231)

Dessert
*Roulette Wheel Dessert Pizza
Ice-Cream Sundae Bar

Poker-tater Chips

Makes: 4 servings

2 medium sweet potatoes, peeled and thinly sliced
2 tablespoons olive oil
Salt, pepper, and paprika, to taste

1. Preheat the oven to 450 degrees.
2. Toss potatoes with olive oil and spread in a thin layer on a cookie sheet.
3. Sprinkle with salt, pepper, and paprika.
4. Bake about 20 minutes, until crispy.

Clams Casino Dip

Makes: 3½ cups

2 5½ ounce cans chopped clams
8 ounces cream cheese
2 cups shredded mild cheddar cheese
1 cup sour cream
1 large garlic clove, minced

4 tablespoons green pepper, chopped
8 tablespoons butter
1 tablespoon lemon juice
½ cup seasoned bread crumbs
Variety of snack crackers and chips

1. Preheat the oven to 350 degrees.
2. Mix clams, cheeses, sour cream, garlic, and pepper; spoon into a 9-inch pie plate.
3 Combine butter, lemon juice, and bread crumbs; sprinkle over dip.
4. Bake for 15 minutes or until cheese melts.
5. Serve with snack crackers and chips.

A Clown's Nose

Makes: 1 serving

1 ounce vodka
1 ounce cherry mix*
2 parts lemonade mix*
1 part cranberry juice
Cracked ice

1. Combine all ingredients and shake well; strain.
2. Pour over ice cubes.

(*To make a mix, dilute lemonade concentrate with ⅛ the required amount of water.)

Razzle Dazzle Raspberry Sherbet

Makes: 2 quarts

3 egg whites
¾ cup sugar
1 cup milk
1 cup half and half
3 cups raspberries in syrup, puréed
2 tablespoons lemon juice
Candy sprinkles for garnish

1. Beat egg whites until stiff, but not dry.
2. Gradually beat in sugar, then milk, half and half, raspberries, and lemon juice.
3. Cover and refrigerate for 30 minutes.
4. Freeze until solid.
5. Spoon the sherbet into cones or sundae glasses and top with candy sprinkles.

Food Service and Decorative Touches

- Serve drinks from a "Ticket Booth" bar setup.
- Create tents or canopies over the buffet tables or serving stations with cloth or plastic drapes in primary colors.
- Add balloons and streamers to table decor.
- Displays circus-related items, such as giant clown shoes, floppy wigs, giant glasses, hats, or trick flowers.
- If using this theme for a birthday party, use colorful mint patties as birthday candle holders.
- Set out snacks in giant popcorn boxes. (See Resources #10.)
- Include cotton candy, Cracker Jack boxes, and cardboard popcorn containers in table decor.
- Serve miniature donuts, popcorn, and peanuts in colorful plastic baskets and buckets.
- Cover tables with circus posters, then overlay with clear plastic.
- Use colorful boxes of Animal Crackers as place cards or seating assignments.
- Rent an electric popcorn maker to add the look, sound, and smell of the circus to your party atmosphere.

COMEDY

This party theme is not just for laughs! This amusing and entertaining theme mixes humor with wonderful food to produce a meaningful tribute to a fan of all things comic. Punch lines, gags, puns, slapstick, and situation comedy can all be represented in a tasteful way—very tasteful, indeed, with this menu.

Party Menu

Snacks
*A "Rarebit" Dip
"Canned" Chips
Mini Corn Dogs

Beverages
Soft Drinks/Mineral Waters
*Punch Line Beer Coctail
Beer/Wine

Buffet
"Take My Rice, Please" Casserole
Sloppy Joe'ks (page 226)
Slapstick Slaw
"On a Roll" Basket

Dessert
*PeaNutty Butter Bars
*Frozen HoHo Dessert
*Wacky Cake

A "Rarebit" Dip
Makes: 1 quart

¼ cup margarine	½ teaspoon salt
½ cup celery, chopped	1 cup milk
½ cup green pepper, chopped	1½ cups American cheese, cubed
2 tablespoons onion, chopped	1 10-ounce can tomatoes with chilies
¼ cup flour	

1. Melt margarine over low heat.
2. Add celery, green pepper, and onion. Sauté until tender.
3. Stir in flour and salt; add milk. Cook, stirring until thickened.
4. Add cheese, stirring until melted. Gradually stir in tomatoes. Cook until heated.
5. Serve hot or cold with potato chips.

Punch Line Beer Coctail
Makes: 1 serving

⅓ once Kahlua	⅓ ounce 151 rum
⅓ ounce amaretto	Beer

1. Fill a 1-ounce shot glass with Kahlua, amaretto, and top off with 151 rum.
2. Light alcohol with a match, then drop the shot, glass and all, into a glass of beer.

PeaNutty Butter Bars
Makes: about 20 squares

½ cup butter	2 cups powdered sugar
1 cup peanut butter	12 ounces chocolate chips or 2 Hershey chocolate bars
1½ cups graham cracker crumbs	

1. Cream butter and peanut butter together.
2. Add graham cracker crumbs and powdered sugar, mixing thoroughly.
3. Press the crust mixture firmly into a 9-by-13-inch pan.
4. Melt chocolate chips or chocolate bars in a double boiler.
5. Pour over the top of the crust mixture and refrigerate until chocolate is firm.
6. Cut into 2-inch squares.

Frozen HoHo Dessert
Makes: 20 servings

2 packages HoHo cakes
1 quart each of 2 ice-cream flavors of your choice, softened
16 ounces Oreo cookies, crushed
12 ounces hot fudge sauce
13-ounce container nondairy frozen topping (like Cool Whip)
Chocolate shavings

1. Cut HoHo cakes in half lengthwise.
2. Line cakes side to side on the bottom of a 9-by-13-inch baking pan.
3. Cover the HoHo layer with one flavor of ice cream.
4. Spread crushed Oreo cookies over ice cream. Freeze until the ice cream is firm.
5. Add a second layer of ice cream. Freeze until the top layer is firm.
6. Pour fudge sauce over the top ice-cream layer, then top with frozen topping.
7. Garnish the dessert with chocolate shavings. Freeze until ready to serve.

Wacky Cake
Makes: 12 to 14 servings

1½ cups flour
1 cup sugar
½ teaspoon salt
1 teaspoon baking soda
3 rounded tablespoons cocoa

1 tablespoon vinegar
1 teaspoon vanilla
5 tablespoons shortening, melted
1 cup cold water
Favorite frosting

1. Preheat the oven to 350 degrees.
2. Sift dry ingredients into a 9-by-13-inch baking dish and spread evenly.
3. Make 3 wells in the dry ingredients. Into the first well, pour vinegar; into the second, vanilla; and into the third, melted shortening.
4. Pour 1 cup cold water over everything; mix well. Bake for 30 minutes.
5. Frost with favorite frosting.

Food Service and Decorative Touches
- Label foods with titles that refer to "corn," "ham," "belly laugh," and "gut-splitting."
- Hang a sign reading "Punch Line" over the bar.
- Cover the buffet and dining tables with comic book pages and covers, Sunday comics, photos of comedians, and cartoon cutouts, then overlay with clear plastic.
- Make paper flowers from all the above-mentioned papers, especially the Sunday comics, to use in decorative arrangements. (See How-To's #13.)
- Thread napkins through the rims of comic nose-and-glasses novelties.
- Order Chinese fortune cookies with riddles and jokes inside. (See Resources #8.)

CRUISE SHIP

Invite your guests to climb the gangway for a luxurious and pampered experience aboard your own improvised cruise ship. Once you festoon your home or rented party space with shipboard decor and set out the deck activity gear, you need only to lay out a lavish (but not necessarily costly) spread, and you're ready to set sail.

Party Menu

Snacks
*Bon Voyage Brie
Tortilla Chips with Salsa
*Potato Chips with Salmon Dip (page 178)
Pita Chips with Cucumber Dip

Beverages
Soft Drinks/Mineral Waters
*Lifesaver
*Sunny Fruit Punch (page 221)
Beers/Wines
Coffees/Teas

Buffet
*Seafood Pasta Salad (page 179)
Piles of Boiled Shrimp over Ice
Large Platter Piled High with Cold Cuts
*Crudites (page 242)
Huge Baskets Filled with Beautiful Fruits and Breads

Dessert
*Chips Ahoy Ice-Cream Pie
Fruit Chunks with Chocolate Dip

Bon Voyage Brie

(Contributed by Alyss Sallerson, You're Cordially Invited, Atlanta, Georgia. See Credits.)

Makes: 6 servings

½ cup apricot jam
1 tablespoon grated orange peel
1 tablespoon brandy or orange juice
1 tablespoon lemon juice

⅛ teaspoon ground cinnamon
1 piece brie cheese (about ½ pound)
Thin baguette slices or water crackers

1. Mix jam, orange peel, brandy, lemon juice, and cinnamon in a shallow microwave-safe serving dish, large enough to also hold the brie.
2. Cover and microwave at full power 1 to 1½ minutes, until the sauce begins to bubble.
3. Set brie into the apricot sauce. Return to microwave and cook, uncovered, until the cheese is hot and slightly melted (about 1 minute); check at 20-second intervals.
4. Scoop cheese and apricot sauce onto baguette slices or crackers

Lifesaver

Makes: 1 serving

2 ounces amaretto	*1 ounce piña colada mix**	*Ice*
1 ounce banana mix*	*1 ounce strawberry mix**	*Lemonade*

1. Combine all ingredients except lemonade; shake well.
2. Pour over ice.
3. Top the glass with lemonade.

(*To make a mix, dilute concentrate with ⅓ the required amount of water.)

Chips Ahoy Ice-Cream Pie

Makes: 12 servings

32 Chips Ahoy chocolate chip cookies	*2 quarts ice cream, any combination of flavors*
¼ cup margarine, melted	*Whipped topping and strawberries or maraschino*
1 cup fudge topping	*cherries for garnish*

1. Crush 20 cookies to fine crumbs.
2. Combine cookie crumbs and margarine and press into bottom of 9-inch springform pan or pie plate.
3. Stand remaining cookies around edge of pan or pie plate.
4. Spread ¾ cup fudge topping over the crust.
5. Freeze for about 15 minutes.
6. While the crust is in the freezer, soften 1 quart of ice cream; spread the softened ice cream over the fudge layer.
7. Freeze for about 30 minutes.
8. Scoop remaining ice cream into small balls; arrange over the ice-cream layer.
9. Freeze until firm, about 4 hours or overnight.
10. Garnish with whipped topping, remaining fudge topping, and strawberries or maraschino cherries. Serve immediately.

Food Service and Decorative Touches

- Serve your dinner buffet style, reminiscent of luxury ocean liners' midnight buffet, complete with ice sculpture.
- For more formal events, cover tables with white linen cloths accentuated with crisp napkins, fresh flowers, candlelight, and your best china and silver.
- If planning a casual gathering with a shipboard theme, use paper and plastic plates and serving ware with a nautical motif in blue, white, gold, and red.
- Hang nautical signal flags as a backdrop for the buffet table, as well as around the edge of the table for a skirt.
- Invert captains hats to hold snacks or decorations.
- Incorporate Styrofoam nautical shapes, such as anchors, portholes, and ship's wheels, into your table decor.
- Tie white rope into nautical knots around royal blue napkins.
- Use white twill (or paper) sailors' hats for name tags, place cards, or seating assignments.
- Fill toy sailboats with candies or nuts to use as place cards or seating assignments (with the names written on the sail) and as party favors.

FAIR, COUNTY OR STATE

Recreate the excitement of a good, old-fashioned fair (state or county) in any locale—with the right menu. Ask anyone what they love about going to a fair, and the tantalizing aromas and tastes will be mentioned every time. This bill of fair fare is designed to satisfy all food lovers, and they won't have to stand in a long line to get it.

Party Menu

Snacks
*People's Favorite Cheese Curds
Spicy Chicken Wings
Popcorn and Peanuts
Hot Pretzels

Beverages
Soft Drinks/Mineral Waters
*Fair Weather Fruity Freeze
*Hot Apple Cider Punch (page 222)
Fresh-Squeezed Lemonade
Beer/Wine

Buffet
Corn Dogs
Foot-Long Hot Dogs
Barbecued Beef Sandwiches
Turkey Drumsticks
French Fries with Melted Cheese

Dessert
*First-Prize Apple Cheese Cobbler
Mini Donuts
Frozen Chocolate-Covered Bananas
Rainbow Ice-Cream Cones

People's Favorite Cheese Curds

(Submitted by Vicki Sachs, Green Bay, Wisconsin.)

Makes: about 32 curd pieces

1 cup flour
2 eggs, well-beaten
2 teaspoons vegetable oil
⅓ teaspoon salt

½ teaspoon baking powder
½ cup milk or beer (your choice)
1 pound cheese curds
Vegetable oil for deep-frying

1. Combine all ingredients except cheese curds and frying oil; mix well.
2. Fill a frying pan with enough oil to cover the cheese curds; heat.
3. Dip curds into the batter and drop into hot oil. Turn and brown lightly.
4. Remove and drain on a paper towel; salt lightly to taste.
5. Serve the curds in paper baskets as at a concession stand.

Fair Weather Fruity Freeze

Makes: 1 serving

⅓ cup lemonade mix*
1 tablespoon sugar
½ cup fresh or frozen strawberries

1 cup ice cubes
Banana chunk (dipped in lemon sauce
  to avoid browning) for garnish

1. Combine all ingredients, except ice and garnish, in a blender; blend until smooth.
2. With blender running, add about 1 cup ice cubes, 1 at a time (keep the lid on until the strawberry mixture becomes slushy).
3. Pour into a tall glass, garnish with a banana chunk, and serve with a tall spoon.

(*To make a mix, dilute lemonade concentrate with ⅓ the required amount of water.)

First-Prize Apple Cheese Cobbler

Makes: 6 servings

Filling

1 cup sugar

¼ cup unbleached flour

¼ teaspoon ground cinnamon

6 cups apple slices (Granny Smith apples work well)

½ cup walnuts, coarsely chopped

Topping

¼ cup sugar

½ teaspoon salt

1 cup unbleached flour

1½ teaspoons baking powder

6 ounces mild cheddar cheese, shredded

⅓ cup butter, melted

¼ cup milk

1. Preheat the oven to 400 degrees.
2. Combine sugar, flour, and cinnamon, then toss with apple slices and walnuts.
3. Pour the apple mixture into a 9-inch square baking pan.
4. To make the topping, combine the dry topping ingredients with cheddar cheese; mix well.
5. Add butter and milk; mix until well blended.
6. Spoon the dough over the fruit mixture.
7. Bake for 30 minutes.

Food Service and Decorative Touches

- Set up serving stations as concession booths; decorate with colorful striped cloths.
- Hang pennants on a string around table edges and from the ceiling to table corners for a carnival/fair atmosphere.
- Serve dry snacks, such as popcorn, pretzels, and potato chips, in large tin containers or carnival food trays.
- Have servers wear concessionaires' paper hats and aprons.
- Use jars of pickles and preserves, sporting first-prize blue ribbons, in table decor.
- Display fresh fruits, vegetables, and home-baked breads and cookies in wicker baskets lined with checked cloths.
- Use individual-sized baskets, boxes, and buckets instead of plates.
- Tie corn husk strips around cloth or paper napkins.
- Place candles in fruit jars or old jelly glasses.
- Stack food containers on top of small crates on the buffet tables.
- Arrange fresh or artificial flowers in large fruit jars, crocks, miniature milk cans, and crockery pitchers.
- Incorporate carnival items, such as straw hats, admission tickets, balloons, and game prizes like plaster statues and stuffed animals, into the table decorations.
- String colored lights around serving areas to create a festive atmosphere.

FARM LIFE

When your guest "farm hands" come in from the "back forty," the meal has to be bountiful to restore their energy after their hard work. But it's not all work on the farm; you can have fun and frolic with friends and family, either to celebrate a holiday or a milestone event.

Party Menu

Snacks
*Deviled Egg Dip with Veggies and
Crackers
Corn on the Cob
Pickled Watermelon Rinds and Pigs' Feet
Biscuits with Ham

Buffet
Variety of Pies
Pick A Sloppy Joe
*Bacon Potato Salad (page 232)
*Wagon Trail Pasta Salad (page 236)
*Crunchy Creamy Slaw (page 231)

Beverages
Soft Drinks/Mineral Waters
*Apple Pie Break
Fresh-Squeezed Lemonade
Beer/Wine

Dessert
*Kountry Kitchen Kake Squares
Home-Baked Pie
Homemade Ice Cream
Fresh Fruit Salad/Watermelon

Deviled Egg Dip with Veggies and Crackers
Makes: 2 cups

½ cup mayonnaise
2 teaspoons lemon juice
2 teaspoons prepared mustard
¼ teaspoon Tabasco sauce

½ teaspoon salt
6 eggs, hard-boiled
1 package whipped cream cheese, plain or with onion
Parsley for garnish

1. In a blender, combine mayonnaise, lemon juice, mustard, Tabasco sauce, and salt.
2. Add 1 egg at a time, blending after each egg.
3. Then blend in whipped cream cheese.
4. Garnish with parsley.
5. Serve with raw vegetables or assorted crackers.

Apple Pie Break
Makes: 1 serving

⅓ part vodka
⅓ part apple juice
⅓ part apple wine

Whipped cream
Cinnamon

1. Mix beverages together and top with whipped cream.
2. Sprinkle with cinnamon.

Kountry Kitchen Kake Squares

(This large cake recipe was developed on the farm for haying time. From *Family Reunions & Clan Gatherings* by Sherri Fiock. See Credits.)

Makes: 48 servings

2½ cups unbleached flour, sifted
3 teaspoons baking powder
½ teaspoon salt
⅛ teaspoon ground nutmeg
2 cups sugar
1 cup vegetable shortening

3 large eggs
1 teaspoon vanilla extract
1 cup milk
⅓ cup brown sugar, packed
1½ teaspoons ground cinnamon

1. Preheat the oven to 350 degrees.
2. Sift flour, baking powder, salt, and nutmeg together and set aside.
3. In a large bowl, cream together sugar and shortening until light and fluffy (use an electric mixer set at medium speed).
4. Add eggs, 1 at a time, beating well after each addition.
5. Blend in vanilla extract.
6. Add the flour mixture to the egg mixture, alternately with the milk, beating well on low speed after each addition.
7. Spread the batter in 2 13-by-9-by-2-inch greased baking pans.
8. Combine brown sugar and cinnamon and blend well; sprinkle over the cake batter.
9. Bake for 15 minutes or until the cake tests done (a toothpick inserted into the center comes out clean).
10. Cool the cakes in the pans on wire racks. Cut each cake into 24 servings.

Food Service and Decorative Touches

- Cover the buffet and dining tables with old-fashioned tablecloths (found at a thrift shop), crochet throws, embroidered runners, and cotton print fabrics.
- Keep drinks cold in galvanized washtubs.
- Give each guest a small paintbrush to use for buttering corn on the cob.
- Fill clean jars with flowers and greens for table decorations.
- Spread quilts, blankets, and tablecloths for picnic dining.
- Use packets of vegetable or fruit seeds as place cards and party favors.
- Decorate tables with small pots of herbs or flowers.
- Display copies of the *Farmer's Almanac* on serving or dining tables.
- Drape plaid shirts or cotton aprons over chairs for covers.
- Incorporate old books, magazines, utensils, toys, bandannas, straw hats, farm gloves, and small tools into decorative arrangements.
- Hang flannel shirts, bib overalls, and cotton aprons as a backdrop for your farmyard buffet table.
- Fill miniature milk cans, authentic antique or modern reproductions, with wheat or corn stalks for quaint table arrangements.
- Light the party with old or new kerosene lamps, hurricane lamps, and old-fashioned candle holders.
- Serve foods and beverages in crockery, enamelware, cut-glass bowls, or pitchers.
- Display jams, jellies, and other homemade goods with prize-winning blue ribbons.
- Fill checkered-cloth-lined baskets with freshly baked goods.

FORTUNE TELLING

Celebrate tomorrow, today! At least take a little look at what the future holds through light-hearted predictions given by readers of tea leaves, palms, handwriting, and cards. Believers and scoffers alike will buy into the "today's the day" menu and, without a doubt, will consider themselves very fortunate.

Party Menu

Snacks
*Hot Tips Dip
Veggies and Crackers
Fruit Kabobs

Buffet
A Perfect Pot "Luck" Menu
*"Crystal" Cheese Ball
*Peppy Prediction Pinwheels

Beverages
Soft Drinks/Mineral Waters
*Peachy Dreams Come True
Wine Coolers
Flavored Coffees/Herbal Teas

Dessert
*Heavenly Hash
Fortune Cookies (Resources #8)

Hot Tips Dip
Makes: about 3 cups

½ pound lean ground beef
16 ounces cream cheese, cut into small pieces
1 can (8 to 10 ounces) green chilies and tomatoes
2 teaspoons Worcestershire sauce
1 packet taco seasoning mix

1. Brown beef well and drain off grease.
2. Add all other ingredients, cover, and cook for about 1 hour, stirring frequently until the cheese is melted, and then occasionally after that.
3. Pour the dip into a clear "crystal" bowl and serve with veggies and crackers.

Peachy Dreams Come True
Makes: 1 serving

1 ounce vodka
1 ounce peach schnapps
1 ounce cherry mix*
1 ounce cream

Ice
Orange juice
Pineapple juice

1. Combine all ingredients except the juices; shake well.
2. Pour into a tall glass and fill the glass with 1 part orange juice and 1 part pinapple juice.
3. Serve with a straw.

(*To make a mix, dilute concentrate with ⅓ the required amount of water.)

"Crystal" Cheese Ball
Makes: 2 balls (1 pound each)

16 ounces cream cheese, softened
10 ounces sharp cheddar cheese, shredded
1 8¼-ounce can crushed pineapple, drained

2 tablespoons green onion, chopped
2 teaspoons Worcestershire sauce
¾ cup walnuts, chopped

1. Thoroughly blend cream cheese and cheddar cheese.
2. Fold in pineapple, chopped onion, and Worcestershire sauce. Chill for several hours.
3. Divide the mixture in half and shape each half into a ball; roll in nuts.
4. Chill overnight (or freeze until needed). Serve with crackers.

Peppy Prediction Pinwheels
Makes: 36 pinwheels

16 ounces cream cheese, softened
1 package Ranch dressing mix
2 green onions, minced
4 12-inch flour tortillas

4 ounces pimento, diced
4 ounces green chilies, diced
1 2.25-ounce can sliced black olives

1. Mix cream cheese, Ranch dressing mix, and minced onions. Spread on tortillas.
2. Drain vegetables, blot dry on paper towels, and sprinkle equal amounts on top of the cream cheese spread. Roll tortillas tightly.
3. Chill the rolls at least 2 hours. Cut into 1-inch pieces; serve with spirals facing up.

Heavenly Hash
Makes: 8 to 10 servings

8½ ounces crushed pineapple with juice
¼ cup sugar (or to taste)
2 cups boiling water
2 3-ounce packages lime Jell-O

2 2-ounce packages Dream Whip, whipped
8 ounces cream cheese, cut into small cubes
1 cup pecans, chopped

1. In a saucepan, bring pineapple, sugar, and water to a boil. Add Jell-O; stir to dissolve.
2. Chill until the mixture begins to thicken, then add Dream Whip, cream cheese, and pecans. Mix well, then chill well.
3. Serve in small crystal bowls.

Food Service and Decorative Touches
- Cover round tables with lace, tapestries, embroidered silks, and fringed shawls.
- Display wizards' hats, crystal balls, tarot cards, tea cups with leaves, and so on.
- Include lace, ribbons, silk flowers, and antique fabrics in table decorations.
- Fill teapots with bunches of flowers for table centerpieces.
- Make charming place cards with individual tea cup and saucer sets.
- Hang a variety of fortune telling items, such as giant tarot cards and gypsy posters, behind the buffet table as a backdrop.
- Use many sizes and types of glasses to hold candles—the more the better. Try to use blue glass candle holders with stars-and-moons designs.
- Arrange tarot cards on the buffet table, then cover with a clear plastic cloth.
- Tie personal horoscopes to napkins with Gypsy silk head scarves. Individual horoscope printouts are a guaranteed ice-breaker.
- Attach silver star and moon ornaments to napkin rings.

KARAOKE/STAR SEARCH

After a lively Karaoke singing and recording session, guests will be revitalized by a backstage buffet of sandwiches, coffee, and desserts fit for rising stars. A delicious variety of foods and beverages will win rave reviews from singers and audience alike.

Party Menu

Snacks
*Sing-Along Spicy Snacks
*"Right on Tuna" Stars
Pretzels/Popcorn/Potato Chips

Beverages
Soft Drinks/Mineral Waters
*Melon-Cooler Babies
*Gold Record Gelatin Shooters
(page 218, #4)
Coffees/Teas

Buffet
*Crooners' Chicken Casserole
Star-Shaped Sandwiches
Top Forty Salad Toss
Rockin' Rolls and Bandstand Breadsticks

Dessert
*"Hum a Few" Bars
Ice-Cream Bars on a Stick (Draw note
designs on the bars with white icing.)
Star-Shaped Cookies

Sing-Along Spicy Snacks
Makes: 8 to 9 cups

½ cup butter
1 to 2 tablespoons Worcestershire sauce
1 cup unsalted mixed nuts
1 cup Ritz Bits

5 cups Crispix cereal
1 cup pretzel sticks and rings
1 cup corn chips, regular flavor
Seasoning salt

1. Preheat the oven to 225 degrees.
2. In a saucepan, melt butter, then add Worcestershire sauce.
3. In a large roasting pan, mix dry ingredients except salt. Pour butter mixture over the dry snacks; mix well, then sprinkle with seasoning salt.
4. Bake in oven for about 30 minutes, stirring occasionally.

"Right on Tuna" Stars
Makes: 4 to 5 dozen

2 6½-ounce cans tuna, well drained
½ cup sharp cheddar cheese, grated
½ cup Monterey Jack cheese, grated
1 cup Ranch dressing
1 2.25-ounce can sliced ripe olives

½ cup fresh mushrooms, chopped
½ cup red pepper, chopped
1 package fresh or frozen won ton wrappers
  (or egg roll wrappers cut in fourths)
Vegetable oil

1. Preheat the oven to 350 degrees.
2. Combine tuna with cheeses, Ranch dressing, olives, mushrooms, and red pepper.
3. Lightly grease a mini muffin tin, press a won ton wrapper into each cup, and brush with oil. Bake 5 minutes, or until golden.
4. Remove the wrappers from tins, place on a baking sheet, and fill with tuna mixture.
5. Bake 5 more minutes, until bubbly.

Melon-Cooler Babies

Makes: 1 serving

2 ounces melon liqueur   1 ounce orange juice
1 ounce Sprite   Ice

Combine all ingredients and shake well. Serve over ice.

Crooners' Chicken Casserole

Makes: 10 to 12 servings

2 16-ounce cans pork and beans   ½ teaspoon soy sauce
3 cups cooked chicken, cut into   ½ cup brown sugar
   bite-sized chunks   4 teaspoons onion, minced
½ cup ketchup   4 tablespoons peach preserves

1. Preheat the oven to 325 degrees.
2. Place beans and chicken in a 4-quart casserole or baking dish.
3. Mix all other ingredients, pour over chicken and beans, cover, and bake for 1¾ hours.

"Hum a Few" Bars

Makes: 35 bars

35 soda crackers, unsalted   1 cup brown sugar, packed
1 cup butter or regular margarine   6 ounces semisweet chocolate pieces

1. Preheat the oven to 375 degrees.
2. Grease a 15-by-10-by-1-inch jelly roll pan, and line the bottom with soda crackers.
3. Combine butter and brown sugar in a saucepan. Cook over medium heat, stirring until mixture comes to a boil. Cook 3 more minutes, stirring constantly.
4. Pour the mixture evenly over crackers.
5. Bake for 15 minutes, then remove from oven. Sprinkle chocolate pieces over the hot crackers and let stand 5 minutes, then spread melted chocolate over crackers.
6. While still warm, cut between crackers making 35 squares. Refrigerate until set.

Food Service and Decorative Touches

- Set up a backstage buffet à la "Star Caterers" for the audience and performers.
- Design place cards to look like backstage passes.
- Create centerpieces using old records, CDs, sheet music, music symbols, autograph books, and microphones together with balloons, streamers, twinkle lights, and star garlands.
- Hang up a shimmery curtain, a "Be a Star" banner, and a red "recording" light.
- Pull napkins through the center holes of 45 records with customized labels.
- Write guests' names on separate sheets of paper, insert the papers into CD boxes, and stand the boxes, opened, next to plates.
- Use sheet music or record album covers as mats under dishes or centerpieces.
- Create flowers from interesting papers, such as sheet music, Mylar, and music-related magazines, to use in decorative arrangements. (See How-To's #13.)
- Unwind discarded cassette tapes, spray the tape and case gold or silver, add glittery touches, and use in decorative arrangements.
- Use LP record albums creatively: Records can be heated and shaped around bowls to create food containers for party snacks or holders for decorative items.

KINDERGARTEN

Kids will be kids . . . and so will most adults, if you just give them the chance. This truly fun and frolic-filled party theme combines activities, decor, costumes, and refreshments reminiscent of kindergarten days. The magic of this party is that no one has to act their age . . . except the truly young kids.

Party Menu

Snacks
*Cheese Puffs
*Freezer Apple 'n' Orange Pops
Carrot and Celery Sticks in Crayola Tin
Dip in a Paste Jar

Beverages
*Banana Punch (page 222)
*Oreo Spin the Bottle
Kool-Aid

Buffet
Peanut Butter and Jelly Mini Sandwiches
Burger and Hot Dog Baskets
French Fries

Dessert
*Pick-Me-Up Cake Cones
*Surprise Bite Cookies
Jell-O Jigglers in Fun Shapes
Ice-Cream Sandwiches and Sundae Bar

Cheese Puffs
Makes: 12 to 15 squares

8 slices white bread
8 ounces old-English cheese slices
¼ cup butter, melted
3 eggs
1 teaspoon salt
½ teaspoon pepper
¾ teaspoon dry mustard
2 cups milk

1. Trim crusts off bread and cut each slice into 1-inch squares.
2. Cut cheese into bite-sized pieces.
3. In a 9-by-13-inch greased casserole, alternate layers of bread and cheese.
4. Pour melted butter on top.
5. Beat eggs well; stir in salt, pepper, mustard, and milk. Combine thoroughly and pour over bread and cheese.
6. Cover and refrigerate for at least 1 hour.
7. One hour before serving, preheat the oven to 350 degrees, and bake for 30 minutes covered, then 30 minutes uncovered, until top is golden and puffy.
8. Cut into 3-inch squares and serve warm on toy plates.

Freezer Apple 'n' Orange Pops
Makes: 24 pops

2 juicy oranges, peeled and sectioned
1 big green apple, washed and cored
1 big red apple, washed and cored
2 teaspoons sugar

1. Cut oranges and apples into chunks and put in a bowl with sugar.
2. Put in the freezer for 30 to 60 minutes, mixing occasionally.
3. Just before serving, poke craft sticks into fruit and arrange "porcupine-style" in a faux sand box. (See How-To's #39.)

Oreo Spin the Bottle
Makes: 2 servings

2 ounces Kahlua
2 scoops vanilla ice cream
3 Oreo cookies, crushed

Combine all ingredients and blend until smooth. Serve in kids' cups.

Pick-Me-Up Cake Cones
Makes: 36 cones

1 box light yellow cake mix
3 dozen 3-inch flat-bottomed ice-cream cones
1 pound light frosting or 1½ cups homemade frosting
Candy sprinkles or other cake decorations

1. Preheat the oven to 350 degrees.
2. Prepare cake batter according to package instructions.
3. Fill each cone half full, and place on a baking sheet (not touching each other).
4. Bake for 25 minutes, or until an inserted toothpick comes out clean. Cool completely.
5. Frost and decorate with sprinkles or other cake decorations.

Surprise Bite Cookies
Makes: 36 cookies

Dough

¾ cup butter	1 egg	1¾ cups flour
½ cup sugar	1 teaspoon vanilla	Gumdrops or malt balls

Icing
½ cup powdered sugar, sifted
⅛ teaspoon vanilla
1½ teaspoons to 1 tablespoon milk

1. In a large bowl, beat butter for 30 seconds. Add sugar; beat until fluffy.
2. Add egg and vanilla, then flour; beat until well mixed. Cover; chill for 1 hour.
3. Preheat the oven to 350 degrees.
4. Shape 1 level tablespoon of dough around a gumdrop or malt ball to form a ball.
5. Place the cookie balls on ungreased cookie sheets.
6. Bake for 15 to 18 minutes, or until the edges are golden. Cool on a wire rack.
7. While the cookies cool, combine icing ingredients and drizzle over the cookies.

Food Service and Decorative Touches
- Use brightly colored paper and plastic serving wear and matching tablecloths.
- Be lavish with balloons, streamers, and miles of brightly colored paper chains.
- Display toys, books, puzzles, and kid headgear in table decor.
- Tie small tags, bearing guests' names, around extra-large crayons with a piece of colorful yarn for seating assignments.
- Use kids' artwork for place mats and as a backdrop for food items.
- Cover tables with paper and draw place settings and guests' names on the table.
- Use mini-Slinkys as napkin holders; create Lollipots Place Cards. (See How-To's #4.)

MAGIC

Houdini himself couldn't conjure up a better party. The magical menu and the dramatic presentation will captivate your guests. The resounding success of this party does not rely on trickery or sleight of hand, and it is done only partly with mirrors.

Party Menu

Snacks
*Abracadabra Mix
*Magic Cheese Poufs
*Salmon-chanted Eating

Beverages
Soft Drinks/Mineral Waters
*Black Magic Mixer
*Troubles Disappear Delight
Coffees/Teas

Buffet
Houdini's Linguini
Hickory Trickery Smoked Turkey
Star-Shaped Gelatin Mold Salads
White and Wheat Wands (Breadsticks)

Dessert
*Pouf, the Magic Ending
Ice-Cream Illusions (Watch 'em
disappear!)

Abracadabra Mix

Makes: 13 cups

6 cups minipretzels (1 9-ounce package)
6 cups Rice or Corn Chex cereal
1 cup shelled peanuts
1 cup brown sugar, packed

½ cup butter or margarine
¼ cup light corn syrup
1 teaspoon vanilla
½ teaspoon baking soda

1. Combine pretzels, cereal, and peanuts in a 4-quart bowl; set aside.
2. In a 2-quart glass bowl, mix together sugar, butter, and syrup.
3. Microwave on high until mixture boils (3 to 3½ minutes). Stir to dissolve sugar.
4. Microwave at 30 percent for 4 minutes, or until the mixture is golden brown.
5. Stir in vanilla and baking soda. Pour over the cereal mixture; toss to coat evenly.
6. Microwave on high uncovered 4½ to 5 minutes, or until lightly glossed; stir twice.
7. Spoon onto wax paper; cool, then break into approximately 2-inch chunks.

Magic Cheese Poufs

Makes: 40 puffs

4 ounces cream cheese
¼ pound sharp cheddar cheese
5 tablespoons butter
½ teaspoon yellow mustard

½ teaspoon Worcestershire sauce
Dash of cayenne pepper
2 egg whites, stiffly beaten
10 slices white bread, crusts removed

1. Melt cheeses and butter over low heat until smooth.
2. Add mustard, Worcestershire sauce, and cayenne. Cool, then fold in egg whites.
3. Preheat the oven to 425 degrees.
4. Cut each bread slice into 4 squares and dip each square into cheese mixture.
5. Arrange bread on a foil-covered cookie sheet; bake 3 to 4 minutes, until browned.
6. Serve immediately on mirrored trays or framed mirrors.

Salmon-chanted Eating

Makes: enough for 36 to 40 crackers

1 8-ounce can red salmon
2 large white onions, finely chopped
2 tablespoons lemon juice
Dash of salt

¼ teaspoon pepper
8 ounces cream cheese
2 tablespoons liquid smoke
¼ cup parsley for garnish

1. Drain salmon, discard bone, and mash with fork until smooth.
2. Add all other ingredients except garnish; mix until smooth and creamy.
3. Pile the spread into a bowl, garnish with parsley, and fit into the cavity of an inverted top hat. Place the hat on a platter and surround with Ritz crackers.

Black Magic Mixer

Makes: 1 serving

1 ounce vodka
1 ounce Kahlua

Ice
Lemonade mix*

Combine vodka, kahlua, and ice; shake well. Pour over ice and fill with lemonade mix.

(*To make a mix, dilute lemonade concentrate with ⅛ the required amount of water.)

Troubles Disappear Delight

Makes: 4 to 5 servings

1 shot glass Kahlua
1 shot glass Malibu rum

1 shot glass amaretto
1 shot glass cream

1 shot glass Bailey's Irish Cream
Ice

Combine all ingredients in a shaker and mix well. Strain into shot glasses.

Pouf, the Magic Ending

Makes: 14 to 16 squares

1 stick margarine
1 cup graham cracker crumbs
1 cup chocolate chips
1 cup butterscotch chips

1 cup walnuts, chopped
1 cup coconut
1 12-ounce can sweetened condensed milk
Whipped cream and star sprinkles for garnish

1. Preheat the oven to 350 degrees.
2. Put margarine into a 9-by-13-inch pan; place pan in the oven to melt margarine.
3. Add graham cracker crumbs and pat lightly to make a crust.
4. Sprinkle with chips, nuts, and coconut, and pour condensed milk on top.
5. Bake for 20 to 30 minutes and cut into 2-inch squares.
6. Serve in champagne glasses. Top with whipped cream and star sprinkles.

Food Service and Decorative Touches

- Use black linens with silver accents. Drape tables with Mylar sheets.
- Display pop-out flowers, top hats, magic wands, mirror boxes, and silk scarves.
- Sprinkle tables with glitter or magic dust and place centerpieces on mirror tiles.
- Group old theatrical posters and photos of magicians behind your buffet table.
- Fill top hats with sparkly tissue; silk, tissue, and feather flowers; and Mylar shred.
- Light tables with silver and crystal candlesticks and battery-operated twinkle lights.
- Tie napkins with small magic tricks.

MYSTERY

You can plan a party with a mystery theme, with or without actually playing a full-scale mystery game. Your guests may be seated for a full-course meal or be invited to graze at a "strolling supper," gathering clues along the way. Whatever your master plan, your menu must intrigue and enthrall your sleuths.

Party Menu

Snacks
*Hidden Clue Cheese Balls
Sherlox and Mini Bagels (with onion and cream cheese)

Beverages
Soft Drinks/Mineral Waters
*Pink Panther Punch
Beer/Wines
Coffees/Teas

Buffet
*Mike HammerBurger Casserole
Super Sleuth's Slaw
Charlie Chan's Chinese Vegetables
Breads and Rolls

Dessert
*Mannix Mandarin Orange Mold
To-Die-For Dessert (detect the most decadent)
Agatha's Crispies (Rice Krispie Bars)

Hidden Clue Cheese Balls
Makes: 36 balls

1 pound extra-sharp cheese, grated
3 cups biscuit mix
1 pound hot sausage
1 teaspoon salt
Variety of stuffings: whole cashews, peanuts, cocktail onions, mushrooms, pitted olives, anchovies, smoked oysters, or pineapple cut into small bits

1. Preheat the oven to 375 degrees.
2. Mix all ingredients except stuffings; shape into 2-inch balls.
3. Make a cavity in each ball and fill with a stuffing ingredient; reshape the ball to hide the stuffing.
4. Bake for 12 minutes. Serve hot.

Tip: These balls may be baked ahead and frozen. To defrost, heat in a 300-degree oven for 10 minutes.

Pink Panther Punch
Makes: 24 4-ounce servings

Ice ring (water, lemon juice, and frozen raspberries)
1 cup Jamaican rum
½ cup brandy

¼ cup sugar
1 quart ginger ale
¼ cup raspberry syrup
¼ cup curaçao

1. Make an ice ring: Freeze a mixture of water, lemon juice, and frozen raspberries in a gelatin mold.
2. Place the frozen ring on the bottom of a punch bowl.
3. Combine the rest of the ingredients and pour over the ice ring.

Mike HammerBurger Casserole
Makes: 8 servings

2 cups brown rice, uncooked
1 cup celery, chopped
¼ cup soy sauce
½ cup fresh mushrooms, sliced

1 can cream of mushroom soup
½ cup onion, chopped
1 pound lean ground beef (or turkey)
4 cups boiling water

1. Preheat the oven to 350 degrees.
2. In a 9-by-13-inch baking dish, mix all ingredients except water.
3. Pour boiling water over mixture.
4. Bake for 30 to 40 minutes.

Mannix Mandarin Orange Mold
Makes: 10 servings

60 Ritz crackers, finely crushed
¼ pound margarine, melted
¼ cup sugar

1 6-ounce can unsweetened frozen orange juice
1 12-ounce can sweetened condensed milk
2 11-ounce cans mandarin oranges, drained
8 ounces frozen dairy topping, thawed

1. Mix cracker crumbs, margarine, and sugar.
2. Press mixture firmly into a 9-by-13-inch baking dish, reserving some crumbs for garnish.
3. Blend thawed orange juice with condensed milk.
4. Fold in mandarin oranges and thawed dairy topping; do not beat.
5. Pour mixture over crust. Top with reserved crumbs.
6. Refrigerate or freeze until serving.

Food Service and Decorative Touches
- Stand hardcover mystery novels on the tables.
- Include toy guns, knives, ropes, and bottles labeled "poison" and marked with skull and crossbones in the table decorations.
- Cover buffet tables with mystery movie posters, and overlay with clear plastic. (See How-To's #19.)
- Cut the title section from covers of paperback mystery novels and form into circles for napkin rings. (See How-To's #27.)
- Serve bread or rolls in inverted "sleuth hats," such as Sherlock Holmes's plaid cap or Mike Hammer's felt fedora.
- Use table linens in black or gray with touches of red to represent the the inevitable bloodshed and to complement prop guns, knives, and bullets.
- Design a table arrangement around the components of the game CLUE, including the game box itself.
- Fashion a napkin holder out of a rope tied in a hangman's knot.

OVER-THE-HILL

This is the all-time staple party theme for milestone birthday parties—thirtieth, fortieth, fiftieth. The decor and costumes are usually drab and dark, and mostly black. The food however, while easy to chew, doesn't have to be drab at all. In fact, it usually features favorites of the guest of honor. These menu selections are designed to poke fun at the idea of getting older and, at the same time, getting a lot better.

Party Menu

Snacks
*Senior Sausage Minis
Hummus Dip with Pita Chips

Beverages
Soft Drinks/Mineral Waters
*Silver Threads
*Melancholy Baby Shooters (page 219)
Coffees/Teas

Buffet
R.I.P. (Real Italian Pizza) Buffet
Tombstone Pizza
Creamed Corn
Old-Favorites Salads

Dessert
*R.I.P. Cookie Pops on a Stick
Variety of Puddings

Senior Sausage Minis
Makes: 32 to 34 minis

1 quart apple cider	*2 teaspoons cornstarch*
¼ cup cider vinegar	*1 package Aidell's Smoked Chicken & Apple*
½ cup chicken stock	*Sausage Minis (See Credits.)*

1. Boil cider, vinegar, and stock down to about 2 cups.
2. Dissolve corn starch in a small amount of cold water or cider and add to sauce
3. Bring back to a boil to thicken the sauce.
4. In a skillet, brown 1 pound of Aidell's sausage.
5. Combine the cider sauce and browned minis.
6. Transfer to a chafing dish or a heat-proof casserole with a warming tray.
7. Serve warm with toothpicks.

Silver Threads
Makes: 4 servings

1 quart vanilla ice cream	*Whipped cream*
⅓ cup white crème de cacao	*Kahlua to drizzle on top*
⅓ cup amaretto	

1. Whip ice cream in a blender; add liquors.
2. Pour into glasses and top with a dollop of whipped cream
3. Drizzle Kahlua on top.

R.I.P. Cookie Pops on a Stick

Makes: 24 cookies

1 cup (2 sticks) butter
1½ cups brown sugar, firmly packed
2 eggs
2½ cups all-purpose flour
2 teaspoons baking powder
¼ teaspoon baking soda
1 teaspoon cinnamon
1 teaspoon nutmeg

½ teaspoon salt
¼ cup milk
1½ cups quick oats, uncooked
Wooden sticks
Sugar
Black food coloring
White icing

1. Cream butter; add sugar and beat until light and fluffy.
2. Beat in eggs.
3. Combine flour, baking powder, baking soda, and spices; add to creamed mixture and mix well.
4. Gradually add milk.
5. Stir in oats. Chill dough 1 to 2 hours.
6. Preheat the oven to 375 degrees.
7. Make 1½-inch balls of dough, shaping with your hands. Place the balls about 3 inches apart on an ungreased cookie sheet.
8. Insert a wooden stick halfway into each ball of dough.
9. Dip a flat-bottomed glass in sugar, then use it to flatten cookies.
10. With fingers, shape dough into gravestone shapes.
11. Bake 13 to 15 minutes, or until golden brown.
12. Cool slightly, then remove from cookie sheet and cool completely on a wire rack.
13. When completely cooled, ice with gray icing (mix black food coloring into white icing). With white icing, write R.I.P. and, if desired, the date.

Food Service and Decorative Touches

- Use black, black, and more black in your decor.
- Drape buffet tables and chair backs with black crepe paper or ribbons.
- Place a papier-mâché R.I.P. tombstone as a focal point on the buffet table.
- Incorporate colorful packaging for "mature" products, such as vitamins, liniments, denture supplies, Geritol and Grecian Formula, into table decorations.
- Spray plastic flowers and greens with black paint and use in table centerpieces.
- Place a sturdy tray on a walker to hold lightweight snacks.
- Fold "retired" eye glasses around black napkins.
- Create silly place cards or seating assignment items with a pair of false teeth chomped on a marshmallow or a small roll.
- Spread out covers of *Mature Living* or *Senior Lifestyles* magazines on the buffet or dining tables, and cover with a clear plastic cloth to protect them.
- Display retirement and senior housing brochures on your tables.

PAJAMA

Remember the wild time you had at those all-night pajama parties? In every case, the experience was unforgettable and well-worth recreating for a group of grownups. Whether your pajama-clad guests stay 'till morning or just spend a great evening, nonstop eating is a big part of the plan.

Party Menu

Snacks
*Pita Party Potatoes
Variety of Chips and Dips
Granola Bars, Pop Tarts, Nuts

Beverages
Soft Drinks/Mineral Waters
*Slumber Smoothies
*P.J.(Pineapple Juice) Punch
Hot Chocolate

Buffet
Raid the Refrigerator Spoils
*Peppy Pizza Pasta
Pick A Salad

Dessert
*Up-All-Night Chocolate Pizza
Bedtime Candy Bars Bar
Insomniac Coffee Drinks

Pita Party Potatoes
Makes: 16 pita wedges

*1 cup mashed potatoes (no milk
  or other liquid added)
3 tablespoons lemon juice*

*3 tablespoons olive oil
3 tablespoons crushed garlic
4 whole-wheat pitas*

1. Combine mashed potatoes with lemon juice, oil, and garlic; mix well.
2. Heat pitas in a dry frying pan, flipping once (or heat in the microwave).
3. Cut the pitas into quarters and dip into the potatoes.

Slumber Smoothies
Makes: 1 serving

*1 ripe banana, peach, or nectarine, peeled and cut into chunks
½ cup milk or ½ cup low-fat yogurt
1 teaspoon honey, sugar, or maple syrup
1 tablespoon natural bran*

Combine all ingredients in a blender and blend until smooth. Serve in a tall glass.

P.J. (Pineapple Juice) Punch
Makes: 6 servings

*3 cups pineapple juice
3 tablespoons superfine sugar
1 lime, cut into 8 wedges*

*3 tablespoons fresh lime juice
¾ teaspoon bitters*

*¼ cup light rum
¾ cup club soda*

1. Combine all ingredients, except club soda, in a covered 2-quart jar; refrigerate
2. Before serving, shake well, add club soda, and pour over ice.

Peppy Pizza Pasta

Makes: 8 to 10 servings

1 pound ground Italian sausage
1 cup onion, chopped
7 ounces elbow macaroni, cooked
8 ounces tomato sauce
4 ounces mushrooms, sliced

15 ounces pizza sauce
2⅓ ounces ripe olives, sliced and drained
3½ ounces packaged sliced pepperoni
　　or 1 cup packaged pepperoni, chopped
8 ounces pizza cheese, shredded

1. Preheat the oven to 350 degrees.
2. Brown sausage and onion; drain.
3. In a bowl, combine all ingredients except cheese.
4. Pour into a 13-by-9-inch baking dish. Sprinkle cheese on top.
5. Cover and bake for 45 minutes.
6. Uncover and bake 5 to 10 minutes longer, or until cheese melts.
7. Serve in small mugs or coffee cups.

Up-All-Night Chocolate Pizza

Makes: 12 servings

1¾ cups semisweet chocolate
　chips, divided
½ cup + 2 tablespoons shortening
½ cup flour
½ cup granulated sugar

2 eggs
1 teaspoon baking powder
2 tablespoons water
Assorted candy for decoration

1. Preheat the oven to 375 degrees.
2. Melt 1 cup chocolate chips and ½ cup shortening in a double boiler; cool.
3. Stir in flour, sugar, eggs, and baking powder; mix well.
4. Spread evenly into a well-greased 12-inch pizza pan. Bake for 15 minutes; cool.
5. Combine ¾ cup chocolate chips, 2 tablespoons shortening, and 2 tablespoons water; stir. Spread the glaze evenly over the cooled chocolate pizza.
6. Decorate as desired with candies.

Food Service and Decorative Touches

- Place sleeping bags, pillows, and cushions on the floor around coffee tables.
- Have guests bring their favorite "blanky" for "social security."
- Use sheets as tablecloths and pillowcases for chair-back covers.
- Place small flower arrangements in bedroom slippers.
- Use Barbie-sized flannel nightcaps as place cards.
- Attach tiny stuffed animals to ponytail holders and use as napkin holders.
- Display stuffed animals everywhere to add to the sleepy-time motif.
- Set up a table of ice cream and toppings for a Slumber Sundae Bar.
- Use "scary" and "spooky" story books or videos as part of table centerpieces or decorative arrangements.
- Display makeup, hair care, or other beauty items at all-girl showers or parties.

STARRY SUMMER NIGHT

Any guest will feel like a star at this party. This elegant and formal theme commands food and drink that sparkles with excitement. Whether the party is a special grand tribute to a guest(s) of honor or just a festive gathering for a happy occasion, it will put a twinkle in every eye. With the accent of silver or gold stars, the theme is perfect for milestone anniversary celebrations.

Party Menu

Snacks
*Caviar-Oyster Canapés
*Ritzy Bits (fit for a star)

Beverages
Soft Drinks/Sparkling Waters
*Starry, Starry Night
*Sparkling Apricot Punch (page 221)
Wines/Champagne
Coffees/Teas

Buffet
*Stroganoff Skillet Supper
Steamed Fresh Vegetables
Sparkling Gelatin Vegetable Salad (in a star-shaped mold)
Hot Crescent Rolls

Dessert
*Sparkling Champagne Dessert
Fresh Star Fruit with Yogurt Dressing

Caviar-Oyster Canapés
Makes: 20 canapés

10 slices white bread	20 smoked oysters
1 3½-ounce jar caviar	Lemon juice

1. Toast bread slices lightly and cut each slice into 2 circles 1½ inches in diameter.
2. Top each circle with caviar, a smoked oyster, and a sprinkle of lemon juice.

Ritzy Bits (fit for a star)
Makes: 8 cups

2 packages Ritz biscuit bits, 1 regular and 1 cheese	1 package Ranch dressing mix
½ cup vegetable oil	1 teaspoon dried dill
	1 teaspoon lemon pepper

1. Preheat the oven to 250 degrees.
2. Put Ritz bits into an oven-proof baking dish.
3. Combine the remaining ingredients and pour over Ritz bits; mix well.
4. Bake uncovered for 20 minutes. Stir 2 or 3 times. Serve.

Starry, Starry Night
Makes: 1 serving

1 ounce tropical schnapps	1 ounce vodka
1 ounce tropical punch	Sprite

1. Combine all ingredients except Sprite; shake well
2. Pour over ice and fill glass with Sprite.

Stroganoff Skillet Supper

Makes: 4 to 6 servings

1 pound lean ground beef	2 tablespoons flour
1 medium onion, chopped	8 ounces tomato sauce
1 clove garlic, minced	4 ounces mushroom pieces, drained
1 teaspoon salt	1 cup sour cream
¼ teaspoon pepper	

1. In a large skillet, brown beef and onion; drain off grease.
2. Add garlic, salt, and pepper; stir in flour, tomato sauce, and drained mushrooms.
3. Simmer for 5 minutes. Stir in sour cream; heat for 3 minutes.
4. Serve over noodles or rice.

Sparkling Champagne Dessert

Makes: 8 servings

1½ cups boiling water	1½ cups seltzer or club soda, chilled
1 8-serving-size package Sparkling White Grape Jell-O	1 cup strawberries, sliced

1. In a large bowl, stir boiling water into gelatin until completely dissolved.
2. Stir in cold seltzer.
3. Refrigerate 1½ hours until thickened.
4. Measure 1 cup thickened gelatin into a medium bowl; set aside.
5. Stir strawberries into the remaining gelatin. Spoon into champagne flute glasses.
6. Beat reserved gelatin with an electric mixer on high speed until double in volume
7. Spoon over gelatin with strawberries. Refrigerate 3 hours or until firm.

Food Service and Decorative Touches

- Sprinkle shiny silver and gold stars and other glittering touches everywhere.
- Set the table with crisp, white linens, fine crystal and china, and silver/gold flatware.
- Light up the dining area, indoors or outdoors, with silver luminary light bags with star cutouts. Weave twinkle lights with flowers and greens.
- Create a centerpiece for a long banquet-style table by arranging long tree branches sprayed with glittery paint down the center of the table. Place fresh white flowers and greens in florist's water tubes and tuck them into the branches. Light the arrangement with crystal-cut votive candle holders or tall tapered candles.
- For an exquisite place card, use a formal, white, professionally printed or hand-written card trimmed with glitter dust, star-shaped confetti, and shiny Mylar ribbon.
- Cover chairs with white pillowcases, pressed crisp with spray starch. Tie Mylar fabric strips around chair backs in big bows.
- Fashion flowers from star-patterned cellophane or tissue paper, then wrap stems around napkins to serve as napkin holders. (See How To's #13.)
- Cover a white linen (or paper) cloth with star-patterned cellophane for an elegant buffet-table treatment. Drape glitter-flecked tulle around table edge.
- Use small star-shaped picture frames for seating assignments or place cards.

SURFIN' USA

The surf's up and so is the excitement and exuberance felt by guests at a party with this popular and easy theme. It won't matter if you are at the beach, pool, or in your backyard—you can produce familiar ocean-side sights, sounds, and, most importantly, tastes that will make any beach bum feel at home.

Party Menu

Snacks
*Salty Nutty "Sand"wiches
Seafood Dip
Fish-Shaped Crackers

Beverages
Soft Drinks/Mineral Waters
*Shark in the Water
*Sunny Fruit Punch (page 221)
Beers/Wines

Buffet
Beach Bum Burgers/Brats Bar
"Moon Doggy" Dogs
Fish 'n' Chips
Seafood Pasta Salad (page 179)

Dessert
*Catch a Wave Cheese Bars

Salty Nutty "Sand"wiches
Makes: 6 servings

2 cups whole pecans or walnuts
   (about ½ pound)
4 ounces cream cheese

4 ounces Stilton or Danish blue cheese
1 tablespoon mayonnaise
½ teaspoon Worcestershire sauce

1. Preheat the oven to 350 degrees.
2. Toast nuts on a baking sheet for 8 to 10 minutes, or until fragrant; cool.
3. In a food processor or by hand, combine cheeses, mayonnaise, and Worcestershire sauce until blended.
4. Refrigerate until firm.
5. Spread about ½ teaspoon of the cheese mixture between 2 nut halves.
6. Refrigerate until serving.

Shark in the Water
Makes: 1 serving

1 ounce vodka
1 ounce curaçao
Cracked ice

Lemonade mix*
½ ounce strawberry mix*

1. Combine vodka, curaçao, and ice; shake well. Strain.
2. Pour over ice into a tall glass.
3. Fill the glass with lemonade mix.
4. Add strawberry mix.

(*To make a mix, dilute concentrate with ⅓ the required amount of water.)

Catch a Wave Cheese Bars

Makes: 24 servings

Crust

¾ cup margarine
¾ cup brown sugar
¼ cup coconut rum

3 cups flour
1 cup almonds, finely chopped

1. Preheat the oven to 350 degrees.
2. Cream together margarine, sugar, and coconut rum.
3. Beat in flour until blended.
4. Stir in nuts.
5. Pat into a 10-by-15-inch pan.
6. Bake for 10 minutes; cool.

Cheese Layer

24 ounces cream cheese, softened
½ cup sugar
3 eggs
¼ cup coconut rum

2 cans crushed pineapple, drained
1 cup almonds, chopped
1 cup shredded coconut

1. Beat cream cheese, sugar, eggs, and coconut rum until creamy.
2. Stir pineapple into the cheese mixture.
3. Pour the cheese/pineapple mixture on top of the baked crust.
4. Combine nuts and coconut; mix well and sprinkle over the cheese layer.
5. Bake at 350 degrees for 20 minutes; cool.
6. Cut into bars.

Food Service and Decorative Touches

- Cover tables with paper or fabric cloths, then overlay with fishnetting.
- Fill seashells of various sizes with snacks, nuts, and tiny candies.
- Fill individual seashells with chocolate candies, wrap with cellophane, and tie with fishnetting. Attach tags with guests' names and use as seating assignments or place cards. The shells also make fun favors.
- Serve food and snacks from plastic pail-and-shovel sets.
- Feature inflated beach balls, floats, and sand pails and shovels of all sizes in either buffet or dining table decorations.
- Create sand blocks to make castles for table decor. (See How-To's #11.)
- Use miniature surf boards as serving trays.
- Search through party catalogs for hundreds of decorative fish, shell, or beach items to use for favors and decorations.
- Drape fishnetting and beach towels on buffet tables or as backdrops for food service areas.
- Set up a beach shack as a bar.
- Cover "beach music" 33 ⅓ record album covers with plastic wrap to make fun snack trays.
- Let guests take home terry-cloth napkins.
- Use tiny inflatable life preservers as napkin holders

TACKY/TASTELESS

Here's the party theme that brings out the worst in everyone. Sporting their least presentable clothing, shoes, accessories, and hairstyles, your guests will show up to show off their very worst behavior. Your task is to serve these fun-loving misfits a variety of foods and beverages that, although presented in a low-brow style, will still be very tasty.

Party Menu

Snacks
*Spam on a Stick
Velveeta or Cheese Wiz on Saltines
Fish Sticks

Beverages
No Name Cola/Tap Water (if drinkable)
*Windex Shots
Cheap Beer/Boxed Wine

Buffet
Pitiful, Poor Excuse Potluck:
Frozen Pizzas
Grilled Cheese Sandwiches
White Castle Hamburgers (or local "gut bomb" favorite)

Dessert
*Drowning Twinkies
Fruit Cake
Ding Dongs/HoHos
Jell-O

Spam on a Stick
Makes: as much as you want

2 cans Spam
Mustard dip of choice (served in tuna can)

1. Preheat the oven to 350 degrees.
2. Cut Spam into 1-inch chunks.
3. Spread Spam chunks out on a cookie sheet and bake for 10 minutes.
4. Spear each chunk with a Popsicle stick.
5. Arrange the spam sticks in an electric frying pan, at the lowest setting. Place on serving table, plug displayed.

Windex Shots
Makes: 1 serving

1 shot vodka
1 shot triple sec
1 shot curaçao
1 shot Rose's Lime Juice
Ice

Combine all ingredients in a glass, mix well, and drink.

Tip: Or you can mix equal parts into a pitcher to make as much as you like

Drowning Twinkies

Makes: 4 servings

6-ounce package orange Jell-O
½ cup pineapple juice
1 quart vanilla ice cream, softened
½ cup 7-Up
8 Twinkies

1. Dissolve Jell-O in boiling water according to package directions.
2. Add pineapple juice, ice cream, and 7-Up.
3. Mix thoroughly (in a blender, if necessary) to dissolve the ice cream, and pour into a deep pan, approximately 9-inch square.
4. Chill until the mixture begins to set.
5. Lay Twinkies, flat side down, in 2 rows on top of the chilled gelatin. (When gelatin is properly chilled, it will resist the Twinkies when you press them in and they will rise a bit.)
6. Chill until fully set; serve.

Food Service and Decorative Touches

- Use any and all tacky, wacky, and tasteless items.
- Cover tables with fabrics of clashing colors and garish prints.
- Use cast-off and garage sale vases filled with dreadful plastic flowers and trimmed with bedraggled lace or ribbons.
- Make place mats of grocery bags, being sure to leave logos in full view.
- Feature a variety of brand-name items, such as serving containers, glasses, paper logo-imprinted products, and advertising specialty gadgets.
- Prominently display white elephant eyesores from the attic and closet.
- Create festive table decorations with supplies from other themes or holidays.
- Serve foods in mismatched dishes, buckets, baskets, or boxes.
- Present each guest with his or her own personalized plastic pocket protector, which can serve as a place card, seating assignment, or napkin holder.
- Pour beverages straight from the container (no crystal pitchers, please) into small fruit or jelly jars and plastic cups or glasses imprinted with logos.
- Lay foods out on the buffet table in original containers: pizza in a cardboard delivery box, chicken in a bucket, and so on.
- Serve food straight from a Crockpot or electric frying pan.
- Label mineral water bottles "Tap Water."

THIS IS YOUR LIFE

Pay tribute to a guest(s) of honor with a meaningful party filled with nostalgia and humor. As the guests express their thoughts and wishes, they can partake of foods and beverages from the guest-of-honor's list of lifetime favorites or those selected just for the event.

Party Menu

Snacks
*"The Big Cheese" Wheel
"Here's to You" Crab Toast
*"Apple of My Eye" and Dip
Life Cereal Party Snacks
Veggies with Dips

Beverages
Soft Drinks/Mineral Waters
*Memories
Beer/Wine

Buffet
*Spice of Life Casserole
Pick A Salad
"Breads of Life" Basket

Dessert
*"Life Is Just a Bowl of Cherries" Bake
Chocolate "Fond a You" Dip
with Fresh Fruit

"The Big Cheese" Wheel
Makes: 24 servings

1 pound Monterey Jack round
3 ounces cream cheese, softened
½ teaspoon dried basil leaves, crushed

¼ cup marinated artichoke hearts,
  drained and chopped
¼ cup pine nuts, toasted

1. Hollow out the cheese round with a knife or spoon, leaving a ½-inch-thick shell on the sides and bottom; reserve the cheese shell.
2. Finely chop 1 cup scooped-out cheese (reserve any extra for another use).
3. Place chopped cheese, cream cheese, basil, artichoke hearts, and 3 tablespoons of pine nuts into a food processor fitted with a steel blade; cover and process until well mixed. Pack mixture into the cheese shell.
4. Sprinkle with the remaining pine nuts; press lightly.
5. Cover and refrigerate until filling is firm, about 3 hours.
6. Cut into thin wedges. Serve with assorted crackers or breads.

"Apple of My Eye" and Dip
Makes: about 3 cups

8 ounces cream cheese, softened
½ cup lemon yogurt
1 tablespoon honey
½ teaspoon vanilla

½ cup coconut, toasted
3 tablespoons milk
Apples, sliced

1. In a small bowl, beat together cream cheese, yogurt, honey, and vanilla until smooth.
2. Stir in coconut and milk. Put into a serving bowl, cover, and chill.
3. Place the bowl of dip on a serving plate and surround with fresh apple slices.

Memories
Makes: 1 serving

1 ounce amaretto	Cracked ice
1 ounce melon liqueur	2 scoops ice cream (optional)

1. Combine amaretto, liqueur, and ice; shake well. Strain.
2. Serve over ice, or mix with 2 scoops of ice cream. (If using ice cream, leave out ice.)

Spice of Life Casserole
Makes: 18 servings

1 pound small shell macaroni	1 16-ounce can tomato sauce, divided
2 pounds ground beef	1 10-ounce jar chili sauce
1 large onion, chopped	1 8-ounce can mushroom pieces
1 16-ounce can kidney beans, drained	1 3-ounce can ripe olives, sliced and drained
1 16-ounce can creamed corn	1 cup cheddar cheese, shredded

1. Cook macaroni according to package directions; drain.
2. Sauté ground beef with chopped onion until done; drain off grease.
3. Transfer the meat to a casserole dish.
4. Stir in beans, corn, tomato sauce, chili sauce, mushrooms, olives, and macaroni.
5. Divide the macaroni mixture into 3 2-quart casseroles and sprinkle cheese on top.

Tip: To serve immediately, bake at 375 for 25 to 30 minutes, or freeze to use later.

"Life Is Just a Bowl of Cherries" Bake
Makes: 18 to 20 servings

2 16-ounce cans cherry pie filling	1 cup pecans, chopped
1 package white cake mix	1 cup butter or margarine, melted
1 cup flaked coconut	Whipped cream for garnish

1. Preheat the oven to 350 degrees.
2. Spread pie filling in 2 8- or 9-inch square baking dishes.
3. Prepare cake mix according to package directions; pour over the pie filling.
4. Sprinkle with coconut and pecans and drizzle melted butter on top.
5. Bake for 40 minutes. Serve warm or cold, topped with whipped cream.

Food Service and Decorative Touches
- Use colors to match the cover of *Life Magazine*—red, black, and white.
- Incorporate guest-of-honor's photos and memorabilia into table decor.
- Collect old copies of *Life Magazine* to use as decorative touches. Use covers as place mats or arrange in collages on table tops. (See How-To's #19.)
- Stand *Life Magazines,* rolled up and secured with ribbon, holding flowers, greens, and other decorative items, in the center of the tables.
- Design a "tributary" buffet backdrop display of photo blowups.
- Make three-inch copies of photos of guest-of-honor's face at different stages of life. Cut out faces in squares or circles, paint with a protective coating, and attach to small plastic or leather-like straps to simulate watches. Label them "The Times of Her/His Life" and use as place cards, napkin rings, or seating assignments.

PREHISTORIC/FLINTSTONES

Now here's a party that takes you waaaaaay back, to a time when a party planner was "between a rock and hard place" when it came to putting together the refreshments for a gala festivity. Today's host, however, will find a whole quarry of options to consider when designing a menu of Flintstones Food Fare or Granite Gourmet Grub for a room full of Prehistoric Party Primates.

Party Menu

Snacks
*Flintstone's Fiery Dip
*Toasted Pita Chips (page 78)
Roots and Berries (veggie and fruit tray)
Kid's Dinosaur Crackers

Beverages
Soft Drinks/Mineral Waters
*Yabba Dabba Doo on the Rocks
Beers/Wines
Coffees/Teas

Buffet
Bone Appetit Buffet:
Dino-Dogs and Barney Burgers
Potato Pebbles and Granite Gravy
Boney Baloney on Stone-Ground Bread
*Jurassic Pork 'n' Pasta Salad
Stone Crabs

Dessert
*Rocky Road So Smooth
Rock Candy
Fresh Berry Bowls
Lava Java

Flintstone's Fiery Dip
Makes: 2½ cups

½ cup Miracle Whip
16 ounces pinto beans, drained and mashed
1 cup cheddar cheese, shredded
4 ounces green chilies, diced
¼ teaspoon Tabasco sauce

1. Preheat the oven to 350 degrees.
2. Combine all ingredients until well blended.
3. Spoon the mixture into a small oven-proof dish.
4. Bake for 30 minutes or until bubbly.
5. Serve with toasted pita chips.

Yabba Dabba Doo on the Rocks
Makes: 1 serving

1 ounce rum
1 ounce strawberry mix*
1 ounce tropical mix*
1 part sweet sour mix
1 part orange juice
Cracked ice

1. Combine all ingredients; shake well. Strain.
2. Serve on the rocks.

(*To make a mix, dilute juice concentrate with ⅓ the required amount of water.)

Jurassic Pork 'n' Pasta Salad

Makes: 6 servings

Salad Ingredients

8 ounces uncooked macaroni shells
1 cup cooked pork, cubed
1 small onion, diced
3 carrots, diced

1 can whole kernel corn
1 cup canned peas
1 stalk celery, chopped
½ cup black olives, chopped

Dressing

Favorite salad dressing, to taste

1. Cook shells according to package directions. Drain, cool, and put into a large bowl.
2. Add the remaining salad ingredients.
3. Pour dressing over the salad and toss well. Refrigerate at least 2 hours.

Rocky Road So Smooth

Makes: 1 serving

1 ounce hazelnut liqueur
1 ounce crème de cacao (dark)
2 scoops Rocky Road ice cream

1. Combine all ingredients and blend until smooth.
2. Serve in stoneware cups.

Food Service and Decorative Touches

- Tie-dye bed sheets and pillow cases gray and black to use as table and chair covers.
- Spray-paint papier-mâché, tin, cardboard, glass, Styrofoam, or plastic containers with faux granite to hold snacks or serve as centerpieces.
- Attach a small toy dinosaur to place cards, name tags, and seating assignments.
- Wrap a few pieces of rock candy in gray netting and tie with a black ribbon. Place at each guest's plate as a place card, favor, or decorative touch.
- Decorate paper napkins, cups, place cards, and seating assignments with dinosaur stickers and rubber-stamp art.
- Paint guests' names on small rocks for place cards or seating assignments. Attach magnet material to the backs, and the rocks can serve as favors.
- Accent the table decor with fabrics or papers in animal-skin-print designs.
- Cut a variety of small bone shapes from Foamcore, spray with granite paint, and attach to ponytail holders to use as napkin holders.

TOGA

This theme is very popular with guests who are college aged or those who wish they were again. Caesar will be honored if you serve one of his salads, but probably not if it is accompanied by Brut wine. Your goal as Palace Party Host is to lay out an "orgy" of foods and beverages fit for the gods and goddesses. Although historically toga has Roman roots, this party menu also pays tribute to the Greeks (college-campus variety), who really know how to toga!

Party Menu

Snacks
*Feta Cheese Dip with Toasted Pita Chips
Mini Lamb/Olive/Onion Kabobs
(on cocktail picks)
Fresh Grapes

Beverages
Soft Drinks/Mineral Waters
*Venus DiMilo Mellow Shooter
Ale in Chalices
Wines of the Gods
Gladiator Gatorade

Buffet
*French Fry Free-for-All
Toppings for Fries
Caesar's Salad Bar

Dessert
*Melon Ball Medley
Bacchanal Baklava

Feta Cheese Dip with Toasted Pita Chips
Makes: about 1 quart

8 ounces cream cheese
10 ounces feta cheese
½ cup milk, divided
10 ounces frozen spinach, thawed
½ onion, finely chopped

5 garlic cloves, crushed
1 teaspoon Worcestershire sauce
¼ teaspoon salt
1 tablespoon honey
¼ cup bread crumbs

1. Mash cheeses with a ¼ cup milk in a blender. Gradually add chunks of spinach
2. In a medium saucepan, combine the cheese mixture with the rest of the ingredients, adjusting the amount of milk to your taste.
3. Bring the mixture to a slow boil and cook until slightly thickened.
4. Transfer the dip to a serving bowl and allow to thicken.
5. Serve with toasted pita chips. (See page 78.)

Venus DiMilo Mellow Shooter
Makes: 1 serving

⅓ part melon liqueur
⅓ part anisette
⅓ part cranberry juice

Layer the ingredients in a shot glass

French Fry Free-for-All

(French fries were invented by Greeks.)

Makes: as much as you like

Potatoes

Seasoning (salt and pepper or other), to taste

Toppings, accompaniments, and garnishes: ketchup, mustard, mayonnaise, vinegar, cheese, gravy, chili, barbecue sauce, tartar sauce, and whatever else strikes your fancy

1. Plug in a bunch of Fry Babies and keep them busy!
2. Prepare a variety of fries: plain cut, crinkle cut, thick cut, cottage, wedge, skin-on, curly, and/or thick.
3. Season fried potatoes with salt or pepper or a variety of seasonings, to taste.
4. Lay out a banquet of toppings, accompaniments, and garnishes.

Important Frying Facts:
- Best potatoes to use for fries are Yukon Gold.
- Canola oil works best. Be sure you use virgin (unused) oil.
- Frying temperature should not exceed 370 to 380 degrees.
- Potatoes should be fried for 9 to 12 seconds, at most.

Melon Ball Medley

Makes: 8 to 10 servings

2 cups cantaloupe melon balls
2 cups watermelon balls
2 cups green seedless grapes

½ cup walnuts, coarsely chopped
½ cup sour cream
½ cup brown sugar

1. Mix fruit, nuts, and sour cream until all the fruit is coated with sour cream.
2. Spoon the fruit mixture into goblets.
3. Sprinkle brown sugar on top.
4. Serve with sundae spoons.

Food Service and Decorative Touches

- Cover tables with white bed sheets, and chairs with pillowcases. Tie and trim with gold braid.
- Wrap small sprays of laurel wreaths around napkins.
- Spray-paint containers of various sizes with gold paint: Use to serve food and beverages.
- Display books, photos, and artwork depicting mythological Roman and Greek gods.
- Create a background display for the buffet table with draped sheets, pedestals, and branch-filled urns.
- Have servers wear custom T-shirts imprinted with Latin slogans and sayings. (See Resources #14.)
- Include holly leaves in all floral arrangements on buffet and dining tables.
- Collect pottery goblets or mugs from thrift stores and spray-paint them gold. Tie gold cords around stems or bases. Use these chalices to serve ale

MEDIEVAL

Revelers in Medieval times weren't too particular about how their food was served to them, but "how much" was a very important detail—food was served on large trays and beverages were passed in tankards. Food that did not find its way to the guests' mouths was enjoyed by some of the earliest party animals, the dogs lying in wait for dropped food morsels.

Party Menu

Snacks
*Toasted Stuffed Brown Rolls
*Parmesan Crisps
Meat Loaf Spread
Whole-Wheat Bread Loaves

Beverages
Fruit Juice/Mineral Waters
*Mulled Spiced Cider Punch
Tankards of Ale and Mead

Buffet
Meat and Potato Pies
Turkey Drumsticks
Vegetable Salads

Dessert
*Rosy Almond Cream
Huge Bowls of Fresh Fruits
Cheeses
Baked Apples

Toasted Stuffed Brown Rolls

Makes: 6 servings

3 whole-meal or whole-wheat brown rolls, halved with bread scooped out
2 ounces butter
4 ounces mushrooms, coarsely chopped
4 ounces fresh spinach, coarsely chopped
2 ounces raisins
Salt, pepper, ground cinnamon, cloves, to taste
1 large egg

1. Put halved rolls into a moderately hot oven for about 10 minutes, or until they are lightly browned and crisp.
2. Melt butter in a pan, add mushrooms, and cook for a couple of minutes.
3. Add spinach and raisins and continue to cook gently for several minutes, or until the butter has been almost absorbed.
4. Season to taste with salt, pepper, cinnamon, and cloves.
5. Beat an egg in a bowl, add to the veggie mixture, and cook gently until the egg slightly binds to the other ingredients.
6. Pile the filling into the halved rolls and serve at once.

Parmesan Crisps

Makes: 18 crisps

6 tablespoons all-purpose flour
4 tablespoons (½ stick) butter, chilled
2 cloves stewed garlic in oil, drained

Pinch of salt
4 tablespoons grated Parmesan cheese,
  preferably imported Reggiano

1. Process all ingredients in a food processor until a dough is formed.
2. Roll the dough into a log about 1½ inches in diameter, wrap in plastic, and chill until firm, about 1 hour.
3. Preheat the oven to 350 degrees.
4. Slice dough ¼-inch thick; place 2 inches apart on a wax-paper-lined baking sheet. Bake for 10 minutes, or until golden brown. Cool on a wire rack.

Mulled Spiced Cider Punch

Makes: 32 4-ounce servings

4 quarts bottled cider
¼ teaspoon bitters
2 teaspoons whole allspice
Brandy or rum (optional)

2 cups orange juice
2 teaspoons whole cloves
½ teaspoon nutmeg

6 tablespoons brown sugar
6 cinnamon sticks for garnish
Orange slices for garnish

1. In a saucepan, combine all ingredients except orange slices. Simmer for 30 minutes.
2. Serve warm in a mug with an orange slice and a cinnamon stick for garnish.

Rosy Almond Cream

Makes: 6 servings

2½ cups milk
2 ounces ground almonds
½ teaspoon ground cinnamon
1 teaspoon ground ginger
1½ ounces rice flour

12 ounces berries or currants, fresh or defrosted
3 ounces sugar
1-2 tablespoons wine vinegar (to emphasize
  the flavor of the fruit), to taste
Crystallized rose or violet petals for garnish (How-To's #32)

1. Put milk in a pan with ground almonds; bring to boil, and simmer for 3 minutes.
2. Meanwhile, mix spices with rice flour in a pan, then gradually add hot almond milk; cook until the mixture thickens slightly. Add berries and sugar. Reserve some berries for garnish.
3. Cook gently until the sugar melts—the fruit should not totally disintegrate, but it should be partially mushed. Add vinegar to taste.
4. Spoon the dessert into glasses and chill for a couple of hours.
5. Serve at room temperature; garnish with berries or crystallized rose petals.

Food Service and Decorative Touches

- Serve dinner on bare wooden tabletops or on tables covered with brown craft paper. Wooden picnic-style tables and benches work well.
- Serve food on pewter plates and beverages in pewter tankards.
- Provide only knives and spoons—forks weren't invented yet!
- Incorporate hand-tooled leathers and soft suede into your table decorations.
- Print individual menus on beige parchment paper, rolled up scroll-style and fastened with a blob of wax and your special seal.
- Drape tables with real or painted tapestries.
- Use candle holders of stained glass, wood, or wrought iron.
- Hang warriors' shields (coats of arms, dragons, griffins) behind food service areas.
- Fill pewter or silver tankards and goblets with fresh wild flowers.
- If you can, rent or create a boar's head for a buffet table centerpiece.
- Pull napkins through wooden, leather, or wrought-iron rings.

VICTORIAN/ GAY NINETIES

Even though the Gay Nineties in the United States and the Victorian era in Britain took place at the same time, they had very different moods and ambiance. Food and drink had some similarity, but not in presentation. This plan includes ideas for both the naughty Nineties and the very proper days of Victoriana.

Party Menu

Snacks
*Shrimp Cheese Pâté
Small Candy Mints
Mixed Nuts

Beverages
Soft Drinks/Mineral Waters
*Raspberry Schnapps Ice Tea
Champagne Punch
Port Wine
Demitasse/Teas

Buffet
*Dining Room Dinner
Tea-Time Sandwiches
Fresh Fruit with Dips
Fresh Vegetables with Dips

Dessert
*Proper Pound Cake
Homemade Ice Cream
Dainty Sugar Cookies
Strawberries and Cream

Shrimp Cheese Pâté
Makes: 34 servings

8 ounces tiny Danish shrimp, drained
8 ounces cream cheese

Black pepper, freshly ground, to taste
2 teaspoon sherry, Madeira, or cognac

1. Combine all ingredients; beat until very smooth.
2. Serve on toast rounds or cucumber slices, or stuff into radishes or celery.

Raspberry Schnapps Ice Tea
Makes: 1 serving

2 ounces raspberry schnapps
Ice

Ice tea
Mint leaf for garnish

1. Pour schnapps over ice in a tall glass.
2. Fill the rest of the glass with ice tea. Garnish with a mint leaf.

Dining Room Dinner
Makes: 8 to 10 servings

2 cups cooked ham, cut into 1½-inch strips
½ pound mushrooms, quartered
½ cup green pepper, cut into 1-inch strips
Dash of thyme
¼ cup butter or margarine
2 10½-ounce cans cream of chicken soup

1 cup water
4 cups cooked rice
18 ounces frozen artichoke hearts, drained
¼ cup sherry
2 tablespoons pimento, chopped
½ cup cheddar cheese, shredded

1. Preheat the oven to 350 degrees
2. In a skillet, brown the ham.
3. Cook mushrooms, pepper, and thyme in butter until the green pepper is tender.
4. Combine soup, water, cooked rice, artichokes, sherry, pimento, and ham; divide the mixture into 2 2½-quart casseroles. Sprinkle cheese around the edges.
5. Bake for 30 minutes. (Or refrigerate until needed.)

Proper Pound Cake

Makes: 12 servings

3 cups self-rising flour	4 eggs
1 cup vegetable shortening	1 teaspoon mace
1½ cups sugar	2 teaspoons vanilla, or 1 teaspoon vanilla
1 cup milk	and 1 teaspoon lemon extract

1. Preheat the oven to 350 degrees.
2. Place flour, shortening, sugar, and milk into a large mixing bowl; beat at medium speed until well blended and smooth.
3. Add eggs, 1 at a time, and continue beating for 5 minutes; add flavorings.
4. Pour the batter into a greased 10-inch tube or loaf pan and bake for 1 hour.

Food Service and Decorative Touches

Victorian:
- Set a true Victorian mood with white wicker furniture or decorator accents.
- Cover tables with linen, lace, crochet, or velvet cloths, doilies, and table runners.
- Set out fine china, silver, and good glassware, as well as silver tea or coffee services.
- Create decorative table arrangements with fresh or silk flowers and greens, especially ferns, trimmed with pastel-colored ribbons.
- Serve food in lovely cut-glass bowls and pitchers and on silver platters.
- Display very ornately framed photos of the era.
- Make beautifully hand-lettered place cards with creamy formal paper.
- Cover chair backs with crisply starched white pillow cases, then tie them back with beautiful ribbons and tuck flowers into the bow knots.
- Tie ribbons and flowers around napkins.
- Gather odd pieces of silverware, bend in half, and use as napkin rings.

Gay Nineties:
- Spread red, black, or gold satin and velvet cloths on the buffet tables.
- Cover the dining tables with red linens accented with black and gold.
- Use cardboard and colored tissue paper to create faux stained-glass Tiffany shades for electric candles.
- Serve food in antique crockery and in cut-glass and china containers.
- Drape fringe trim around the edges of the buffet table.
- Search thrift shops for antique sheet music to use in table decor. Lay a collage of sheet music on the buffet table and cover with clear plastic (See How-To's #19.)
- Find or create era-appropriate pieces of clothing, accessories, or shoes to enhance your table decor.
- Cover two-inch-wide cardboard tubes with satin and trim with fringe to make napkin holders.

ROARING TWENTIES

Roll up the rug and lock the door for a members-only "what's-the-password?" speakeasy party. Your guests, all dolled up in their glamorous garb will rave on and on about your "neat eats" and "devoon drinks." Fill the bathtub with gin, crank up the Victrola, and get ready to have so much fun that you oughtta get raided!

Party Menu

Snacks
*Password Passarounds
Goldfish Crackers

Beverages
Soft Drinks/Mineral Waters
*Bathtub Gin Punch in a Coffee Cup
Coffees/Teas

Buffet
Midnite Menu of Speakeasy Specials
Ham and Potato Scallop
Waldorf Salad (page 65)
Green Beans and Mushrooms

Dessert
*Charleston Chocolate Chiller
Chocolate After-Dinner Mints
Struttin' Strawberry Shortcake

Password Passarounds
Makes: 32 to 36 servings

1 12-ounce package corn-muffin mix
¼ cup grated Parmesan cheese
2 3-ounce cans potted meat
3 4-ounce Vienna sausages

28 cocktail onions
½ cup sweet pickles, sliced
½ cup stuffed olives, sliced

1. Preheat the oven to 400 degrees.
2. Prepare corn-muffin mix according to package directions and spread evenly in a well-buttered 15½-by-10½-by-1-inch jelly-roll pan or bake-broil serving tray.
3. Sprinkle the top with Parmesan cheese.
4. Spoon potted meat in 3 narrow rows crosswise and at each end of the pan.
5. Cut Vienna sausages in half lengthwise; arrange V-shaped rows between rows of potted meat.
6. Place cocktail onions between each sausage V.
7. Arrange rows of sliced pickles and olives in the remaining spaces.
8. Bake for 20 to 25 minutes, or until browned.
9. Cut into small rectangles.

Bathtub Gin Punch in a Coffee Cup
Makes: 30 coffee cups

30 maraschino cherries
Juice for ice cubes (your choice)
3 cups cranberry juice
1 cup orange juice

1 cup pineapple juice
½ cup grapefruit juice
2 2-liter bottles ginger ale, ice cold
Gin or vodka (optional)

1. The day before the party, put a maraschino cherry into each ice-cube compartment and fill with fruit juice; freeze.
2. Combine all fruit juices and mix well.
3. Put the fruit juice ice cubes into a punch bowl and pour the juice mixture on top.
4. Fill the punch bowl with ice-cold ginger ale. Add gin or vodka, if you like.
5. Ladle ice cubes and punch into coffee cups.

Charleston Chocolate Chiller

Makes: 6 servings

1 large chocolate almond bar, chopped
¼ cup hot coffee
1 10-inch graham cracker pie shell
1 quart coffee ice cream
1 quart chocolate ice cream
Hot fudge sauce

1. Place the chocolate bar into hot coffee and stir until chocolate melts (heat the coffee if necessary).
2. Spread the chocolate/coffee mixture on the pie shell; freeze until chocolate hardens.
3. Spread a layer of coffee ice cream and a layer of chocolate ice cream over the hardened chocolate.
4. Freeze until ready to serve.
5. Serve with hot fudge sauce.

Food Service and Decorative Touches

- Create an intimate night club atmosphere with white linens and candles.
- Drape red, black, and silver satin and fringe around the buffet table.
- Make centerpieces of real or artificial flowers in recycled glass or silver vases.
- Use red, black, silver, and white for your color scheme.
- Trim vases and food containers with strings of faux pearls and satin ribbons in theme colors.
- Set a fancy headpiece (New Year's Eve-style) with feather and glitter trim at each lady's place and a satin ribbon bow tie at each man's place.
- Trim small lampshades with red fringe and place them on top of battery-operated candles.
- Place a string of battery-operated twinkle lights around the bottom of a fish bowl filled with water and either live or plastic fish.
- Place centerpieces on top of mirror tiles.
- Serve all drinks in coffee cups.
- Design and produce a papier-mâché twenties hollow bathtub to hold a punch bowl.
- Set deco-framed or matted photos of twenties movie stars among your table decorations.

FORTIES/WARTIME

Nostalgia fans will love this "those were the days" theme of big band music, vintage costumes, and samples of once-rationed modest food provisions. The authentic wartime recipes included may not qualify as favorites today, but your guests will enjoy the adventure of tasting them alongside other popular foods and beverages.

Party Menu

Snacks
*Cream Cheese in Sour Dough Loaf
Cheese and Sausage Biscuits
Victory Garden Veggies with Dip

Beverages
Soft Drinks/Mineral Waters
*Sparkling Red Slush Punch
Beers/Wines
Coffees/Teas

Buffet
*1943 Meat Puff
*Mum's Impossible Pie (savory filling)
SOS (creamed chipped beef on toast points)
Assorted Sandwiches

Dessert
*Mum's Impossible Pie (sweet-filling)
Canteen Donuts

Cream Cheese in Sour Dough Loaf

Makes: 8 servings

8 ounces cream cheese
8 ounces sour cream
1 jar dry beef, chopped
Dash of Lea & Perrins sauce
Garlic, to taste

4 ounces cheddar cheese, grated
3 green onions, chopped
Tabasco sauce, to taste
1 round sour dough bread loaf

1. Preheat the oven to 350 degrees.
2. Combine all ingredients except the bread; mix until well blended.
3. Hollow out the center of the sour dough loaf (reserving the removed bread chunks) and fill with the cheese mixture.
4. Wrap the loaf in foil and bake for 4 to 5 minutes.
5. Use scooped-out bread chunks for dipping.

Sparkling Red Slush Punch

Makes: 2 gallons

2 cups sugar
1 cup boiling water
32 ounces pineapple juice

2 quarts cranberry juice
Lemon-lime soda (1 gallon maximum)

1. Stir sugar into boiling water; cool.
2. Add juices and freeze.
3. Remove from the freezer ½ hour before serving.
4. Scoop out slush into a punch bowl.
5. When the bowl is ½ full, slowly add the lemon-lime soda; stir gently.

1943 Meat Puff

Makes: 4 servings

1½ cups flour
2 teaspoons baking powder
½ teaspoon salt
2 egg yolks, well beaten
1 cup milk

1 to 1½ cups leftover meat, coarsely chopped
2 teaspoons onion, minced
¼ cup carrot, grated
2 tablespoons shortening, melted
2 egg whites, beaten until stiff

1. Preheat the oven to 425 degrees.
2. Sift together flour, baking powder, and salt.
3. Mix together egg yolks and milk and add them to the sifted ingredients; stir.
4. Add meat, onion, carrot, and shortening; mix well. Fold in egg whites.
5. Pour the mixture into a well-greased 1-quart baking dish. Bake for 45 minutes.
6. Serve with gravy.

Mum's Impossible Pie

(This wartime pie recipe can be used as a main dish or dessert.)

Makes: 4 servings

Crust

4 eggs
16 ounces milk
⅙ cup all-purpose flour

½ teaspoon baking powder
½ teaspoon salt
4 ounces margarine, melted

Savory Filling

1 onion, finely chopped
1 ounce cheese, grated
6 ounces condensed milk
Black pepper, to taste

1 7-ounce can tuna or salmon, drained
4 ounces mixed vegetables, frozen or canned
2 tablespoons parsley, chopped

Sweet Filling

5 ounces sugar
2 teaspoons vanilla
1 egg

3½ ounces coconut
6 ounces condensed milk
2 tablespoons sour cream

1. Preheat the oven to 375 degrees.
2. In a large bowl, beat together the crust ingredients.
3. Combine the crust batter with the ingredients for the chosen filling.
4. Pour the mixture into a lightly greased 10-inch pie plate; bake for 35 to 40 minutes.

Food Service and Decorative Touches

- Drape white linens with red, white, and blue bunting.
- Serve food on trays, cafeteria-style, or in antique or replica tins or packaging.
- Display framed photos of forties movie and musical celebrities. (See Resources #4.)
- Create a backdrop with Uncle Sam and other wartime posters and flags.
- Festoon the area with red, white, and blue balloons and crepe paper streamers.
- Wrap dog tags, personalized with guests' names, around napkins.
- Display military items, such as medals, hats, gloves, belts, and scarves.
- Light tables with flashlights or air-raid-warden lighted helmets.
- Print ration coupons or stamps to be redeemed for drinks and food.

FIFTIES

A "fab" party theme for those who are either reaching the age of fifty or whose high-school "heydays" were in the 1950s. This spectacularly popular party scheme will generate lots of high spirits and enthusiasm. Although you can serve almost anything, foods and beverages from the "rock and roll" era will please any "bopper"—big or little.

Party Menu

Snacks
White Castle Pâté with Bread and Crackers (page 10)
*Hot Pot Chili-Mac Snack
Cocktail Wieners
Potato Chips with Onion Dip
Veggies and Dips

Beverages
Soft Drinks/Mineral Waters
*Hula-Hoop
*Bubble Gum '57 Chevy Shooter
Beer/Wine
Coffees/Teas

Buffet
Pick A Sloppy Joe
Big Bopper Build-Your-Own Burger Bar
French-Fried Potatoes and Onion Rings
Pick A Slaw

Dessert
*Elvis's All-Time Favorite Sandwich
Brownies with Ice Cream
Soda Fountain Favorites

Hot Pot Chili-Mac Snack
Makes: 16 to 18 ½-cup servings

4 cups cooked macaroni
2 cans chili with beans
½ cup onion, chopped
½ cup celery, finely chopped
1 cup beef broth
¾ cup cheddar cheese, shredded

1. Place all the ingredients, except cheese, into a saucepan and cook on low heat for 1 hour.
2. Sprinkle cheese on top during the last 15 minutes of cooking.
3. Serve as a snack in fifties diner-style coffee cups with teaspoons.

Hula-Hoop
Makes: 1 serving

⅓ ounce lemonade mix*
⅓ ounce orange juice
⅓ ounce cranberry juice
1 ounce vodka
1 ounce peach schnapps
Cracked ice

1. Combine all ingredients; shake well. Strain.
2. Serve over ice.

(*To make a mix, dilute lemonade concentrate with ⅓ the required amount of water.)

Bubble Gum '57 Chevy Shooter

Makes: 2 servings

1 ounce vodka   1 ounce bubble gum mix*
⅓ ounce sweet sour mix*   ⅔ ounce orange juice
Cracked ice

1. Combine all ingredients and shake well. Strain.
2. Serve over ice.

(*To make a mix, dilute concentrate with ⅛ the required amount of water.)

Elvis's All-Time Favorite Sandwich

Makes: 4 servings

Creamy peanut butter   6 squares milk chocolate
2 slices white bread   Ice cream or whipped topping
6 ¼-inch-thick banana slices

1. Slather peanut butter on one side of both bread slices.
2. Layer banana slices on top of peanut butter on 1 slice.
3. Lay chocolate pieces on top of the banana layer, and cover with the second bread slice, peanut butter side down.
4. Grill the sandwich on both sides until golden brown. Cut in quarters.
5. Serve each quarter topped with ice cream or whipped topping.

Food Service and Decorative Touches

- Serve food in plastic or paper drive-in burger baskets.
- Cover tables with black-and-white-checked plastic or linen cloths.
- Make napkin holders out of plain or fancy ponytail holders.
- Cover food/snack containers with faux black leather for a decorative "greaser" look, or cut leather into strips to trim drinking glasses.
- Incorporate typical fifties decor into the table decorations: sunglasses, roller skates, 45 rpm records, album covers, fuzzy dice, Chevy motifs, musical notes, musical instruments, soda fountain accessories.
- Hang "cool" white, pocketed T-shirts over chairs: Roll ciggie packs into the sleeves and tuck black plastic combs into the pockets.
- Stand framed or matted photos of fifties icons on the buffet and dining tables: Elvis, Marilyn, James Dean, Bill Haley, and so on.
- Use soda fountain pink, Day-Glo chartreuse, lilac, and black-and-white colors.
- Create a unique soda-fountain centerpiece with flowers: Fill a tall soda glass with white carnations, and place a red carnation in the middle, for a cherry.
- If you can find them, use original or replica classic Coca-Cola bottles as candle holders. In general, Coca-Cola memorabilia is readily available and will add greatly to your fifties decor.

SIXTIES

No one will protest the enjoyment experienced at a nostalgic love-in, patterned after the memorable era of the sixties. Make sure that the setting for your hippie-health-nut feast is vividly tie-dyed, beaded, and fringed. And if you are doing this party potluck, you'd better check the brownies!

Party Menu

Snacks
*Baked Cheddar Olives
Sprouts and Veggie Sandwiches
Variety of "Health" Nuts

Beverages
Juices/Mineral Waters
*Flower Power Punch
Herbal Teas

Buffet
Whole-Grain Baked Goods
*Spicy Stuffed "Magic" Mushrooms
Soy/Nut Burgers
Tofu Dogs

Dessert
*Peach on Earth Pie
Granola Bars/Brownies
Fresh Fruit

Baked Cheddar Olives
Makes: 24 olives

24 pimiento-stuffed olives (1 3-ounce jar)
1 cup cheddar cheese, grated
2 tablespoons unsalted butter, softened
½ cup flour
⅛ teaspoon cayenne pepper

1. Preheat the oven to 400 degrees.
2. Drain olives and pat dry with towels.
3. Combine cheese and butter in a bowl.
4. Add flour and cayenne pepper and blend until well mixed.
5. Drop the dough by tablespoons onto wax paper and wrap each piece of dough around an olive, covering it completely.
6. Arrange wrapped olives on a baking sheet, and bake in the middle of the oven for 15 minutes, or until golden.
7. Serve warm.

Flower Power Punch
Makes: 10 4-ounce servings

1 cup vodka
1 cup melon liqueur
½ cup orange juice mix*
½ cup pineapple juice mix*
Ice ring with edible fresh flowers frozen inside
1 quart sparkling apple cider
Edible flowers for garnish

1. Pour alcohol and juices over the ice ring.
2. Add cider just before serving. Float edible flowers on top for garnish.

(*To make a mix, dilute juice concentrate with ⅓ the required amount of water.)

Carrot Cashew Commune Slaw

Makes: 12 ½-cup servings

4 cups green cabbage, shredded
1 cup carrots, shredded
½ cup cashew halves
½ cup raisins
⅓ cup creamy dressing

1. Combine all ingredients and mix well.
2. Serve help-yourself family-style.

7-Layer (1 for each decade) Bars

Makes: 12 bars

1 cup graham cracker crumbs
1 cup flaked coconut
1 can condensed milk
1 cup pecans, chopped

½ stick butter or margarine, melted
6 ounces butterscotch chips
6 ounces chocolate chips

1. Preheat the oven to 325 degrees.
2. Layer all ingredients in a 9-by-13-inch pan in the order listed. Do not mix or stir.
3. Bake for 30 minutes. Cool.
4. Cut into bars.

Food Service and Decorative Touches

- Create a disco atmosphere with bright neon-colored linens and decorations.
- Use neon items for table decor and favors.
- Create a backdrop for your buffet table with movie, record, and concert posters.
- Hang a disco-ball light over the buffet table.
- Put seventies record album covers under food containers or centerpieces.
- Use strips of old polyester fabrics to trim food containers and vases, or tie them around napkins.
- Spray eight-track tapes in neon colors and incorporate them into your table decor.
- Go crazy with funny foods and beverages named after seventies movie/TV hits, such as "True Grits in Grease," "Archie Bunker Burgers," "The Sting-ers," "Roots Beer," "Rocky Road Ice Cream," "Godfather's Goodies," and a big bowl of "Jawsbreakers."

WARTIME/M*A*S*H

Invite the troops for a rerun of the award-winning movie and television program, and you'll find stars in your midst. Whether gathering in the mess hall for K.P rations or standing in line at the makeshift gin still for a *M*A*S*H* martini, your party enlistees will be active enough to earn a furlough. If done right, this party theme will surely win you a medal of honor.

Party Menu

Snacks
*Mashed Potato Martinis
Chips/Dips
Popcorn

Beverages
*M.(edicinal) A.(lcohol-based) S.(anity)
H.(elpers) Shooters (page 219)
*Artillery Punch
Martinis
Coffee/Tea

Buffet
*S.O.S. Casserole
*Bivouac Beef Bundles
*Crunchy Creamy Slaw (page 231)

Dessert
*Frosty Furlough Chocolate Drink
Cookies and Cake from Home

Mashed Potato Martinis
Makes: 20 servings

8 cups mashed potatoes
1 cup sour cream
1 cup chives, chopped
1 cup garlic butter

1 cup cheese, grated
1 cup bacon bits
1 cup caviar
1 cup horseradish sauce (clearly labeled!)

1. Serve ½ cup mashed potatoes in martini glasses with a small spoon.
2. Make a topping bar with the rest of the ingredients, 1 ingredient per container, and let the guests fix their "martinis" any way they like them.

Artillery Punch
Makes: enough for a battalion

1 quart strong black tea
1 bottle red wine
½ pint dry gin
1 jigger Benedictine
½ pint lemon juice
1 quart rye whiskey

1 pint Jamaican rum
½ pint brandy
1 pint orange juice
Block of ice
Simple syrup, to taste
Twists of lemon peel for garnish

1. In a large punch bowl, combine all ingredients except lemon peel; mix well.
2. If you find the punch too dry, add simple syrup, to taste.
3. Serve in small tin cups, and garnish with twists of lemon peel.

S.O.S. Casserole

Makes: 6 servings

1½ pounds lean ground beef
¼ cup onion, chopped
½ cup celery, chopped
½ teaspoon salt
4 cups herb stuffing cubes

1½ cups milk
2 large eggs
1 can (10¾ ounces) cream of mushroom soup
1 teaspoon dry mustard
1 cup cheddar cheese, shredded

1. Preheat the oven to 350 degrees.
2. Brown meat, onion, and celery in a large skillet; drain off excess fat. Stir in salt.
3. Arrange stuffing cubes in a greased baking pan and top with the meat mixture.
4. Beat together milk, eggs, soup, and mustard and pour over the meat.
5. Sprinkle with cheese and bake uncovered until a knife inserted in the center comes out clean (about 30 to 40 minutes).
6. Cool for 5 minutes, then cut into squares and serve.

Bivouac Beef Bundles

Makes: 4 servings

1 pound ground beef
4 carrots, sliced
2 potatoes, cubed

1 medium onion, sliced in ¼-inch pieces
Butter, melted
Salt and pepper, to taste

1. Form 4 hamburger patties and place each on a sheet of aluminum foil; add individual servings of carrots, potatoes, and onions to the foil.
2. Brush everything with melted butter and sprinkle with salt and pepper.
3. Fold foil over food and place on charcoal or open fire.
4. Cook for 1 hour, turning every 15 minutes. Serve on foil or tin plates.

Frosty Furlough Chocolate Drink

Makes: 1 large or 2 medium servings

2 cups milk
2 tablespoons chocolate syrup
1 ounce cream of coconut

2 scoops chocolate ice cream
Canned whipped cream
1 tablespoon pecans, chopped

1. Blend milk, syrup, and cream of coconut. Add ice cream and blend until smooth.
2. Pour into a soda fountain glass, top with whipped cream, and sprinkle with pecans.

Food Service and Decorative Touches

- Create mess-hall seating with picnic tables and benches, metal trays, and tin cups.
- Cover tables with camouflage or army-green paper or fabric.
- Make miniature road signs to label foods on the buffet table. (See How-To's #15.)
- Display toy helicopters, military gear, hospital equipment, and canteens.
- Float helium-filled camouflage-design balloons.
- Hang small kerosene lamps and flashlight swags over table areas.
- Serve snacks, display serving utensils, and create centerpieces in bedpans, tin buckets, medical supply boxes, and inverted helmets and/or army boots.
- Hang twinkle lights behind the buffet table (use IV stands as supports).
- Use metal military dog tags as place cards or napkin holders.

FUTURISTIC FANTASIES

Until the day when we can all climb aboard a space shuttle, we will have to settle for a simulation. This theme will send groups of all ages, from grade school to the geriatric set, into orbit, with its "gala-ctic" enhancements. "Houston, we are having an incredible party—no problems!"

Party Menu

Snacks
Moon Cheese and Crackers
Sun Chips and Dip
Fresh Fruit-uristic Tray

Buffet
*Lunar Noodles with Beef
"Corn"stellation Bread
Star Trek Spinach Salad

Beverages
Solar Cola/Mineral Waters
*Plutonium Q 26 Space Modulator
Starbucks Coffees
Trekkie Teas

Dessert
*Tang Dessert
*Milky Way Wonder Cake
Big Dipper Ice Cream
Mars Bars, L'il Orbit Donuts

Plutonium Q 26 Space Modulator
Makes: 1 serving

⅓ part orange juice
⅓ part lemonade mix*
⅓ part Coke

1 ounce cherry mix*
1 ounce vodka
Cracked ice

1. Combine all ingredients; shake well. Strain.
2. Serve over ice.

(*To make a mix, dilute lemonade and cherry concentrates with ⅓ the required amount of water.)

Lunar Noodles with Beef
Makes: 10 servings

2 pounds ground beef
12 ounces flat noodles, cooked and drained
4 onions, chopped
2 green peppers, chopped

1 stalk celery, chopped
2 cups tomato soup
2 cups mushroom soup
1 pound cheddar cheese, cubed

1. Preheat the oven to 350 degrees.
2. Brown ground beef and put into a 4-quart casserole.
3. Add noodles, onions, green peppers, and celery.
4. Simmer soups and cheese together until the cheese melts. Pour over beef and noodles and stir.
5. Bake uncovered for 30 minutes.

Tang Dessert

(This recipe is a prize winner! Mary Kelley of Gillette, Wyoming, won "Best of the Chamber" at a local Wyoming Events tasting event. See Credits.)

Makes: 8 ½-cup servings

8 ounces cream cheese, softened	2 eggs
¼ cup sugar	12 ounces Cool Whip
¼ cup Tang powder	11 ounces mandarin oranges

1. Beat cream cheese, sugar, and Tang well.
2. Add eggs, 1 at a time, beating well after each addition.
3. Add Cool Whip and mandarin oranges. Mix well and freeze.
4. Take out of the freezer 1 hour before serving time. Serve this simple dessert in elegant chocolate cups. (See Resources #7.)

Milky Way Wonder Cake

Makes: 6 servings

6 regular-sized (or 13 individual-sized) Milky Way candy bars	2½ cups all-purpose flour
	½ teaspoon baking soda
2 sticks (1 cup) butter or margarine	1¼ cups buttermilk
2 cups sugar	1 teaspoon vanilla
4 eggs	1 cup nuts, chopped

1. Preheat the oven to 350 degrees.
2. In a heavy saucepan over low heat, melt candy bars with 1 stick of butter, stirring frequently until smooth. Remove from heat and allow to cool.
3. Beat remaining stick of butter and sugar until light and fluffy.
4. Add eggs, 1 at a time, beating well after each addition.
5. Stir together flour and baking soda and add to butter alternately with buttermilk, mixing just until dry ingredients are moist.
6. Blend in cooled Milky Way mixture, vanilla, and nuts.
7. Turn the batter into a greased and floured 10-inch bundt or tube pan.
8. Bake for 1 hour and 20 minutes, until a toothpick inserted into the center comes out clean. (The top will be quite dark.)
9. Cool 10 minutes before removing from the pan; finish cooling on a wire rack.

Food Service and Decorative Touches

- Cover tables with Mylar cloth or paper, and accent with paper mats imprinted with computer graphics and laser art.
- Add touches of silver stars and lunar shapes to all decor.
- Incorporate hologram glasses, mirrored globes, clear tubing, mirror tiles, *Star Trek* memorabilia, and silver wire into the table decor and floral arrangements.
- Place serving containers on clear acrylic pedestals to simulate floating in space.
- Hang space ship and flying saucer models, moons, stars, and lunar circles over the tables with clear wire.
- Use novelty head gear (Martian-style with antennae) as place cards and favors.
- Light tables with laser lights, neon, twinkle lights, and chase lights in clear tubes.
- Create flowers of silver Mylar tissue (How-To's #13) and mix with branches sprayed silver and dusted with glitter to create out-of-this-world centerpieces.

ARTS AND CRAFTS

This is a duo party theme since it can be used as a tribute to an artsy-craftsy type of person or as an activity event at which the guests participate in creative crafts. In either case, this creative cuisine will result in a prize-winning menu.

Party Menu

Snacks
*Crafter's Cheese 'n' Bacon Crusts
*Artistic Party Palette
"Clean Fingers" Dry Snacks

Beverages
Soft Drinks/Mineral Waters
*The Mona Lisa
*"Proud o' Your Project" Punch
Coffees/Teas

Buffet
Patchwork Lasagna (varied-colored pasta)
Gelatin Mold Salad Wreath
Rolls, Breadsticks, and Breads (shaped to form hosts' monograms)

Dessert
*Creativity's Reward Chocolate Dip
Fresh Fruit Chunks for Dipping (on short craft sticks)
Home-Decorated Cake
Homemade Candy

Crafter's Cheese 'n' Bacon Crusts
Makes: 12 servings

6 slices bacon, crumbled
½ cup walnuts, chopped
½ cup mayonnaise
1 cup olives, chopped
½ cup green onion tops, chopped
1½ cups cheddar cheese, shredded
12 slices whole-wheat or white bread

1. Combine all ingredients except bread; mix well.
2. Toast 12 slices of bread (sandwich style, crusts removed) and cut into assorted shapes with a knife or cookie cutters.
3. Spread the cheese mixture on the toast shapes.
4. Broil until the tops are crusty brown; serve immediately.

Tip: If preparing this snack days before the party, follow the instructions to Step 3, then wrap the snacks and freeze them until ready to use.

Artistic Party Palette
Makes: as much as you like

Carrots
Celery
Green pepper
Jicama
6 colors of food coloring
2 to 3 vegetable dips to fill 6 small (3-inch maximum) round containers

1. Cut vegetables into pieces ½-inch thick and 4 to 5 inches long.
2. Make small vertical cuts on 1 end of each vegetable stick to create a "brush."
3. Dye each dip with a food coloring.
4. Stand the vegetable sticks, brushes up, in a tall ceramic pot place on a platter.
5. Arrange dip containers around the edge of the platter.

The Mona Lisa

Makes: 1 serving

2 ounces amaretto
1 ounce cream

Cracked ice
Pineapple juice

1. Combine amaretto, cream, and ice; shake well. Strain.
2. Pour over ice into a tall glass.
3. Fill the rest of the glass with pineapple juice.

"Proud o' Your Project" Punch

Makes: 36 punch-cup servings

1 12-ounce package frozen pink
lemonade concentrate
2 liters diet ginger ale

12 ounces frozen fruit of choice
1 gallon rainbow sherbet

1. In a very large punch bowl, make lemonade according to package instructions.
2. Add ginger ale and frozen fruit.
3. Scoop the entire package of sherbet into the punch to float on top.

Tip: The frozen fruit and sherbet will keep the punch cold. However, you may have to add ice if you serve this outdoors in very hot weather.

Creativity's Reward Chocolate Dip

Makes: 1½ cups

⅔ cup light corn syrup
½ cup whipping cream
8 ounces semisweet or German sweet chocolate

1. Microwave corn syrup and whipping cream in a microwave-safe bowl on high for 90 seconds or until the mixture comes to a boil.
2. Add chocolate and stir until melted.
3. Serve warm as a dip for fruit, cake, or cookies.

Food Service and Decorative Touches

- Decorate place cards, name tags, or party favors with yarn, feathers, rubber stamp art, buttons, beads, and drawings.
- Fashion napkin holders of yarns, lace, ribbons, and craft trims.
- Pile arts-and-crafts supplies and decorative scraps in the center of the table, and have guests make centerpieces.
- Display arts-and-crafts supplies, books, and finished projects on the buffet table.
- If possible, serve foods and beverages in craft-project containers, such as tole (lacquered or enameled, elaborately painted metalware), decoupage, woven baskets, or ceramics.
- Wrap cloth or paper around the bottom of a flower pot and make a band over it with an embroidery hoop. Line the pots with plastic or aluminum foil and use them as snack containers.
- Cover the table with white paper and provide a cupful of markers for guests to demonstrate their creativity.
- Tuck a small paintbrush or crayon into each knotted napkin.

BOARD GAMES

A challenging and competitive session of playing parlor games calls for a menu of food and beverage items that can be enjoyed while concentrating on individual or team strategies. Except for a grand finale of dessert and coffee, refreshments must be served and enjoyed "single-handedly" over the game boards.

Party Menu

Snacks
*Parcheesi Parmesan Popcorn
*Pictionary Pickle Pickups
Scrabble Mix Snacks ("checkerboard" cereals, nuts, dried fruits)
Dealer's Choice Chips 'n' Dips

Beverages
*Red-and-Black Checkerboard Sangria
Soft Drinks
Coffees/Teas

Buffet
"Trivial Pursoup"
"Mo-Napoli" Pasta Salad
"Backgamm-onion" Rings
"Toss the Diced" Carrot Salad
Board of Bread

Dessert
*C.L.U.E. Cake (Chocolate Lovers' Unbelievable Edible)
Fruit and Cheese Kebabs
(on pick-up sticks)

Parcheesi Parmesan Popcorn

(From *For Popcorn Lovers Only,* by Dianne Pfeiffer. See Credits.)

Makes: 8 cups

½ cup uncooked popcorn
3 tablespoons olive oil, divided
1 tablespoon butter

3 cloves fresh garlic, pressed
3 tablespoons grated Parmesan cheese

1. Pop popcorn using 2 tablespoons olive oil instead of cooking oil. Set aside in a large bowl.
2. Melt butter in a small pan over low heat. Stir in remaining olive oil.
3. Add garlic to pan and sauté briefly.
4. Dribble melted butter over popcorn. Toss with hands to coat thoroughly (careful—the oil may still be hot).
5. Sprinkle with Parmesan cheese.

Tip: Substitute 1 tablespoon of bottled garlic oil and 1 tablespoon of butter for coating mixture.

Pictionary Pickle Pickups

Makes: almost a peck!

1 quart dill pickles, sliced thinly
1¾ cups all-purpose flour
2 teaspoons cayenne pepper
2 teaspoons paprika
2 teaspoons pepper

2 teaspoons garlic salt
1 teaspoon salt
3 dashes Tabasco sauce
1 cup beer
Vegetable oil for deep-frying

1. Drain pickle slices well and dredge them in 1 cup of flour; set aside.
2. Combine the remaining ¾ cup flour with the rest of the dry ingredients.
3. Add Tabasco sauce and beer; mix well.
4. Dip pickle slices in batter and deep-fry in hot (375-degree) oil until golden.
5. Drain on towels and serve warm. (Would be cute served on a checkerboard covered with clear plastic wrap.)

Red-and-Black Checkerboard Sangria
Makes: 4 to 6 servings

2 cups cherries, blackberries, and black grapes　　*1 bottle dry red wine*
Peel of 1 lemon (in 1 long strip, if possible)　　*Club soda, to taste*
½ cup strongly brewed black tea　　*Ice*

1. Place fruits, lemon peel, tea, and enough wine to cover the fruit completely into a 2½-quart pitcher. Chill the rest of the wine.
2. Just before serving, pour remaining chilled wine into the pitcher; stir.
3. Add club soda and ice.

C.L.U.E. Cake (Chocolate Lovers' Unbelievable Edible)
Makes: 8 to 10 servings

1 18½-ounce package chocolate,　　*4 eggs*
*　double chocolate, or fudge cake mix*　　*½ cup salad oil*
1 3½-ounce box instant chocolate　　*½ cup warm water*
*　pudding mix*　　*½ cup walnuts, finely chopped*
½ cup sour cream　　*6 ounces semisweet white chocolate morsels*

1. Preheat the oven to 350 degrees.
2. Place cake mix, pudding mix, sour cream, eggs, salad oil, and warm water into a large bowl. Mix at low speed until ingredients are well blended. Beat 3 minutes more at medium speed.
3. Gently mix in walnuts.
4. Turn batter into a lightly greased and floured bundt or tube pan.
5. Bake 45 to 55 minutes or until a toothpick inserted into the cake comes out clean.
6. Let the cake stand 5 minutes. Turn out of the pan onto a cooling rack.
7. Melt chocolate pieces over double boiler or in a microwave. Drizzle on top of cake. (See How-To's #34.)

Tip: Cake can be eaten warm or cool.

Food Service and Decorative Touches
- Trim name tags or place cards with colorful game pieces: checkers, dominos, or Scrabble tiles.
- Tie napkins with blue ribbons and trim with prize medals.
- Collect boxed games at thrift stores or garage sales. Stack game boxes to create bases and pedestals for bowls, baskets, or boxes of snacks.
- Cover game boards with clear plastic wrap to make trays for serving or passing around appetizers.
- Make napkin holders out of toy paper money. (See How-To's #27.)

BOOKS

Your guest(s) of honor will find volumes of enjoyment in menu items that you have selected from popular cookbooks or family recipe file boxes. From a "table of delicious contents" you can serve guests in style—by the book, or according to your own imaginative authoring.

Party Menu

Snacks
*Chapter One Chili Cheese Roll
Dip of Fools
Chippers by the Dozen (dippables of choice)

Beverages
Soft Drinks/Mineral Waters
*Library Limeade Punch
Grape Expectations (wines)
Ale of Two Cities (beers)
Coffees/Teas

Buffet
Pelican Beef
War 'n' Pizza
Pickwick Peppers
Breads of Madison County

Dessert
*Happy Ending Banana Nut Cheesecake
Huckleberry "Finnish" Pie
3 Musketeers Candy Bars

Chapter One Chili Cheese Roll

Makes: 40 pieces

8 ounces American cheese, grated
3 ounces cream cheese, softened
⅛ teaspoon garlic powder

¼ cup chopped pecans
2 tablespoons chili powder
Crackers or Melba toast

1. Mix cheeses until well blended. Stir in garlic powder and pecans.
2. Form the cheese mixture into a roll about 10 inches long.
3. Spread chili powder on a sheet of wax paper and roll the cheese log over the paper. Chill.
4. Slice the log and serve with crackers or Melba toast.

Library Limeade Punch

Makes: 30 to 35 punch-cup servings

1 12-ounce can frozen limeade concentrate, thawed and undiluted
1 6-ounce can frozen orange juice concentrate, thawed and undiluted
Ice block or ring
1 750-milliliter bottle Chablis or other dry white wine, chilled
1 large bottle lemon-lime soda, chilled
Lemon, lime, or orange slices for garnish

1. In a glass or plastic pitcher, dilute frozen juices according to directions.
2. Pour juices over an ice block or ring into a large punch bowl.
3. Add wine and soda, and garnish with fruit slices.

Happy Ending Banana Nut Cheesecake

Makes: 10 servings

1 cup chocolate wafer crumbs	2 large eggs
¼ cup margarine, melted	¼ cup chopped walnuts
16 ounces cream cheese, softened	⅓ cup milk chocolate chips
½ cup sugar	1 tablespoon margarine
½ cup ripe bananas, mashed	2 tablespoons water

1. Preheat the oven to 350 degrees.
2. Combine crumbs and margarine; press onto the bottom of a 9-inch spring form pan and bake for 10 minutes.
3. Combine cream cheese, sugar, and banana, mixing at medium speed on electric mixer until well blended.
4. Add eggs, 1 at a time, mixing well after each addition.
5. Stir in walnuts, pour over crust.
6. Bake for 40 minutes.
7. Loosen the cake from the pan rim; cool before removing the rim.
8. Melt chocolate pieces and margarine with water over low heat, stirring until smooth. Drizzle over cheesecake. Chill.

Food Service and Decorative Touches

- Design seating assignments or place cards as bookmarks, decorated according to the honoree's reading preference: use ribbons, lace, medals, flowers, and so on.
- Create a greeting-card-style menu, with the title of the event on the front and the menu written as a table of contents inside.
- Stack and arrange attractive books on the buffet table to serve as bases for serving containers (place something between the container and the book to protect the book).
- Obtain display boxes from your local bookstore and line them with plastic or foil to hold snacks or bunches of flowers for centerpieces.
- Place lovely books between interesting bookends as centerpieces. Add flowers, greens, or other decorative materials.
- Fold pages from discarded books into two-inch strips, then staple the ends to form three- to four-inch rings to hold napkins.
- Create a buffet table backdrop with promotional posters for current best-selling books (available at bookstores or local distributors).
- Illuminate your buffet or dining table with mini book lites, which can also be given as door prizes at the end of the party.

CARD GAMES

As your guest card players enthusiastically engage in games of skill, with a bit of luck thrown in, ply them with food and beverages fit for a King or Queen, or even a Jack or two. Deal out a menu that will be aces high with your crowd.

Party Menu

Snacks
*Puffy Rice Diamonds
Finger Sandwiches (shaped like hearts, diamonds, clubs, and spades)
Veggies with Dip

Beverages
Soft Drinks/Mineral Waters
*Gin Game Fizz
*Royal Flush Shooters (page 218, #2)
Coffees/Teas

Buffet
*High "Steaks" Casserole
Triple-Deck Gelatin Salad
Breads and Rolls

Dessert
*Lucky Lemon Custard Squares
Rummy Cake
Nuts 'n' Mints Bridge Mix

Puffy Rice Diamonds
Makes: 40 diamonds

2 cups short-grain rice
4 cups water

Salad oil for frying
Salt, to taste

1. Combine rice and water in a 3-quart pan; bring to a boil. Cover, lower the heat, and simmer on low heat about 25 minutes.
2. Preheat the oven to 275 degrees.
3. Spread the cooked rice ¼-inch thick on a slightly greased cookie sheet.
4. Cut into 2-inch diamonds and separate.
5. Bake uncovered for about 2 hours, until thoroughly dry; cool.
6. In a 3-quart pan, pour 1 inch of oil and heat to 375 degrees.
7. Fry rice pieces until puffy and golden (about 1 minute).
8. Drain and season to taste. Serve warm or cooled.

Gin Game Fizz
Makes: 1 serving

Juice of ½ lemon
2 ounces dry gin
Cracked ice

1 teaspoon powdered sugar
Carbonated water
Cherry or orange slice for garnish

1. Combine lemon juice, gin, ice, and sugar; shake well.
2. Strain into a chilled 7-ounce highball glass, and fill the glass with carbonated water.
3. Stir and garnish with a cherry or an orange slice.

High "Steaks" Casserole

Makes: 6 to 8 servings

2 pounds 1-inch-thick round steak
2 teaspoons salt
Dash of pepper
Flour
6 medium onions, sliced

¼ cup vegetable oil
3 large potatoes, peeled and halved
1 can cream of tomato soup
16-ounce can French-cut green beans

1. Preheat the oven to 350 degrees.
2. Cut round steak into serving-sized pieces.
3. Season with salt and pepper.
4. Roll in flour.
5. Cook onions in oil until tender, but not brown; remove onions from the pan.
6. Brown steak pieces slowly on both sides; place into a 3-quart casserole.
7. Add onions and potatoes; pour soup on top.
8. Bake covered for 1 hour and 45 minutes, or until steak is tender.
9. Add green beans and bake for 10 to 15 minutes longer.

Lucky Lemon Custard Squares

Makes: 16 2-inch squares

Crust

½ cup butter
1 cup flour
¼ cup icing sugar

1. Preheat the oven to 350 degrees.
2. Combine all ingredients and pat into an 8-by-8-inch pan. Bake for 10 minutes.

Custard Topping

¾ cup sugar
½ teaspoon baking powder
3 tablespoons lemon juice
2 tablespoons flour

2 eggs, beaten
Rind of 1 lemon
Icing sugar for garnish

1. Combine all ingredients except icing sugar; mix well. Pour over the baked crust.
2. Bake at 350 degrees for 20 minutes.
3. Sprinkle with icing sugar while still warm.

Food Service and Decorative Touches

- Decorate place cards or name tags with tiny playing cards, poker chips, cribbage pegs, score pads, and so on.
- Display all kinds of playing cards—in the pack, fanned out, or scattered about.
- Give each guest a playing card for a seating assignment. Seat all of one denomination (all Aces, all Kings, all Jacks) at one card table.
- Use table linens, serving ware, and accessories in red and black and in shapes of hearts, clubs, diamonds, and spades.
- Incorporate colorful how-to books on card playing into your table decor.
- Tuck each napkin into an empty cardboard deck container.
- Make a house of cards centerpiece for the buffet table.

COMPUTERS

Pay tribute to your favorite "geek" with a party based on the world of computers and technology. Your tech-inspired menu will offer "bytes" of delicious foods and nectars fit for the G.O.D.s (Geek of the Day). Naturally, apples share this program.

Party Menu

Snacks
*Jicama Hacker Snackers
Micro-Meatballs
Veggies and Dips

Buffet
"Build Your Own Mighty Mac"
Burger Bar
*Mac 'n' Mayo Pasta Salad

Beverages
*Apple o' Lemon (AOL) Punch
Hot Apple Cider
Apple Juice and Seltzer Spritzers
Coffees/Cinnamon Apple Tea

Dessert
*Internutty Bars
*Chocolate Mouse (page 46)
Cheese and Apple Slices

Jicama Hacker Snackers
Makes: 6 servings

½- to 2-pounds jicama (a root vegetable)
Juice of 2 limes
Chili powder, to taste

1. Cut jicama in half crosswise.
2. Cut each half into ½-inch-thick slices, then cut the slices into ½-inch-long spears. Trim off the skin.
3. Refrigerate until needed.
4. About an hour before serving, bathe spears in lime juice and sprinkle with chili powder. Serve chilled.

Apple o' Lemon (AOL) Punch
Makes: 12 servings

Thick apple slices　　　*1⅓ cups pineapple juice*
1½ quarts apple juice　　*2 pints orange juice*
2 cinnamon sticks　　　*½ cup lemon juice*
8 whole cloves　　　　　*28 ounces ginger ale*

1. A day before the party, arrange thick apple slices in a Jell-O mold; fill with water and freeze.
2. The day of the party, pour apple juice into a nonaluminum kettle.
3. Tie cinnamon sticks and cloves in a cheese cloth, add to the apple juice, and simmer uncovered for 15 minutes; discard the spice bag.
4. Mix spiced juice with remaining fruit juices.
5. Place the frozen apple ice ring in a large punch bowl and pour the cooled fruit juice mix and ginger ale on top.

Mac 'n' Mayo Pasta Salad

Makes: 6 to 8 servings

Salad Ingredients

1 pound uncooked elbow macaroni

½ cup onions, chopped

½ cup green pepper, chopped

6-ounce can tiny shrimp

6-ounce can water-packed tuna, drained and flaked

½ cup celery, chopped

Dressing

Mayonnaise, to taste

¼ cup Catalina salad dressing

¼ cup green relish

1. Cook macaroni according to package directions. Drain, cool, and put into a large bowl.
2. Add the remaining salad ingredients.
3. In a small bowl, mix the dressing ingredients. Pour the dressing over the salad and toss well to evenly coat all ingredients. Refrigerate at least 2 hours before serving.

Internutty Bars

Makes: 12 3-inch squares

½ cup margarine, softened

¾ cup brown sugar

1½ cups flour

¼ teaspoon salt

1 can (9.5 ounces) mixed nuts

6 ounces butterscotch chips

½ cup light Karo syrup

2 tablespoons butter

12 walnut halves

1. Preheat the oven to 350 degrees.
2. Combine margarine with brown sugar and mix well.
3. Add flour and salt to the sugar mixture; mix well.
4. Press into a 9-by-13-inch pan.
5. Bake for 10 minutes; cool.
6. Spread mixed nuts on top.
7. Melt butterscotch chips, Karo syrup, and butter over low heat; pour over nuts.
8. Bake for 10 minutes.
9. Mark the cake into 12 3-inch squares and press a walnut half into the center of each square.
10. Cool and cut into squares.

Food Service and Decorative Touches

- Cover the buffet table with tractor-feed computer paper.
- Place mouse pads under serving containers or centerpieces.
- Use computer disk storage boxes as containers for dry snacks or centerpieces.
- Set out each guest's utensils and napkin in a diskette envelope.
- Hot-glue small computer chips onto metal pins. Attach pins to ponytail holders to make napkin rings or party favors.

GARDENING

The task of planning a festivity for a green-thumbed garden enthusiast is fertile with great party possibilities that will surely include a harvest of fantastic food and flowers, whether from your own garden, or the neighborhood farmer's market. Indoors or outdoors, your party is destined to blossom and flourish.

Party Menu

Snacks
*Mulched Mushroom Dip
*Cucumber Slices with Tasty Toppings
Garden Fresh Veggies
Fruit Chunks on Floral Picks
Fruit Dip

Buffet
Fresh Vegetable Soup
Baked Stuffed Artichokes
Ratatouille
*Rainbow Garden Pasta Salad (page 236)
Vegetable and Berry Breads and Muffins

Beverages
*Frosty Floral Lemonade
Fruit Juices and Shakes
Coffees/Fruit Teas

Dessert
*Sweets in the Soil
Berries and Cream

Mulched Mushroom Dip

Makes: about 2½ cups of dip

1 pound white button mushrooms, diced
1 cup Monterey Jack cheese, shredded
¼ cup bacon, finely crumbled, or
    ¼ cup Imitation Bacon Bits
½ cup sour cream

1 teaspoon Worcestershire sauce
4 drops hot sauce
½ cup seasoned bread crumbs
Cherry tomatoes, bell and chili peppers, and
    breadsticks

1. Preheat the oven to 350 degrees.
2. Combine diced mushrooms, Monterey Jack cheese, and bacon.
3. Stir in sour cream; blend well.
4. Blend in Worcestershire sauce and hot sauce.
5. Place the mixture in a 1-quart casserole and top with bread crumbs.
6. Bake for 15 minutes, or until cheese melts.
7. Place the dip in a chafing dish and serve hot with cherry tomatoes, bell pepper strips, chili peppers, and breadsticks for dipping.

Cucumber Slices with Tasty Toppings

Makes: as much as you want

Cucumbers, sliced
Sour cream or cream cheese, to bind the toppings
Suggested toppings: caviar, bacon bits, chopped olives, chopped/whole nuts

Place a dab of sour cream or cream cheese on each cucumber slice and top with topping of your choice.

Frosty Floral Lemonade
Makes: 6 to 8 servings

5 cups distilled water, divided
1½ cups sugar
6 large strawberries, hulled, or ¼ cup
   pink hibiscus flowers, dried
   (pesticide free)

¼ cup lavender leaves, chopped, or
   1 tablespoon dried lavender flowers
2¼ cups lemon juice
Ice cubes with a fresh flower frozen in each cube
Fresh lavender flowers for garnish

1. In a medium saucepan, combine 2½ cups water, sugar, and hulled strawberries (or hibiscus flowers). Bring to a boil; stir to dissolve sugar.
2. Reduce heat and simmer for 5 minutes to extract pink from flowers.
3. Remove from heat; stir in lavender leaves, cover, and cool.
4. Strain cooled herb liquid into a large pitcher or jar (if using strawberries, gently press juice from the berries).
5. Add lemon juice and the remaining 2½ cups water; stir and taste. Adjust sugar.
6. Just before serving, add flower ice cubes.
7. Pour into chilled glasses and garnish with lavender flowers.

Sweets in the Soil
Makes: 10 to 12 servings

1 pound Oreo cookies
¼ cup butter or margarine, softened
8 ounces cream cheese, softened
1 cup powdered sugar
3½ cups milk

2 packages (3½ ounces each) instant
   French vanilla pudding
12 ounces frozen whipped topping
1 8-inch clay flowerpot (new and washed)
Plastic flowers (or fresh in florist's water tubes)

1. With a food processor or blender, crush cookies and set aside. (You can also put them in a plastic bag and smash them with a rolling pin.)
2. Cream together butter or margarine, cream cheese, and powdered sugar.
3. Combine milk, pudding, and whipped topping, and stir into the creamed mixture.
4. Place alternate layers (about 2 inches thick) of crushed cookies and pudding mixture in the flowerpot, ending with a thick layer of cookie crumbs on top.
5. Refrigerate until serving time.
6. Insert fresh or plastic flowers into the "soil" and set the pot on the table as a grand finale centerpiece. At dessert time, scoop out the dessert with a trowel.

Food Service and Decorative Touches
- Serve food in large plastic-lined clay flower pots and seedling trays.
- Pour alcoholic beverages from misting bottles.
- Arrange utensils and napkins in gardening tool carriers on the buffet table.
- Use tiny clay pots holding a napkin and a garden marker for place cards.
- Assign a plant for each table and make corresponding seating assignments. (For example: "Sit at the Radish table.")
- Make place mats of floral prints, magazine art, gift-wrap, or wallpaper.
- Use tablecloths and napkins in floral/garden prints.
- Decorate all tables and party areas with plants, flowers, tools, misting bottles, flowerpots, gloves, aprons, bags of soil, and gardening books and magazines.
- Place vials of fresh flowers next to each place setting. (See How-To's #14.)

GOURMET COOKING

When planning a menu for a gourmet cook, you may want to consult with the guest(s) of honor. The food and beverages should be special (no meat loaf, please) and beautifully arranged. The service and presentation all contribute to the success of the event.

Party Menu

Snacks
*Clinton Castle Crackers
*Apple Chicken Toasts
Silver Spoon Appetizers (How-To's #38)
*Crudites Tray (page 242)

Beverages
Soft Drinks/Bottled "Designer" Water
*Limoncello à la Limoncello
Fine Wines
Cocktails
French Roast Gourmet Coffees/Teas

Buffet
Crab Meat with Pasta
*Spinach LaBelle
Herbed French Bread

Dessert
*Pears Belle Helene
*Orange Sorbet
*Chocolate Mousse (page 46)
Fresh Fruit and Cheese Tray
Coffee with Liqueurs

Clinton Castle Crackers

(From *Breton's Best at Zabars*, by Debra Chapman. See Credits.)

Makes: ½ cup of cheese mixture

¼ pound cream cheese, softened
¼ pound brie, rind removed
1 box Breton crackers, any variety

1 small bunch green grapes
4 ounces pecan halves
4 ounces salmon pastrami, cut in strips

1. Blend together cream cheese and brie until soft.
2. Using a pastry bag fitted with a star tip, pipe cheese mixture onto crackers. (You can use a melon scoop instead of pastry bag.)
3. Slice a grape lengthwise three-quarters of the way down; insert pecan half into the grape, and place in center of each cracker.
4. Curl piece of salmon pastrami around each cracker. (If the pastrami is not long enough, wrap it around the grape only, and put the bundle on top of the cracker.)

Apple Chicken Toasts

Makes: 32 pieces

8 slices raisin toast, each cut diagonally into 4 triangles
1 cup sour cream
2 Delicious apples, each cut into 16 slices
½ pound smoked chicken, broken into bite-sized pieces
Scallions, curled, for garnish

1. Place a smear of sour cream on each toast piece.
2. Top each with an apple slice, chicken piece, and a scallion curl.

Limoncello à la Limoncello

(An after-dinner classic featured at Limoncello Café in New York City. You must begin preparations for this drink 2 weeks before the party. See Credits.)

Makes: 2 quarts

1 quart 80-proof vodka
Peel of 5 lemons
Peel of 3 limes

1 quart distilled water
3 cups sugar

1. Mix vodka with lemon and lime peels and let stand in a jar or bottle for 2 weeks.
2. Make simple syrup by mixing water and sugar and bringing it to a boil.
3. Cool syrup to room temperature.
4. On the day of the party, add the syrup to the vodka mixture, strain through a cheesecloth, and transfer to a bottle.
5. Chill in the freezer and enjoy as a delightful after-dinner cocktail.

Spinach LaBelle

Makes: 6 servings

2 packages frozen spinach
¼ pound butter
1½ cups herb stuffing

1 envelope onion soup mix
1 cup sour cream

1. Preheat the oven to 325 degrees.
2. Cook spinach until tender. Drain and blot out excess water.
3. Melt butter in a sauce pan; add stuffing.
4. Combine soup mix and sour cream; add spinach.
5. Spread half the stuffing in a 1½-quart casserole.
6. Spoon the spinach mixture on top; cover with remaining stuffing.
7. Bake for 30 minutes.

Pears Belle Helene

(The preparations for this dessert must begin a day before the party.)

Makes: 4 servings

1 quart water
2½ cups sugar
4 pears, peeled
4 ounces dark sweet chocolate

1 teaspoon vanilla extract
½ cup whipping cream
French vanilla ice cream

1. Combine water and sugar; heat to boiling.
2. Add pears, reduce heat, and cook gently until tender (about 30 minutes).
3. Refrigerate pears and syrup for 24 hours.
4. The day of the party, melt chocolate in a heavy pan over low heat, stirring frequently until the chocolate is smooth and glossy.
5. Add vanilla extract and whipping cream; bring to a boil, stirring constantly.
6. Remove from heat.
7. To serve, place each pear into an individual dessert bowl, place a scoop of ice cream alongside pear, and spoon chocolate sauce over top.

Orange Sorbet

Makes: 6 servings

1 egg white
¾ cup sugar
2 cups fresh orange or mandarin juice
1 cup Asti Spumante or other sparkling wine (nonalcoholic works as well)

1. Beat egg white until foamy.
2. Gradually add sugar and beat until thick and creamy.
3. Put all ingredients into an ice-cream maker, process according to manufacturer's instructions, and freeze.

Tip: Do not store for more than 2 days.

Food Service and Decorative Touches

- Set an elegant table with linens, real plates, glasses, and utensils (not necessarily china, crystal, and sterling silver, but not plastic).
- Use all kinds of gadgets or containers, books, and elegant food packaging identified with gourmet cooking to create centerpieces and to decorate the tables.
- Arrange wine bottles, fancy breads, and fresh fruits and vegetables on chopping blocks for buffet table decor.
- Place pretty wine bottles and glasses in arrangements with flowers and candles for an elegant look on buffet or dining tables.
- Tie a ribbon around a small bunch of herbs, then tie around napkins.
- Display exotic spices or herbs in fancy bottles with raffia ribbon tied around the neck.
- Write each guest's name on a tag and hang the tag on the neck of a wine bottle. This will make a great place card and a party favor.
- Use small pots of herbs, decorated with ribbons and guests' names, as another delightful favor/place card.
- Type or hand-print elegant menu(s) to stand on each table, greating-card style or in fancy frames.

HAY/SLEIGH RIDE

After a raucous time out on a hay or sleigh ride, the crew will have worked up an appetite for good, tasty, warm-up fare. Start them off with hot drinks, and follow with hearty and satisfying party eats to give your guests a "great ride."

Party Menu

Snacks
*Puffy Pizza Squares
*Curried Meatballs (page 229)
Veggies with Dip

Beverages
*Hot Buttered Cranberry Punch (page 223)
Hot Toddies
Coffees/Teas

Buffet
Pick A Sloppy Joe
*Cran-Orange Slaw (page 231)
Gelatin Salad

Dessert
*Warm Berry Pie à la Mode
*Hot Chocolate Royale
Fruit and Cheese

Puffy Pizza Squares
Makes: 8 servings

Filling
1½ pounds lean ground beef or pork
1 cup onion, chopped
1 cup green bell pepper, chopped
1 garlic clove, finely chopped
½ teaspoon oregano

Dash of salt
½ cup water
⅛ teaspoon hot sauce
1 8-ounce can tomato sauce
1½ ounces spaghetti sauce mix

1. In a large skillet, brown ground meat; drain off excess grease.
2. Stir in remaining ingredients; simmer about 10 minutes, stirring occasionally.

Topping
7 ounces cheese, sliced (Monterey Jack or mozzarella)
½ cup grated Parmesan cheese

Batter
1 cup milk
1 tablespoon oil
2 eggs

1 cup all-purpose flour
½ teaspoon salt

1. In a bowl, combine milk, oil, and eggs; beat 1 minute on medium speed.
2. Add flour and salt; beat 2 minutes or until smooth.

Assembly
1. Preheat the oven to 400 degrees.
2. Pour hot filling mixture into a 13-by-9-inch pan. Top with cheese slices.
3. Pour batter over cheese slices, covering completely. Sprinkle with Parmesan cheese.
4. Bake for 25 to 30 minutes, or until puffed and brown. Cut into squares.

Warm Berry Pie à la Mode

Makes: 8 servings

2 medium cooking apples, peeled, cored, and thinly sliced
1 tablespoon lemon juice
Vegetable cooking spray
10 ounces frozen raspberries in light syrup, thawed
1 cup regular oats, uncooked

3 tablespoons margarine
1 teaspoon ground cinnamon
½ cup walnuts, chopped
2 tablespoons honey
½ teaspoon ground nutmeg
Ice cream or whipped topping

1. Preheat the oven to 375 degrees.
2. Combine apples and lemon juice; toss gently.
3. Place the apples into a 10-by-6-by-2-inch baking dish coated with cooking spray.
4. Top with raspberries.
5. Combine oats and remaining ingredients except the ice cream; sprinkle evenly over raspberries.
6. Bake for 30 minutes, or until lightly browned and apples are tender.
7. Cut into squares and serve warm, topped with a small scoop of ice cream or a dollop of whipped topping.

Hot Chocolate Royale

Makes: 2 servings

1 ounce chocolate, unsweetened
¼ cup sugar
Dash of vanilla
Dash of ground cinnamon

Dash of salt
3 cups milk
Whipped cream or mini marshmallows

1. Carefully melt chocolate over very low heat, or in the top of a double boiler over simmering water.
2. Add sugar, spices, and milk; stir to mix well.
3. Heat until scalding, but not boiling.
4. Pour into mugs and top with a dollop of whipped cream or a few marshmallows.

Food Service and Decorative Touches

- Set the table casually—plastic and paper table covers, serving ware, and utensils.
- Decorate in colors to match your overall theme. If you use this theme for a shower, use wedding/baby colors.
- Light the room with lanterns, battery-operated lights, and, if allowed, candles. (Some venues do not allow candles on the premises because they are a potential fire hazard.)
- For a western setting, use bandannas as napkins, accents, and trim for centerpieces, and even spread them out as place mats. (Two bandannas can be knotted together and draped over a chair back for a great decorative touch.)
- Serve foods, breads, and snacks in baskets, wooden buckets, or small barrels.
- Create mini hay-bale boxes and fill them with fresh or straw flowers; trim with bandannas or gingham ribbons. (See How-To's #12.)

MAKEOVER/MINISPA

This is an ideal theme for a wedding shower, an all-girl birthday party, or a gals' gab fest. Every guest gets a beauty makeover and has a relaxing and rejuvenating time filled with laughter, friendship, and, of course, the latest gossip. The foods and beverages for this event must be light and tasty and convenient to eat in the midst of the various spa activities.

Party Menu

Snacks
*Crab and Avocado Melts
Fresh Vegetables
Pick A Dip

Beverages
Mineral Waters/Juices
*Apricot Wine Coolers
Champagne and Orange Juice
Iced Coffee Smoothies
Herbal Teas

Buffet
*Chicken Waldorf Salad in Stems
Fresh and Healthy Salad Bar
Rice Crackers with Sesame Spread

Dessert
*Peaches and Cream Cheese Bars
Fruit Kebabs

Crab and Avocado Melts
Makes: 20 servings

⅔ cup sour cream
½ cup mayonnaise
Salt and pepper, to taste
3 cups cheddar cheese, shredded
6 slices bacon, cooked and crumbled

6 ounces crab meat, rinsed, drained, and flaked
⅓ cup green bell pepper, finely chopped (optional)
5 English muffins, split and lightly toasted
2 avocados, seeded, peeled, and sliced

1. In a large bowl, combine sour cream, mayonnaise, salt and pepper, 1 cup cheddar cheese, bacon, crab meat, and green pepper.
2. Spoon the crab mixture onto toasted muffin halves.
3. Top each muffin with 2 avocado slices and remaining cheddar cheese.
4. Broil 3 to 5 minutes, or just until cheese melts.
5. Cut each muffin half into 2 pieces and serve warm.

Apricot Wine Cooler
Makes: 1 serving

2 ounces apricot schnapps
½ cup Sprite
½ cup white wine
Cracked ice

1. Combine all ingredients and shake well. Strain.
2. Serve over ice.

Chicken Waldorf Salad in Stems

Makes: 8 to 10 stemmed-glass servings

2 cups celery, chopped
4 tablespoons raisins
4 tablespoons light raisins
½ cup walnuts, chopped

4 cups cooked chicken breast, diced
2 cups red apple, unpeeled and diced
1 cup mayonnaise (fat-free, if you like)
Lettuce and green grapes for garnish

1. In a large bowl, combine all ingredients except garnish; mix well.
2. Refrigerate until serving.
3. Serve in stemmed glasses lined with lettuce.
4. Garnish with green grapes.

Peaches and Cream Cheese Bars

Makes: 12 3-inch bars

1½ cups graham cracker crumbs
¼ cup brown sugar
⅓ cup butter, melted
8 ounces cream cheese

½ cup peach jelly
1 egg
¼ cup flaked coconut
¾ cup nuts, chopped

1. Preheat the oven to 350 degrees.
2. Combine crumbs, sugar, and butter; press into the bottom of a 9-by-13-inch pan.
3. Bake for 5 minutes.
4. Combine cream cheese, jelly, and egg; mix until well blended.
5. Spread the cream cheese mixture over the baked crust.
6. Sprinkle coconut and nuts on top and press lightly into the cream cheese.
7. Bake for 25 to 30 minutes, or until lightly browned.
8. Cool before slicing and serving.

Tip: Use low-fat, low-sugar, and low-sodium ingredients whenever possible for a really healthy dish.

Food Service and Decorative Touches

- Set up long tables as makeup centers, setting a place for each guest with her own supplies and mirror.
- Provide terry cloth napkins, face cloths, or towels.
- Tie face cloths around bottles of mineral water, and label each bottle with a guest's name.
- Display mirrors of various sizes and shapes.
- Place fresh fruits and vegetables in pretty baskets and bowls, arranged with fresh greens and trimmed with ribbons.
- Lay white paper in front of each guest for the makeover session; replace with place mats when serving refreshments.
- During the makeover, serve beverages in tall glasses with flexible straws for easy sipping.

MUSIC

This theme plays well with music lovers, and it will include a medley of menu items to please any guest—even the tone deaf and monotone. From chorus to verse to big ending, from snacks to sweets, this party fare is really something to sing about.

Party Menu

Snacks
*Overture Cheese Spread
Crackers and Bread Rounds
"Minuet"ure Meatballs

Beverages
Soft Drinks/Mineral Waters
*Perfect Pitch Shooters
Bubbles in the Wine Champagne Punch
(page 166)
Coffees/Teas

Buffet
*Chicken Chip Concerto Bake
*Symphony in Sausage and Eggs
Spinach Salad with Strawberries and
Mandarin Orange Slices
Rhapsody in Rolls

Dessert
*Easy Encore S'mores
*Melony Melody Cake
Sweet-A-Long Ice-Cream Dessert Bar

Overture Cheese Spread

(Begin preparing this spread a day before the party.)

Makes: 1 cup

6 ounces cream cheese, softened
¼ cup butter, softened
1 teaspoon sweet paprika
1 teaspoon capers, drained

2 anchovy fillets, rinsed, dried, and minced
1 shallot, minced
½ teaspoon caraway seeds
Salt and pepper, to taste

1. In a bowl, cream together cream cheese and butter.
2. Add remaining ingredients and mix well.
3. Pack into a crock and chill, covered, for 1 day to meld flavors.
4. Serve cheese with crackers or toast points.

Perfect Pitch Shooters

Makes: 1 serving

1 ounce vodka
1 ounce peach schnapps
Ice

1. Shake together all the ingredients.
2. Strain into a 2-ounce shot glass.

Chicken Chip Concerto Bake

Makes: 4 servings

2 cups cooked chicken, diced
1½ cups celery, diced
½ cup almonds, blanched and chopped
4 cups potato chips, divided

½ cup mayonnaise
½ small onion
1 lemon slice, peeled
1 cup cheddar cheese, cubed

1. Preheat the oven to 375 degrees.
2. Put chicken and celery into a greased 2-quart casserole. Top with chopped almonds.
3. Put 2 cups of potato chips into a blender, cover, and process 4 cycles at "stir"; empty the potato chips onto wax paper and set aside.
4. Repeat with remaining chips.
5. Put remaining ingredients into the blender, cover, and process at "blend" until smooth; add to chicken and mix well.
6. Sprinkle potato chip crumbs over the top and bake for 30 minutes.
7. Serve in mugs or coffee cups.

Symphony in Sausage and Eggs

(This dish is great for a brunch-time party, or any time. Begin preparing this dish a day before the party.)

Makes: 6 servings

12 cups herb-seasoned croutons
1½ + ½ cups sharp cheddar
  cheese, grated
1½ pounds mild bulk sausage
4 eggs

2½ + ½ cups milk
¾ teaspoon dry mustard
½ teaspoon salt
Dash of pepper
1 can cream of mushroom soup

Day Before
1. Place croutons on the bottom of a greased casserole; top with 1½ cups of cheese.
2. Brown and drain sausage; put on top of cheese.
3. Beat eggs with 2½ cups milk and seasonings; pour over the cheese.
4. Refrigerate overnight.

Next Day
5. Preheat the oven to 300 degrees.
6. Dilute soup with ½ cup milk; pour over the cheese.
7. Spread the remaining ½ cup of cheese on top.
8. Bake for 1½ hours.

Easy Encore S'mores

Makes: 48 squares

⅔ cup light corn syrup
2 tablespoons margarine or butter
1 11½-ounce package chocolate chip morsels
1 teaspoon vanilla
1 10-ounce package Golden Grahams cereal (about 8 cups)
3 cups miniature marshmallows

1. In a 3-quart saucepan, heat corn syrup, margarine, and chocolate morsels to boiling, stirring constantly.
2. Remove from heat and stir in vanilla.
3. Place cereal in a large mixing bowl and pour chocolate mixture on top; toss quickly until the cereal is completely coated with chocolate.
4. Fold in marshmallows, 1 cup at a time.
5. Using the buttered back of a spoon, press the mixture evenly into a greased 13-by-9-by-12-inch baking pan. Let stand until firm, at least 1 hour, then cut into about 1½-inch squares.

Melony Melody Cake

Makes: 10 servings

1 watermelon (7 to 9 inches in diameter)
8 ounces frozen whipped topping, thawed
8 ounces nonfat lemon yogurt
Fresh fruit for garnish (kiwi, strawberries, grapes, blueberries)

1. Cut a 3-inch-thick cross section from the watermelon.
2. To remove rind from the watermelon cross section, cut 4 vertical slits through the rind without cutting the flesh. This will divide the rind into 4 equal sections.
3. Cut between the rind and the red flesh to remove the rind. You will now have a circle of watermelon.
4. Fold together whipped topping and yogurt.
5. Pat the watermelon circle dry with paper towels; place on a flat serving plate.
6. Frost top and sides with whipped topping mixture.
7. Decorate as desired with fresh fruit.
8. Refrigerate until ready to serve—several hours or overnight. Cut into wedges.

Food Service and Decorative Touches

- Use a black-and-white color scheme.
- Cover tables with sheet music (chart side up) and overlay with clear plastic. (See How-To's #19.)
- Feature novelty items shaped like music notes and clefs in your table decor.
- Wrap napkins in paper rings made of sheet music paper, customized with the name of the event or the guest of honor.
- Display attractive music-related books.
- Use a rubber stamp or hand-crafted potato stamp of a four-inch music note to decorate plain bed sheets and pillowcases to use as table and chair covers.
- Incorporate decorative musical instruments into the buffet table decor.
- Fashion a seating chart on a poster/banner to emulate a music staff, with guests' names written on music notes. (See How-To's #1.)

NIGHT AT THE . . .
(THEATER, BALLET, OPERA)

This theme is perfect to honor a fan of any of the three entertainment forms, or as a pre- or post-theater gathering. The suggested menu is designed for an entire evening at home, but it can easily be altered for a pre- or post-theater gala.

Party Menu

Snacks
*Best Wurst Pâté Spread
Cocktail Rye Bread, Lahvosh Crackers
Verdi's Veggies and Diva's Dips

Beverages
Soft Drinks/Mineral Waters
*Phantom Champagne Punch
*Hamlet's Martini (page 224)
Coffees/Teas

Buffet
*Turkey "Bing" Salad
Puccini's Fettuccine
Tosca Tossed Salad
Toast "Pointes" and Bread Twirls

Dessert
*Fat Lady Finale Pie
Nutcracker Sweets
Fruit and Cheese Finale

Best Wurst Pâté Spread
Makes: about 1¾ cups of dip

1 cup liverwurst
½ cup sour cream
1 teaspoon Dijon mustard

1 teaspoon dill pickle relish
¼ cup white onion, minced
½ teaspoon white pepper

1. Blend liverwurst and sour cream until smooth and creamy.
2. Add all the other ingredients; blend well.
3. Chill or serve at room temperature.

Phantom Champagne Punch
Makes: 14 servings

2 6-ounce cans frozen lemonade
5 cups water, divided
14 whole strawberries

14 pineapple chunks
1 cup triple sec or other orange-flavored liqueur
2 bottles (750-milliliter size) champagne, chilled

1. Preferably the day before serving, mix 1 can frozen lemonade concentrate with 3 cups water; pour into ice cube trays, and freeze.
2. Thread toothpicks with 1 whole strawberry and 1 pineapple chunk; arrange on a plate, cover, and refrigerate.
3. Immediately before serving, combine the second can of lemonade, 2 cups water, liqueur, and prepared ice cubes in a punch bowl.
4. Gently add chilled champagne; stir.
5. Serve in champagne glasses and garnish each glass with a fruit skewer.

Turkey "Bing" Salad

Makes: 6 servings

1¼ pounds smoked turkey breast, diced
1 cup green onions, chopped
¾ cup celery, chopped
⅓ cup low-fat mayonnaise
3 tablespoons fresh thyme,
   chopped, divided
Salt and pepper, to taste

6 tablespoons olive oil
3 tablespoons white wine vinegar
8 ounces mixed baby greens
2⅓ cups pitted Bing cherries, coarsely chopped
½ cup hazelnuts, husked, toasted,
   and coarsely chopped

1. Mix turkey, green onions, celery, mayonnaise, and 2 tablespoons chopped thyme in a medium bowl.
2. Season with salt and pepper.
3. In a large bowl, whisk oil, vinegar, and remaining 1 tablespoon chopped thyme until well blended.
4. Season with salt and pepper.
5. Add greens to the vinaigrette and toss well. Divide among plates.
6. Add cherries and nuts to the turkey salad; mix.
7. Spoon the salad on top of the greens.

Fat Lady Finale Pie

(Actually, this dessert is just the opposite, since it is low in fat and sugar.)

Makes: 8 servings

1 4-ounce package Jell-O sugar-free
   instant vanilla pudding mix
⅔ cup nonfat dry milk powder
1¼ cups water
½ teaspoon mint extract

Green food coloring
1 cup light dessert topping
2 tablespoons mini mint chocolate chips
1 6-ounce ready-made chocolate-flavored pie crust

1. Combine pudding mix, milk powder, and water; mix well with a wire whisk.
2. Fold in mint extract, green food coloring, and dessert topping.
3. Gently stir in chocolate chips.
4. Pour the mixture into the pie crust and refrigerate until ready to serve.

Food Service and Decorative Touches

- For an all-evening party, serve the complete menu.
- For a preperformance party, serve appetizers, drinks, and smaller portions of dessert.
- For a postperformance party, serve appetizers, drinks, a minibuffet, and dessert.
- Use top hats, white gloves, opera glasses, and theater programs as decorative accents. Add props from specific shows, if you like.
- Design place cards to look like theater tickets.
- Create table centerpieces to represent specific shows, and decorate each table accordingly.

PETS

Your party will go to the dogs . . . or cats, gerbils, goldfish, or even iguanas . . . when you devote the event to the love of pets. Feed your pet lover and guests "chow" that even their pets would obediently sit up and enjoy.

Party Menu

Snacks
*Rin Won Ton Cheese Tarts
Doggie-Bone-Shaped Sandwiches with
Cat-Treat Tuna Salad
Goldfish and Animal Crackers

Beverages
Soft Drinks/Mineral Waters
*Hair o' the Dog Cocktail
Coffees/Teas

Buffet
*Spuds Mexkenzie
Chili Dogs
Classic Pet-tato Salad

Dessert
*Kitty Litter Cake
Doggie-Biscuit-Shaped Cookies
Chocolate Turtles, KitKat Bars

Rin Won Ton Cheese Tarts
Makes: 16 servings

7½ ounces crab meat
8 ounces cream cheese
Vegetable oil for deep-frying

2 teaspoons soft bread crumbs
2 drops sesame oil
1 package won ton skins

1. Combine all ingredients except skins. Fill squares with 1 teaspoon of mixture.
2. Fold the filled skins to make triangles; moisten edges to seal.
3. Fry in oil heated to 370 for 3 minutes, or until brown and puffed, turning once.
4. Serve with mustard or sweet/sour sauce.

Hair o' the Dog Cocktail
Makes: 1 serving

4 ounces clamato juice
   (tomato/clam juice mixture)
Dash each of salt and pepper
Dash of Worcestershire sauce

Dash of Tabasco sauce
Splash of beer (for a bit of of fizz)
Shrimp, celery heart, and lime wedge
   for garnish

1. Combine all ingredients except garnish; serve in a salt-rimmed soda glass over ice.
2. Garnish with ½ a shrimp, a celery heart, a lime wedge, and 2 straws.

Spuds Mexkenzie
Makes: 4 servings

2 tablespoons vegetable oil
4 medium red potatoes (about 1½
   pounds), cut into ¾-inch chunks
½ medium red onion, coarsely chopped
½ medium green bell pepper, chopped

¼ cup Mexican cooking sauce
1 15-ounce can black beans, drained
1 cup cheddar cheese, shredded
1 cup (or more) salsa, mild or medium
Guacamole, sour cream, and cilantro for garnish

1. Heat oil in a large nonstick skillet; add potatoes and sauté over medium-low heat until potatoes are tender, stirring and turning potatoes frequently.
2. Add chopped onions and bell peppers; sauté 2 to 3 minutes longer, or just until vegetables are crisp-tender, but retain their color.
3. Reduce heat to lowest setting; drizzle vegetables with Mexican sauce and toss.
4. Add black beans and cheese; toss again to combine ingredients and to heat thoroughly, until cheese melts.
5. Divide the mixture among 4 plates; spoon salsa on top.
6. Garnish with guacamole, sour cream, and a sprig of cilantro.

Kitty Litter Cake
Makes: 24 servings

1 package spice cake mix *1 package white sandwich cookies*
1 package white cake mix *Green food coloring*
1 package vanilla pudding mix *12 small Tootsie Rolls*

1. Prepare and bake cake mixes according to package directions.
2. Prepare pudding mix and chill until ready to assemble.
3. Crumble white sandwich cookies in small batches in a blender (scrape often). Set aside ¼ cup of the cookie crumbs. To the ¼ cup cookie crumbs, add a few drops green food coloring and mix with a fork.
4. When cakes are cooled to room temperature, crumble them both into a large bowl.
5. Gently toss the cake chunks with half the remaining uncolored cookie crumbs and the chilled pudding.
6. Line a new, clean kitty litter box with plastic wrap or aluminum foil. Put the cake mixture into the litter box.
7. Put 3 unwrapped Tootsie Rolls in a microwave-safe dish and heat until soft and pliable, ends curving slightly. Bury in the cake mixture.
8. Sprinkle the remaining untinted cookie crumbs over top.
9. Scatter green cookie crumbs lightly over the top (to look like chlorophyll).
10. Heat remaining Tootsie Rolls, 3 at a time, in the microwave until almost melted.
11. Scrape them onto the top of the cake and sprinkle with cookie crumbs.
12. Serve with a new pooper scooper.

Food Service and Decorative Touches
- Cover tables with brown craft paper and make paw prints all over it with potato or rubber stamps.
- Serve snacks in new, clean pet bowls.
- Arrange lots of stuffed animals on tables for centerpieces and buffet table decor.
- Make place cards by writing guests' names on dog tags (metal or cardboard).
- Put flowers in a clear dog snack jar; use dry dog food to hold the flowers in place.
- Feature all manner of clean (new preferred) pet paraphernalia: Wrap collars around serving bowls or bottles; lay leashes down the center of buffet table; arrange pet toys in baskets along with flowers or greens as centerpieces; display colorful pet-food packages. (No used litter boxes, please!)
- Have fun with food labels: Fido's Favorites, Bowzer's Burgers, Kitty's Klassics, Puppy Chow Mein, Paws That Refreshes, Vet's Vittles, or Rover's Refills.

PHOTOGRAPHY

I know you can picture this! A festive party held for a camera carryin' photography enthusiast that has all the guests posing for Kodak moments. The selected menu items will look like they belong on a magazine page—and will still be good enough to eat and drink!

Party Menu

Snacks
*Darkroom Mushroom Munchies
*Black-and-White Bread Strips
"See What Develops" Veggies with Dip
(served in a developer pan)

Beverages
Soft Drinks/Mineral Waters
"Shutter Bug" Gelatin Shooters
*Kodachrome
Coffees/Teas

Buffet
*Quick-as-a-Flash Casserole
*Kodakolor Konfetti Kole Slaw (page 231)
Rolls and Breads

Dessert
*Pretty-as-a-Picture "Say Cheese" Cakes
Photo Finish Fruit Bowl
Ginger Snaps

Darkroom Mushroom Munchies
Makes: 25 stuffed mushrooms

1 small onion, finely chopped
8 mushroom stems, finely chopped
4 to 6 strips of bacon, fried and
  crumbled (reserve fat)

8 ounces cream cheese, softened
25 large mushrooms, stems removed

1. Preheat the oven to 350 degrees.
2. Sauté onion and mushroom stems in bacon fat until tender; drain off excess fat.
3. Combine the bacon, onion, and stems mixture with the softened cream cheese; mix well and stuff into each mushroom cap.
4. Bake for 10 to 15 minutes. Place under the broiler until tops are golden.

Black-and-White Bread Strips
Makes: 32 servings

8 ounces cream cheese
¼ cup sour cream
½ teaspoon celery salt
½ teaspoon garlic powder

1 teaspoon sesame seeds
8 slices black bread, crusts trimmed
8 slices white bread, crusts trimmed

1. Mix cream cheese, sour cream, seasonings, and seeds to make a creamy spread.
2. Spread mixture on black bread slices and top with white bread slices.
3. Cut each sandwich into 4 strips. Arrange on trays made of framed black-and-white photos.

Denver Pizza Squares

Makes: 8 servings (2 squares per serving)

*1 11-ounce can Pillsbury Crusty
  French Loaf
2 tablespoons prepared mustard
2 cups (12 ounces) ham, finely diced
½ cup onion, chopped*

*¾ cup green bell pepper, chopped
1 cup fresh tomato, diced
1¼ cups fresh mushrooms, chopped
1½ cups (6 ounces) mozzarella cheese, shredded
2 teaspoons dried parsley flakes*

1. Preheat the oven to 375 degrees.
2. Pat dough into a 11-by-16-inch baking pan, along the bottom and up the sides.
3. Bake 8 to 9 minutes and remove from oven.
4. Spread mustard evenly over crust.
5. Layer ham, onion, green pepper, tomato, and mushrooms over the mustard.
6. Sprinkle cheese and parsley flakes evenly over the top.
7. Bake 20 minutes, or until cheese is bubbly.
8. Cool 4 to 5 minutes, then cut into 16 squares.

Un-Baked Alaska

Makes: 12 servings

*1 angel food cake
10 chocolate sandwich cookies,
  broken into small pieces*

*1 quart strawberry ice cream, slightly thawed
8 ounces frozen nondairy whipped topping, thawed
Cocoa powder for garnish*

1. Turn the cake small end up. With a long sharp knife, cut out the cake's center from top to bottom, leaving about ½ inch from outer edge.
2. Carefully lift out the center cylinder. Place the shell onto a serving plate.
3. Cut a ½-inch-thick slice off the bottom of the cylinder. Place the slice into the shell to partially cover the bottom opening, and use the rest of the cylinder to cover up the remaining hole. (You won't need remaining cylinder.)
4. Stir cookie pieces into ice cream. Spoon the ice cream into the cake shell, rounding the top.
5. Spread whipped topping decoratively over the cake and ice cream.
6. Sift cocoa over cake.
7. Freeze the cake for at least 3 hours for ice cream to harden.
8. When the topping is hard, you can wrap the cake and freeze up to 2 days.

Food Service and Decorative Touches

- Lay out a collage of maps, magazine covers, and travel advertisements on tables and cover with clear plastic. (See How-To's #19.)
- Set up a bar to represent a travel/ticket counter, dress the bartender in uniform.
- Have guests bring potluck foods representing their travels.
- Serve snacks in small suitcases, bags, and baskets labeled with baggage claim tickets. For buffets, serve food on airline trays.
- Use luggage tags for napkin rings or place cards.
- Laminate travel pictures and maps to use as place mats.
- Create centerpieces of small suitcases or duffel bags filled with flowers, branches, and greens accented with candles and electric lights.
- Create centerpieces representing the guest-of-honor's favorite places of travel.

BOWLING

When your guest of honor is the King or Queen Pin of the alley—bowling alley, that is—the party you create will take on a nice roll with a menu of delicious refreshments that will make a perfect score in a league of their own.

Party Menu

Snacks
*Sassy Spare Ribs
Cheese Spread in Bowling Pin Shape
(trimmed with pimento stripes)
Bowling Ball Black Olives (pitted)
Ed Norton's Nachos
Snack Crackers

Beverages
Soft Drinks
*Bowlin' Bouillon
Beer

Buffet
"Bowl 'em Over" Sandwich Bar
(See Food Service suggestions for sandwich name ideas.)
*Turkey Beer Balls
Super Tossed Salad Bowl

Dessert
*Banana Split Bowls
Strike Your Fancy Bowl of Fruit
Bowling Banquet Bon Bons

Sassy Spare Ribs

(The ribs must be marinated overnight.)

Makes: 30 to 40 pieces

1 tablespoon dry mustard
1 teaspoon chili powder
1 teaspoon sage
1 tablespoon salt

10 pounds spareribs, cut in 3-inch pieces
1 bottle beer
1 cup honey
1 tablespoon lemon juice

1. Mix spices and rub on the ribs.
2. Combine beer, honey, and lemon juice; mix well, pour over ribs, and marinate overnight.
3. Preheat the oven to 350 degrees.
4. Roast the ribs, uncovered, for 2 hours, basting with leftover marinade.

Bowlin' Bouillon

Makes: 1 serving

3 ounces cold beef bouillon
Ice

1 ounce vodka or gin
Beef jerky stick

1. Pour bouillon over ice into an old-fashioned glass.
2. Add vodka or gin.
3. Add a small beef jerky swizzle stick.

Turkey Beer Balls

Makes: 30 balls

2 pounds ground turkey
2 small onions, chopped
1 green pepper, chopped
¾ cup flour

Oil for frying
2 cans or bottles beer
4 tablespoons chili sauce

1. Mix turkey, onion, and pepper; form into 2-inch balls.
2. Sprinkle flour over meatballs and brown in a bit of oil.
3. Drain off fat, leaving meatballs in the pan; add beer and chili sauce.
4. Simmer until warm; serve in a chafing dish.

Banana Split Bowls

Makes: 4 servings

2 medium bananas
4 ½-cup scoops vanilla ice cream
½ cup chocolate sauce
½ cup fresh strawberry sauce
½ cup pineapple sauce

½ cup whipped cream
½ cup walnuts, chopped
4 maraschino cherries
12 small ice-cream wafers

1. Cut bananas in half lengthwise, then cut in half crosswise.
2. Place 2 sections of banana in the bottom of a small dessert bowl.
3. Place a scoop of ice cream on top of the bananas.
4. Drizzle ⅛ cup of each sauce on top of the ice cream.
5. Top with ⅛ cup whipped cream topping.
6. Sprinkle nuts on top of cream, and garnish with a cherry.
7. Serve with ice-cream wafers.

Food Service and Decorative Touches

*   Use cleaned and spray-painted bowling pins for table decorations.
*   Arrange flowers and candles in the finger holes of bowling balls.
*   Use score sheets as place mats.
*   Fill large trophy cups with snacks or flowers.
*   Fill small trophy cups with dry snacks and use them as place cards.
*   Tie colorful bowling-shoe strings around napkins.
*   Trim place cards with bowling-theme stickers.
*   Hang thrift-store bowling shirts over chair backs.
*   Have fun with food labels for your sandwich bar: The Lois Lane, The Alley McGraw, Ralph and Ed's Pick-up Piler, and so on.

FISHING

There are definitely two "angles" for this party—a celebration honoring an avid fisher-person or a get-together for a group of "fishing widows." Either way, your guests should go for the food and beverage offerings . . . hook, line, and sinker.

Party Menu

Snacks
*Deep Sea Salmon Dip
Crackers, Cocktail Bread Rounds, and
Veggies to Dip
Goldfish Crackers

Beverages
Soft Drinks/Mineral Waters
*Fish House Punch
Beer (from the cooler)
Coffees/Teas

Buffet
Fish Fry
Au Gratin Potato Bake
*Seafood Pasta Salad
Seaweed Salad
Rolls and Breads in a Fishing Basket

Dessert
*"The Big One" Cookie
Frozen Yogurt with Toppings

Deep Sea Salmon Dip
Makes: about 3 cups

1 15½-ounce can Alaska salmon
2 8-ounce packages cream cheese, softened
1½ tablespoons lemon juice

2 teaspoons horseradish
2 to 3 drops liquid smoke
½ cup green onions, thinly sliced

1. Drain salmon, reserving 2 tablespoons salmon liquid; flake the salmon and set aside.
2. Mix together cream cheese, salmon liquid, lemon juice, horseradish, and liquid smoke.
3. Fold salmon and green onions into the cheese mixture.
4. Refrigerate until chilled, to allow flavors to combine.
5. Serve the dip in a fish-shaped dish.

Fish House Punch
(This punch will be best if you allow it to stand overnight.)
Makes: 6 quarts

1 quart fresh lemon juice
1 cup sugar
2 quarts water
2 quarts Jamaican rum

1 quart brandy
¼ cup peach brandy
*Fish-shaped ice block (frozen in a fish-shaped
    gelatin mold)*

1. Strain lemon juice into a large bowl.
2. Add sugar and water, and stir until the sugar dissolves.
3. Add rum, brandy, and peach brandy.
4. Let stand at least 4 hours or overnight.
5. Pour punch into a clear punch bowl over a fish-shaped ice block
6. Float fish-shaped ice cubes in the bowl.

Seafood Pasta Salad

Makes: 6 servings

Salad Ingredients

3 cups cooked 3-color spiral pasta, drained and cooled
1½ cups small shrimp, cooked (You can also use lobster, crab, or tuna—or a mixture.)
½ cup green pepper, diced
½ cup carrots, sliced
½ cup zucchini, sliced

Dressing

½ cup Lea & Perrins white wine Worcestershire sauce
½ cup mayonnaise
Salt and pepper, to taste

1. Combine all the salad ingredients in a large bowl.
2. In a small bowl, mix the dressing ingredients. Pour the dressing over the salad and toss well. Refrigerate at least 2 hours before serving.

"The Big One" Cookie

Makes: 10 chunk servings

1 cup walnuts
2½ cups all-purpose flour
1 cup granulated sugar
1 cup butter or margarine, cold
Powdered sugar (optional)

1. Preheat the oven to 350 degrees.
2. Finely grind nuts in a blender, processor, or grinder.
3. Mix nuts, flour, and sugar.
4. Cut in butter with a pastry blender until the mixture is crumbly.
5. Spread the mixture onto a greased, flour-dusted 12-inch pizza pan; do not press down.
6. Bake until lightly browned (35 to 40 minutes); let cool in the pan on a wire rack.
7. Slide the cookie from the pan onto a rack and sprinkle with powdered sugar, if desired.
8. Wrap the cookie in plastic wrap until ready to serve, to keep it moist. Break into chunks to eat.

Food Service and Decorative Touches

- Decorate flower centerpieces with clean bobbers, lures, reels, and other small fishing equipment or supplies.
- Spread out fishnetting on top of newspapers as table covers.
- Fill lure-festooned hats, fish buckets, or baskets with snacks, breads, or serving utensils.
- Tie each napkin around a floppy toy fish from a novelty store.
- Float a few goldfish, real or plastic, in a bowl as a centerpiece.
- Add colorful fishing pamphlets, books, or posters to your buffet table, or use them to create a backdrop.

GOLF/TENNIS

Hunger and thirst are two byproducts of a lively round of golf or a brisk set of tennis. Both activities are reputed to turn gentle players into ardent game addicts. However, if you use the menu and recipes below, you are sure to win over even the most fervent golf or tennis "nuts."

Party Menu

Snacks
*Creamy on the Green Sticks
*Cheesy Pickle Cart Wheels

Beverages
Soft Drinks/Mineral Waters
*Sports Day Sunset Sipper
Wine Coolers/Beer
Coffees/Teas

Buffet
Golf: Country Club Sandwiches, Birdie Burgers, Glorious Greens Salad
Tennis: Backhand Burgers, Love 'n' Quiches

Dessert
*Knickers Snickers Cake
*Love and Spoonful Whipped Lemon Hole-in-One Donuts

Creamy on the Green Sticks
Makes: about 1 cup

2¼ ounces deviled ham (canned)
⅛ teaspoon salt
1 teaspoon Dijon-style mustard

5 ounces smoky cheese spread (1 jar)
2 tablespoons sweet pickle relish
Celery stalks, cut in 2-inch sections

1. Combine all ingredients except celery stalks; mix thoroughly and stuff into celery.
2. Arrange the stuffed pieces on a tray or platter lined with green Astroturf material.

Cheesy Pickle Cart Wheels
Makes: 36 wheels

1 jar dill pickles (about 6 pickles)
8 ounces cream cheese
3 ounces smoked meat, thinly sliced

1. Roll each whole pickle in cream cheese, covering completely.
2. Wrap each cheese-covered pickle in 1 layer of meat. Chill for at least 1 hour.
3. Slice rolls crosswise into wheels and arrange on either a golf- or tennis-design tray.

Sports Day Sunset Sipper
Makes: 1 serving

2 teaspoons grenadine
Ice
⅓ cup orange juice

⅓ cup pineapple juice
Lemon slice for garnish

1. Pour most of the grenadine into a large, stemmed glass. Fill glass with ice.
2. Pour equal amounts of orange and pineapple juice over the ice.
3. Top with a lemon slice, add a dash of grenadine, then watch the sunset.

Knickers Snickers Cake

Makes: 10 servings

16 1½-ounce Snickers bars,
  cut into small pieces
¼ cup water
2 tablespoons smooth peanut butter
2 cups flour, unsifted
¾ teaspoon baking soda
¼ teaspoon salt

1 cup butter
2 cups sugar
4 eggs, separated
3 teaspoons vanilla
1¼ cups buttermilk, divided
Whipped cream or nondairy topping for garnish

1. Preheat the oven to 350 degrees.
2. In the top of a double boiler, combine cut-up Snickers bars, water, and peanut butter; heat, stirring until melted and blended. Cool.
3. Mix flour, baking soda, and salt. Set aside.
4. In a large bowl, cream butter thoroughly; gradually add sugar and beat until fluffy.
5. Beat in 4 egg yolks into the butter mixture. Add vanilla.
6. Add cooled candy bar mix and ¼ cup buttermilk to the butter; mix until smooth.
7. Stir in the flour mix alternately with the remaining 1 cup buttermilk; mix only until blended. Gently fold in 4 stiffly beaten egg whites.
8. Divide the batter between 2 greased and floured 9-inch square pans.
9. Bake 45 to 55 minutes.
10. Cool in the pans for 5 minutes; then remove from the pans to the cooling rack.
11. Serve the cake with whipped cream or nondairy topping.

Love and Spoonful Whipped Lemon

Makes: 6 servings

1 angel food cake
2 3-ounce boxes lemon pudding

4 cups milk
8 ounces nondairy topping

1. Break angel food cake into bite-sized pieces and put into a 9-by-13-inch pan.
2. Cook pudding and milk according to package directions. While still hot, pour the pudding over the cake pieces. Let set until cool, then refrigerate.
3. When ready to serve, spread with nondairy topping.

Food Service and Decorative Touches

Golf:
- Cover the cake or dessert table with Astroturf.
- Mark foods with small flags bearing each dish's name.
- Serve nuts or candies in golf ball boxes, and chips or popcorn in buckets.
- Wrap each guest's utensils in a terry cloth fingertip towel; use golf tees to secure paper napkins around utensils or to trim name tags, place cards, or party favors.
- For both: Spray-paint balls, buckets, golf clubs, tennis rackets, visors, gloves, or trophies, to match your decor. Use gold or silver as formal accents.

Tennis:
- Use terry wrist bands as napkin rings and score cards as seating or place cards.
- Spread a tennis net over the tablecloth on your buffet table.
- Use ball canisters to hold flowers, and invert the canisters to hold chunky candles.
- Have servers pass appetizers on paper-lined tennis rackets.

HEALTH AND FITNESS

Even health nuts like to party. This party menu is ideal for a celebration dedicated to a person who has made a commitment to lead a healthy life. However, even the guests who are fast-food freaks will be satiated.

Party Menu

Snacks
*Fresh Fruit Forkfuls with Yogurt Dip
*Cool Down Cottage Cheese Dip
Pita Bread Triangles and Veggies for Dipping

Beverages
Mineral Water
*A+ Apple-Apricot Smoothies
Decaffeinated Coffees/Herb Teas

Buffet
Hopelessly Healthy Salad Bar
(Vegetable and Pasta)

Dessert
*No-Guilt Chocolate Toffee Bars
Low-Cal Coffee Smoothies

Fresh Fruit Forkfuls with Yogurt Dip

Makes: as much as you want

Fresh pineapple, cantaloupe, watermelon, banana, and kiwi, cut into chunks
Whole strawberries, grapes, blueberries, and raspberries
Yogurt, favorite flavors, for dipping

1. Spear a fruit chunk or a whole fresh fruit onto the end of a fork.
2. Cut florist's oasis to fit a large tray or platter.
3. Completely cover the oasis with fresh moss.
4. Poke the handle of each fork into the moss, covering the platter with the forkfuls.
5. Place bowls of dip among or next to the fruit, and let guests help themselves.

Note: Provide an attractive receptacle for used forks.

Cool Down Cottage Cheese Dip

Makes: 4 servings

¼ cup cucumber, chopped
¼ cup green onion, chopped
  (the green and the white parts)
¼ cup radish, chopped

½ cup sour cream
½ cup cottage cheese
½ teaspoon celery salt
¼ teaspoon black pepper

1. Mix together cucumber, green onion, and radish.
2. Add sour cream and cottage cheese; mix well.
3. Add seasonings.
4. Scoop the dip into a small dish; place the dish on a large platter and surround it with dippables.

A+ Apple-Apricot Smoothies
Makes: 2 servings

1 apple (Golden Delicious), peeled, cored, and chopped
1 cup apple juice
4 fresh apricots, pitted (peeled or not, as you like)
1 banana, peeled and broken into chunks
¾ cup plain yogurt
10 to 12 ice cubes
1 tablespoon honey
Apple and apricot slices for garnish

1. In a blender, combine all ingredients except garnish; blend well.
2. Pour into tall glasses and garnish with apple and apricot slices.

No-Guilt Chocolate Toffee Bars
Makes: 16 servings (2 bars per serving)

1 8-ounce can Pillsbury refrigerated crescent rolls
¼ cup Brown Sugar Twin
⅓ cup reduced-calorie margarine
½ cup (2 ounces) walnuts, chopped
⅔ cup (4 ounces) mint chocolate chips

1. Preheat the oven to 350 degrees.
2. Pat rolls out to cover the bottom of an ungreased 10-by-15-inch baking pan, sealing perforations between the rolls.
3. In a small saucepan, combine Brown Sugar Twin and margarine and boil 1 minute; pour the mixture evenly over the dough.
4. Sprinkle with walnuts.
5. Bake 12 to 16 minutes, or until the dough is golden brown.
6. Remove the pan from the oven and sprinkle with chocolate chips—move pieces around as they melt to create an uneven pattern.
7. Cool on a wire rack and cut into 32 bars.

Food Service and Decorative Touches
- Use terry wristbands as napkin rings, personalized with guest-of-honor's name or initials.
- Group small exercise paraphernalia, such as barbells, jump ropes, and ankle weights, in the center of dining tables; accent with vitamin and health-food packages.
- Wrap sports headbands around boxes, pots, and baskets for table decor.
- Spread covers, ads, and photos from fitness and health magazines on tabletops and cover with clear plastic. (See How-To's #19.)
- Make centerpieces of fresh flowers, plants, and herbs in clay pots or natural baskets.
- Serve a variety of beverages in water bottles.
- Print customized labels for recycled vitamin bottles. Fill with sugarless candy and use as place cards or table assignments.

HUNTING

Ah, the great outdoors and the life of a rugged sportsman. A life filled with daring challenge and, yet, rest and relaxation. This party pays homage to a persistent dweller of the "blind" or the woods who patiently waits to bag the "big one." This menu will save you the time of hunting down a bounty of the perfect recipes and serving ideas.

Party Menu

Snacks
*Dare Ya' Duck Sauce with Quackers
Venison-Stuffed Mushrooms
Fresh Fruit and Cheese Tray

Beverages
Soft Drinks/Mineral Waters
*Hot Hunt Cup
Wild Turkey Shooters
Coffees/Teas

Buffet
*Pheasant Wild Rice Casserole
Whole-Grain Rolls
Spinach and Citrus Salad

Dessert
*"Happy Hunting Grounds" Pie
Decorated Cookies in Duck, Turkey, and
Deer Shapes

Dare Ya' Duck Sauce with Quackers

Makes: 1 cup of sauce

8 ounces cream cheese, softened
1 teaspoon chili powder
1 teaspoon garlic powder

1 drop hot sauce
¼ cup Chinese duck sauce
Triscuits, Wheat Thins, or Melba Toast Rounds

1. Combine all ingredients except duck sauce; mix well.
2. Pile the dip into a serving dish and cover generously with duck sauce.
3. Serve with Triscuits, Wheat Thins, or Melba Toast Rounds.

Hot Hunt Cup

Makes: 10 to 12 punch-cup servings

4 cups cranberry juice
4 cups apple juice
1 cup pear juice
4 whole cloves

1 cinnamon stick
1 lemon, thinly sliced
Brandy or rum (optional)
Apple wedges for garnish

1. In a saucepan, combine all ingredients except alcohol and garnish.
2. Bring to a boil, lower the heat, and simmer 2 to 3 minutes.
3. Strain the liquid into coffee cups.
4. Add liquor, if desired.
5. Garnish with apple wedges.

Pheasant Wild Rice Casserole

Makes: 6 servings

1 cup uncooked wild rice	1½ cups milk
1 medium onion, chopped	2 cups pheasant, cooked and diced
1 stick margarine or butter	1 2-ounce jar pimento, diced (optional)
¼ cup flour	2 tablespoons parsley flakes
1 3-ounce can sliced mushrooms	Salt and pepper, to taste
1½ cups chicken broth	½ cup slivered almonds

1. Prepare wild rice according to package directions.
2. Preheat the oven to 350 degrees.
3. In a large pan, sauté onion in butter until tender; remove from heat and stir in flour.
4. Drain mushrooms, reserving liquid. Add enough broth to the mushroom liquid to measure 1½ cups, then gradually stir the broth into the flour mixture.
5. Add milk and cook, stirring constantly, until thick.
6. Transfer the sauce to a 2-quart casserole and add rice, mushrooms, pheasant, pimento, parsley, salt, and pepper. Sprinkle with almonds.
7. Bake for 25 to 30 minutes. Serve in mugs or as an entrée.

"Happy Hunting Grounds" Pie

Makes: 12 3-inch squares

Crust

18 graham crackers, crushed	¼ cup powdered sugar
¼ cup butter	½ cup pecans, chopped

Filling

5 cups milk, divided	2 packages (3⅛-ounce) French vanilla instant pudding
5 cups vanilla ice cream, divided	2 packages (3⅛-ounce) chocolate instant pudding
	1 package (3⅛-ounce) butter pecan instant pudding

Garnish

Whipped topping
Graham cracker crumbs
Pecans, finely chopped

1. To prepare the crust, combine all crust ingredients, mix well, and press into a 9-by-13-inch pan.
2. Blend together 3 cups milk and 3 cups ice cream with 1 package vanilla and 2 packages chocolate pudding; pour onto crust.
3. Mix the remaining vanilla and butter pecan pudding with 2 cups milk and 2 cups ice cream; pour over the chocolate layer.
4. Garnish with whipped topping, then sprinkle with graham cracker crumbs and chopped pecans. Chill until the ice cream is firm.

Food Service and Decorative Touches

- Create a centerpiece around a duck decoy, duck call, pussy willows, and branches.
- Use camouflage fabric for tablecloths, napkins, or accent touches.
- Make centerpieces out of greens and flowers arranged in inverted hunting hats.
- Use feathered objects or anything hunter-orange in color as decorative accents.
- Display colorful hunting pamphlets, books, or posters, or use them for a backdrop.

ICE SKATING

This is another "do it" or "about it" theme that is designed around the activity through food, beverage, and decoration selection. If your party follows a brisk session of ice skating, your guests will be instantly warmed by the heat and spice of your menu. However, a gathering without the activity will skim along just as smoothly.

Party Menu

Snacks
*Zesty Sausage Ryes
Tasty Trail Mix
Figure-8 Warm Pretzels
Hot Popcorn

Beverages
Soft Drinks/Mineral Waters
*Cheery Crock of Cider
Coffees/Teas

Buffet
*Spicy Brats and Beans Warm-Up
Pick A Slaw
Hot Rolls and Breads

Dessert
*Frost on the Pumpkin Pie
Spicy Cake Bars with Cream Cheese
Icing
Coffee Drinks

Zesty Sausage Ryes
Makes: 80 slices

1 pound hot bulk sausage
1 pound mild sausage
1 onion, chopped

2 pounds processed cheese, grated
1 teaspoon Italian seasoning
2 loaves party rye bread

1. Preheat the oven to 350 degrees.
2. Sauté sausage and onion together, stirring often.
3. Add cheese and seasoning; continue cooking until cheese melts.
4. Arrange bread slices on a cookie sheet and spread mixture on each.
5. Bake for 15 minutes.

Tip: If preparing this dish days ahead of time, follow steps 2 to 4, then wrap the slices well and freeze.

Cheery Crock of Cider
Makes: as much as you want

Cran-(anything) juice
Apple juice (low-cal works fine)
Cinnamon sticks, broken into
  1- to 2-inch pieces

Whole cloves
Lemon or orange peel (optional)
Brandy or rum (optional)

1. Pour equal amounts of both juices into a crock pot.
2. Wrap the cinnamon sticks, a few whole cloves, and citrus peel in a piece of cheese cloth. Add the spice bundle to the juices.
3. Bring to a low simmer, and simmer for at least 1 hour.
4. Take out the spices to prevent the liquid from getting bitter.
5. Serve hot in mugs with or without a shot of brandy or rum.

Spicy Brats and Beans Warm-Up

Makes: 12 servings

1 31-ounce can pork and beans
1/4 cup onion, chopped
1/4 cup ketchup
1/4 teaspoon chili powder
2 drops cumin

3/4 pound kielbasa, sliced and slightly browned
1/4 cup brown sugar, firmly packed
2 tablespoons green pepper, chopped
Dash of garlic powder
Shredded cheddar cheese for topping (optional)

1. Preheat the oven to 350 degrees.
2. Place all ingredients, except cheese, in a greased 2-quart casserole dish; mix well.
3. Cover and bake for 35 minutes.
4. Serve in heavy mugs. Sprinkle cheddar cheese on top if desired.

Frost on the Pumpkin Pie

Makes: 6 to 8 servings

1 9-inch baked pie shell or graham cracker crust
1 pint vanilla ice cream, softened
1 cup canned pumpkin
1 cup sugar
1 teaspoon pumpkin pie spice
1/2 teaspoon ground ginger
1/2 teaspoon salt
1/2 cup walnuts, chopped
1 cup whipping cream, chilled

1. Spread ice cream in the pie shell. Freeze until ice cream is solid.
2. Mix pumpkin, sugar, pumpkin pie spice, ginger, salt, and walnuts.
3. In a chilled bowl, beat whipping cream until stiff; fold into pumpkin mixture.
4. Pour into the pie shell over ice cream and freeze several hours.
5. Remove from freezer 10 to 15 minutes before serving.

Food Service and Decorative Touches

- Lay mirrors, framed or tiles, on tables to simulate ice.
- Use very clean or new skating gear on tables as decorative accents.
- Fill skates (may be sprayed gold or covered with glitter or decoupage) with arrangements of winter flowers or snowflake flowers.
- Use earmuffs, small scarves, or mittens to hold napkins.
- Arrange fresh, silk, or paper flowers in thermos bottles or jugs.
- Place big paper or crystal-like snowflakes under a clear plastic tablecloth.
- Hang snowflakes from white-frosted branches arranged in large Lucite or glass vases or buckets.
- Arrange white, fluffy, silk or paper flowers with battery-operated twinkle lights in glass-block vases.
- Put tea-lite candles in small square votive holders or glasses.
- Make paper flowers, snowflakes, and other decorative items from iridescent tissue and cellophane for a snow-like effect.

KITE FLYING

For kids of all ages—2 to 92—kite flying provides an entertaining and exhilarating activity or an excellent party theme. After a glorious day of high-flying fun, your guests will be brought back to earth by a pleasing array of party refreshments.

Party Menu

Snacks
*Kite Kuties
Flyin' Fryin' Onion Rings
Veggies and Dips

Beverages
Soft Drinks/Mineral Waters
Higher Than a Kite Gelatin Shooters
Old-Fashioned Lemonade
Coffees/Teas

Buffet
Kite-Shaped Pizza Pieces with String Cheese Tails
*Fiesta Pasta Salad
Stack-Your-Own Sandwiches
Watermelon Fruit Boat

Dessert
*Mile-High Strawberry Pie
Kite-Shaped Cake (How-To's #33)
Homemade Ice Cream in Cones

Kite Kuties

Makes: as many as you like

Rye bread slices, crusts removed
Cream cheese
Deviled ham
Deviled egg mix
Jicama strips, curled

1. Trim the corners of bread slices to create kite shapes.
2. Cover half of each slice with cream cheese, and the other half with deviled ham.
3. Use a pastry bag filled with deviled egg mix to divide sections.
4. Add "tails" of curled jicama strips.
5. Serve on a kite-shaped tray. (See Decorative Touches.)

Fiesta Pasta Salad

Makes: 6 servings

Salad Ingredients
8 ounces uncooked 3-color pasta spirals
6 small tomatillos, each cut into 8 wedges
½ jalapeño pepper, seeded and finely chopped
20 ounces pineapple chunks, drained (reserve ½ cup juice)

Dressing
½ teaspoon lime peel, grated
¼ teaspoon salt

1 tablespoon fresh cilantro, snipped
2 tablespoons vegetable oil
½ cup reserved pineapple juice

1. Cook pasta according to package directions. Drain, cool, and put into a large bowl.
2. Add the remaining salad ingredients.
3. In a small bowl, mix the dressing ingredients. Pour the dressing over the salad and toss well to evenly coat all ingredients.
4. Refrigerate at least 2 hours before serving.

Mile-High Strawberry Pie

Makes: 6 servings

10 ounces frozen strawberries, thawed
1 cup sugar
2 egg whites
1 tablespoon lemon juice
1½ teaspoons salt
½ cup whipping cream
1 teaspoon vanilla
1 10-inch baked pie shell

1. Combine strawberries, sugar, egg whites, lemon juice, and salt in a large mixing bowl.
2. Beat with a mixer at medium speed for 15 minutes or until stiff.
3. In a separate bowl, whip cream, then add vanilla.
4. Fold the cream into the strawberry mixture.
5. Pile everything lightly into the pie shell and place into the freezer for several hours or overnight.

Food Service and Decorative Touches

- Make small kites using tissue paper and pipe cleaners to use as place cards or trims for name tags.
- Hang a display of kites as a backdrop for the buffet table, and wherever else possible.
- Cover picnic tables and serving surfaces with bright fabrics.
- Match all serving ware, plastic or paper, to table colors
- Have guests bring blankets for picnic-style service.
- Create centerpieces of small kites, interspersed with puffy clouds made of tissue paper. Anchor kites into green-painted Styrofoam to represent grass.
- Cover kite-shaped cardboard with white paper and then with colored plastic wrap. Add a ribbon tail trimmed with ribbon bows. Use this tray to serve kite-shaped snacks.

OLYMPICS/ATHLETICS

Whether you have gathered your guests to watch the games on television or to actually participate in energetic activities, choose an athletic motif in both the content and the service of your food and drink selections. Then, let the fun and games begin!

Party Menu

Snacks
*Pregame Pizza Peppies
*Cheese Medals
Chips for the Champs
Veggies for the Victorious
Dips for the Defeaters

Beverages
Soft Drinks/Mineral Waters
*Golden Glow Punch (page 222)
*Gold Medal Shooters (page 218, #4)
Beer/Sports Drinks

Buffet
*Beefed Up Javelins
Pasta with Shrimp
Crisp French Bread

Dessert
*Finish Line Chocolate Cake
Golden Fruit Gelatin Ring

Pregame Pizza Peppies
Makes: 32 pieces

4 English muffins
1 cup pizza sauce
½ cup onions, finely chopped

8 green pepper rings, quartered
16 slices pepperoni, cut in half
1 cup mozzarella cheese, shredded

1. Split muffins in half and toast them in the toaster.
2. Spread pizza sauce on both halves of the muffins. Top with onions.
3. Cut each muffin half into 4 pieces.
4. Place 8 muffin pieces in a circle around the edge of a paper plate (use 4 plates).
5. Lay a section of green pepper and half a slice of pepperoni on top of each muffin.
6. Top evenly with mozzarella cheese.
7. Place each plate, uncovered, in the microwave, and cook on high for 1 minute; rotate each plate half a turn after 30 seconds. Serve warm.

Cheese Medals
Makes: 36 servings

½ cup butter or margarine
3 ounces sharp cheddar cheese, grated
1 cup flour

⅛ teaspoon crushed red pepper
¼ teaspoon salt

1. Preheat the oven to 400 degrees.
2. Cream together butter and cheese; add remaining ingredients.
3. Shape the mixture into a 1½-inch roll; wrap in foil. Chill well, then slice ⅛-inch thick.
4. Bake for 6 minutes.
5. While warm, make an imprint on each slice with a toy medal.

Beefed Up Javelins

Makes: 4 servings (1 meat skewer and 1 vegetable skewer per serving)

1 pound sirloin	12 pearl onions	1 zucchini, cut into small wheels
2 pounds mushrooms	8 cherry tomatoes	1 green pepper, cut into squares

Marinade Sauce

2 tablespoons brown sugar	½ teaspoon salt	½ cup soy sauce
2 tablespoons sesame seeds	½ cup onions, chopped	¼ teaspoon black pepper
2 tablespoons peanut oil	1 teaspoon lemon juice	

1. Combine marinade ingredients and set aside.
2. Cut and cube sirloin and add it to the marinade; marinade for 2 to 3 hours.
3. Preheat the oven to broil.
4. Arrange meat on skewers. Arrange vegetable chunks on separate skewers.
5. Broil meat 4 inches from heat. Brush with marinade; turn every 2 or 3 minutes.
6. After 5 minutes, add vegetable skewers. In total, the meat should cook for about 10 minutes and the vegetables for about 5 minutes.

Finish Line Chocolate Cake

Makes: 16 servings

2 cups sugar	1 cup water	2 eggs
2 cups flour	½ cup buttermilk	1 teaspoon cinnamon
1 stick margarine	1 teaspoon soda	1 teaspoon vanilla
4 ounces baking chocolate		

1. Preheat the oven to 400 degrees.
2. Sift together sugar and flour.
3. Place margarine, chocolate, and water in a saucepan and bring to a rapid boil.
4. Pour the chocolate mixture over the sugar and flour mixture; stir well.
5. Combine buttermilk with baking soda, then add eggs, cinnamon, and vanilla; mix well and add to the flour mixture, mixing until well blended.
6. Pour batter into a greased and floured 10-by-15-by-1-inch pan. Bake for 20 minutes.

Frosting

1 stick margarine	1 pound powdered sugar	1 cup pecans
4 ounces baking chocolate	2 teaspoons vanilla	1 cup coconut (optional)
6 tablespoons milk		

1. Before cake is done, mix margarine, chocolate, and milk in a small saucepan.
2. Bring to a boil, then pour into a large bowl over powdered sugar. Add vanilla, pecans, and coconut, if desired; mix well. Spread the frosting over the still-hot cake.

Food Service and Decorative Touches

- Create a backdrop with posters, banners, and other symbols of Olympic games.
- Fasten napkins (paper or cloth) with sports medals or ribbon pins.
- Decorate tables with red, white, and blue flags, streamers, and balloons.
- Utilize sports equipment packaging as snack containers.
- Hang or drape uniforms over chair backs.
- Incorporate sports medals, ribbons, trophies, and awards into centerpieces and buffet table decor. Accent with Olympic-logo hats and mugs.

ROLLER SKATING

After a rollicking roller-skating event, your guests will be ready for cooling and refreshing foods and beverages. This menu is designed for the after-skating gathering or for a party honoring a roller-skating enthusiast. Wheels or blades—you'll have it made.

Party Menu

Snacks
*Mini-Mex Cheese Rolls
*Cheesy Pickle Wheels (page 180)
Chips and Dips

Buffet
Sandwich Fixins on a Skateboard
Speedo Slaws and Salads
Crispy Onion "Rinks"

Beverages
Soft Drinks/Mineral Waters
*Endless Summer Punch
Sippables in Sports Bottles
Hot and Iced Coffees/Teas

Dessert
*Pepper-Upper Peppermint Pie
Assorted Ice-Cream Bars
Skate-Shaped Iced Sugar Cookies

Mini-Mex Cheese Rolls

Makes: 3 dozen

1 4-ounce jar pimiento
1 4-ounce can green chilies
1 2.25-ounce can black olives
1 package Ranch dressing mix

16 ounces cream cheese, softened
2 green onions, minced
4 12-inch flour tortillas

1. Dice pimiento and chilies. Slice black olives. With a paper towel, blot all vegetables dry.
2. Mix dressing mix, cream cheese, and green onions. Divide the mixture evenly among 4 tortillas.
3. Sprinkle equal amounts of pimiento, chilies, and olives on top of the cream cheese.
4. Roll tortillas tightly.
5. Chill at least 2 hours.
6. Cut rolls into 1-inch pieces. Discard ends.
7. Arrange on a serving plate with spirals facing up.

Endless Summer Punch

Makes: 8 punch-cup servings

1 cup vodka
1 cup orange juice
1 cup lemonade mix*

¼ cup peach juice or mix*
Ice cubes or ice ring
Orange slices for garnish

1. Combine all ingredients except garnish; mix well.
2. Pour over ice cubes or ice ring.
3. Garnish with orange slices.

(*To make a mix, dilute lemonade and peach juice concentrate with ⅓ the required amount of water.)

Pepper-Upper Peppermint Pie

Makes: 12 servings

⅔ cup butter	2 graham cracker pie crusts
2 cups powdered sugar	2 cups whipping cream
4 eggs	6 cups mini marshmallows
4 squares chocolate, melted	⅓ cup peppermint candy, crushed

1. Combine butter, powdered sugar, and eggs; whip with a mixer.
2. Blend in melted chocolate.
3. Pour into crusts.
4. Whip cream and add in marshmallows.
5. Smooth the cream on top of the chocolate layers.
6. Top with crushed peppermint candy.
7. Chill well before serving.

Food Service and Decorative Touches

- Arrange either spray-painted and decorated castoffs or clean and/or new skating gear with silk flowers, greens, plants, and other decorative materials.
- Tuck bunches of fresh or plastic flowers into skates, then attach balloons and streamers to create table centerpieces.
- Secure blades or wheels of skates in Styrofoam bases.
- Write guests' names on sun visors to use as favors, place cards, or table assignments.
- Cover tables with plain white paper, and decorate the center area of the paper with magazine and newspaper ads for roller skating supplies or centers. Outline the pictures with a Neon highlighter. Place a centerpiece on top of this artwork.
- Use inexpensive water bottles for place cards, table assignments, or party favors.
- Display other clean equipment, such as pads and hats, and skating instruction books.
- Use lined equipment packaging cartons as snack and flower containers.

SKIING/SLEDDING/ SLEIGHING

In the good old wintertime, you will find that the best way to endure the cold weather is to celebrate it! So help your guests survive the chill of a frosty outing by serving them a party menu that's hot, hot, hot.

Party Menu

Snacks
*Chalet Cheese 'n' Chili Chews
*Zesty Sausage Ryes (page 186)
Cheese Fondue Pot with Bread Squares
for Dipping

Beverages
*Snowflake
*Snowshoe
*Mulled Cider (page 127)
Hot Toddies

Buffet
Pick A Sloppy Joe
*Warm Potato Salad Julienne (page 233)

Dessert
*Snowy Wonder Cake
Hot Chocolate with Whipped Cream
Mochas and other Coffee Drinks

Chalet Cheese 'n' Chili Chews

Makes: 36 1½-inch squares

4 tablespoons butter
5 eggs
¼ cup flour
½ teaspoon baking powder
⅛ teaspoon salt

Dash of cayenne pepper
2 cups (8 ounces) Monterey Jack
   or cheddar cheese
1 cup small-curd cottage cheese
1 4-ounce can green chilies, diced

1. Preheat the oven to 400 degrees.
2. Melt butter in a 9-inch square baking pan in the oven.
3. In a large bowl, whisk eggs until well blended.
4. Stir in flour, baking powder, salt, and cayenne pepper.
5. Tip the baking pan to coat bottom and sides with the melted butter; add the excess butter to the flour mixture.
6. Add cheeses and chilies to the flour mixture; blend well.
7. Pour the mixture into the buttered pan and bake for 15 minutes.
8. Reduce oven temperature to 350 degrees and bake 30 to 35 minutes longer, until the top is lightly browned and a knife inserted into the center comes out clean.
9. Let cool on a rack at least 10 minutes.
10. Cut into 1½-inch squares. Serve warm or at room temperature.

Tip: This dish can be made in advance and kept in the refrigerator, covered, up to 2 days. If preparing longer in advance, freeze it.

Snowflake

Makes: 1 serving

1 ounce hazelnut liqueur
1 ounce crème de cacao (white)

Ice or ice cream
Cream

1. Pour liqueurs over ice.
2. Fill the rest of the glass with cream.

Tip: If you like, blend 2 scoops of ice cream with the liqueurs and the cream.

Snowshoe

Makes: 1 serving

1 ounce tequila
1 ounce peppermint schnapps

1. Pour tequila and schnapps into a glass—do not mix.
2. Serve this drink over ice or straight up.

Snowy Wonder Cake

Makes: 8 to 10 servings

1 package white cake mix
1 3-ounce box vanilla instant pudding
8 ounces cream cheese, softened
1 large can crushed pineapple, drained

Large container frozen nondairy topping,
   room temperature
4 ounces walnuts, crushed

1. Mix and bake cake according to package directions.
2. While the cake is baking, mix pudding according to package directions.
3. Combine the pudding with cream cheese; mix on low for about 1 minute, then on high until mixed thoroughly.
4. Cover the cooled cake with the pudding and cream cheese mixture.
5. Top with crushed pineapple; reserve some pineapple for garnish.
6. Cover the entire top with frozen topping.
7. Garnish with walnuts and bits of pineapple.
8. Refrigerate until serving.

Food Service and Decorative Touches

- Since snow is the theme, choose white tablecloths, napkins, candles, and dishes.
- Heap mounds of artificial snow in the center of the table and add silver and clear glass ornaments or a twelve-inch evergreen tree with twinkle lights to create a wintery centerpiece.
- Make a runner of mirror squares down the center of the buffet table, sprinkle with sparkly snow, and add candles or twinkle lights for a dramatic effect.
- For a more casual motif, use ski caps, ear muffs, mittens, and goggles in your centerpieces and table decor. Accent with travel brochures, pamphlets, and sport books.
- For additional serving and decor ideas, see page 187.

Treat your "star-gazing" guests to an evening of wonderful entertainment—the awards—and food and drink to match. Since gazing goes smashingly with grazing, place your food stations strategically to create an easy traffic flow and to encourage your guests to help themselves while they keep a sharp eye on the silver screen.

Party Menu

Snacks
Double Feature Popcorn
*Ham Oscar "Roles"
Premier Pretzels
Mogul's Meatballs
"Variety" of Veggies with Dip

Beverages
Soft Drinks/Mineral Waters
Champagne Fountain with Real
Champagne or with
*Celebrity Champagne Taste-Alike
Shooters for the Stars
Coffees/Teas

Buffet
Box-Office Beefcake Bake (favorite
hamburger/beef casserole)
Best Supporting Salad
"Serious Earned Bread" and Rolls

Dessert
*People's Choice Popcorn Bars
Critic's Choice Cheesecake
StarBursts Candies
Kudos Candy Bars

Ham Oscar "Roles"
Makes: 12 servings

10 ounces asparagus, fresh or frozen
16 ounces light cream cheese, softened
2 teaspoons horseradish

2 teaspoons Dijon mustard
½ teaspoon Worcestershire sauce
1 pound ham, thinly sliced

1. Snap off the woody base of the asparagus and cook spears covered in a small amount of boiling water for 4 to 8 minutes or until crisp-tender. Drain and cool.
2. Mix cream cheese, horseradish, mustard, and Worcestershire sauce.
3. On each slice of ham, spread a thin layer of the cheese mixture.
4. Place one spear of asparagus at one end of ham slice, and roll up, jelly-roll style.
5. Cut each roll into bite-sized pieces.

Tip: These rolls can be made up to 24 hours before the party.

Celebrity Champagne Taste-Alike
Makes: 10 servings

2 quarts white grape juice
2 liters diet 7-Up
1 liter club soda

1. Combine all the ingredients and mix well.
2. Serve well-chilled for a great champagne taste-alike

People's Choice Popcorn Bars

Makes: 16 bars

4 cups miniature marshmallows
1 cup butterscotch chips
3 tablespoons butter
3 quarts popped popcorn
1 12-ounce jar hot fudge sauce

1. In a large Dutch oven, over low heat, melt marshmallows with butterscotch chips and butter; stir occasionally until smooth.
2. Add popcorn; toss until well coated.
3. Press half of the mixture firmly into a greased 9-inch square pan.
4. Spread fudge sauce evenly over the popcorn layer.
5. Press remaining popcorn mixture over the fudge.
6. Allow mixture to cool and harden.
7. Slide a spatula under the entire mixture, slide onto a cutting board, and cut into bars.

Food Service and Decorative Touches

- Fill the tables and surrounding area with "fit-for-a-star" razzle dazzle, glamour, glitter, and glitz.
- Purchase or make papier-mâché award statuettes to use as decorative touches wherever needed.
- Lavishly use the standard Tinsel Town decor: movie clapboards, film cans, director's chairs, and photography equipment. (See How-To's #25.)
- Spruce up the tables with star cutouts of every size, shiny tinsel, battery-operated twinkle lights, mirror tiles, and Mylar fabrics.
- Duplicate the famous HOLLYWOOD sign for your main buffet table backdrop.
- Label your grazing stations Movie Star Munchies Station, That's Entertainment Entrée Station, Screen Sirens Sweets Stop, Leading Man Liquor Saloon, and so forth.
- Have food passed on silver trays by formally attired servers (white gloves required).
- Display eight-by-ten-inch glossies of classic movie stars.
- Create customized movie passes to direct your guests to their assigned tables.
- Use small pin spotlights to highlight your centerpieces.

ELECTION RETURNS

A group of political party-goers will work up quite an appetite as they anxiously await the outcome of an election. A generous array of "pick-'em-up" and "eat-'em-up" treats will keep your pollsters occupied and satisfied during the exciting wait.

Party Menu

Snacks
*"Wait 'n' See" Food Spread
Crackers, Bread Rounds, and
Veggies for Dipping

Beverages
Soft Drinks/Mineral Waters
*Campaign Champagne Punch
Election Elixirs
Coffees/Teas

Buffet
Pollsters Do-It-Yourself Pizza Piling
(individual pizza crusts and
assorted toppings)

Dessert
*Post-Election Peach Pecan Pastries
Sweet Success Bar (variety of dessert
bars and cookies)

"Wait 'n' See" Food Spread
Makes: 3 cups of dip

16 ounces cream cheese, softened
8 ounces crab meat
½ cup bottled horseradish sauce

2 tablespoons green onions, finely chopped
½ cup almonds, sliced
Paprika (optional)

1. Preheat the oven to 375 degrees.
2. Beat cream cheese until smooth, 1 to 2 minutes.
3. Blend in the remaining ingredients, except almonds and paprika.
4. Spread mixture in a 9-inch pie plate.
5. Top with almonds and sprinkle with paprika, if desired.
6. Bake uncovered for 20 minutes.
7. Serve with assorted crackers and vegetables.

Campaign Champagne Punch
(Begin preparations the day before the party.)
Makes: 36 punch-cup servings

1 quart cranberry juice cocktail
1 cup cognac

1 bottle sweet white wine, chilled
4 ⅘-quart bottles champagne, chilled

1. Day before: Pour cranberry juice cocktail into a quart heart-shaped or ring-shaped mold and freeze overnight.
2. Just before serving: Place the cranberry mold into a large punch bowl. Stir in the rest of the ingredients.

Post-Election Peach Pecan Pastries
Makes: 35 bars

2 8-ounce cans Refrigerated Crescent Dinner Rolls
½ cup butter
⅓ cup peach preserves
2 cups pecans, chopped
1 cup sugar
Confectioners' sugar (optional)

1. Preheat the oven to 375 degrees.
2. Unroll the dough into 2 large rectangles.
3. Press both rectangles, side to side, into an ungreased 15-by-10-by-1-inch baking pan to form a crust.
4. Melt butter in a medium saucepan over low heat; cook and stir 4 to 5 minutes or until light golden brown.
5. Add preserves, pecans, and sugar; stir to coat.
6. Smooth the nut, preserves, and sugar mixture over the dough.
7. Bake for 10 to 15 minutes, or until crust is deep golden brown.
8. Cool for 30 minutes before cutting into squares.
9. Serve warm or cool. Sprinkle with confectioners' sugar, if desired.

Food Service and Decorative Touches
- Drape red, white, and blue bunting around buffet tables.
- Skewer appetizers with toothpicks decorated with U.S. flags.
- Set up a food station to look like a voting booth, with curtains pulled aside.
- Cover the dining tables with white paper, and provide pens for guests to reserve their seat by writing their names at a place setting.
- Fasten napkins with large campaign buttons.
- Use replicas of small ballot boxes as bases for food containers.
- Serve snacks in inverted campaign-style straw hats, with red, white, and blue bands.
- For more serving and decor ideas, see page 11.

EMMY AWARDS

This television viewing event rates a prize-winning menu of its own. Between the suspense of waiting for the awards results and watching the tempting food and beverage commercials, your guests are bound to be ravenous, so your "boob tube" buffet will get a great reception. There is nothing remote about this party.

Party Menu

Snacks
*Made-for-TV Seafood Specials
Couch Potato Chips
*Cable-Ready Crudités (page 242)
Pick A Dip

Beverages
Soft Drinks/Mineral Waters
*TV Tea Punch
Sitcom Shooters
Coffees/Teas

Buffet
*Rerun Turkey and Stuffing Pie
Cranberry Gelatin Salad
Freshly Baked Crescent Rolls

Dessert
*Top Banana Flambé Finale (with performance presentation)

Made-for-TV Seafood Specials
Makes: 8 servings (4 wedges per serving)

*1 cup crab meat
¼ cup green stuffed olives, sliced
½ cup tomato sauce*

*8 ounces mild cheddar cheese, cut into small cubes
4 English muffins, split
Pimento and olive pieces for garnish*

1. Combine all topping ingredients except muffins and garnish; mix well.
2. Refrigerate for at least 1 hour to blend the flavors.
3. Spread the crab mixture on English muffin halves, and broil until cheese melts.
4. Cut each muffin half into quarters.
5. Decorate each piece with small bits of pimento and olive. Serve hot.

TV Tea Punch
Makes: 50 servings

*4 cups black tea, cold
4 cups orange juice
Juice of 4 lemons
4 oranges, thinly sliced*

*2 cups sugar (or to taste)
16 cups cracked ice
12 cups ginger ale*

*4 cups soda or sparkling water
Whole strawberries for garnish
1 bunch fresh mint*

1. Combine tea, juices, orange slices, and sugar. Stir until the sugar dissolves. Chill.
2. Pour into a large punch bowl over ice. Add ginger ale and soda just before serving.
3. Ladle the punch into tall tea glasses or champagne flutes.
4. Garnish with strawberries and mint; add sipping straws.

Rerun Turkey and Stuffing Pie

Makes: 6 servings

2 cups cooked turkey, diced
½ teaspoon seasoned salt
1 cup prepared turkey stuffing
¼ cup green onions (with tops), sliced

½ cup cooked green peas
1 cup milk
2 eggs
½ cup biscuit mix

1. Preheat the oven to 400 degrees.
2. Arranged diced turkey in a greased 9-inch pie plate.
3. Sprinkle with seasoned salt.
4. Separate stuffing into small pieces and arrange on top of turkey.
5. Top with onions and peas.
6. Beat the remaining ingredients in a blender until smooth (about 15 seconds).
7. Pour onto the pie plate.
8. Bake for 30 to 35 minutes, or until a knife inserted into the center comes out clean. Cool 5 minutes.
9. Serve with hot turkey gravy.

Top Banana Flambé Finale
(with performance presentation)

Makes: 8 servings

¼ cup butter
8 medium ripe bananas, cut
   lengthwise then crosswise
⅓ cup peach jam

⅓ cup orange juice
½ cup white rum or heated brandy
Ice cream or whipped cream for garnish

1. Gather your audience.
2. In a large pan, melt butter over medium heat.
3. Add bananas and cook for 3 to 4 minutes, then carefully turn bananas over and cook 1 to 2 minutes more, until just tender.
4. Transfer the bananas to a large platter.
5. Add peach jam and orange juice to the pan; bring to a boil and cook about 2 minutes until the sauce thickens; return bananas to the pan.
6. Add rum or brandy; light with a match and stand back, admiring the flame.
7. When the flame goes out, place 4 pieces of banana on each plate and divide the sauce evenly among the plates; top with a scoop of ice cream or a dollop of whipped cream.

Food Service and Decorative Touches

- Serve a variety of snack foods on TV trays.
- Provide aluminum TV dinner trays for buffet dinners.
- Set up serving stations of popular brand-name commercial food displays.
- Use *TV Guides* generously in your decorating scheme. Cut titles from cover pages to use as napkin rings. (See How-To's #27.)
- Make a silly decorative object for the buffet table of old rabbit ears sprayed gold or wrapped in aluminum foil, then trimmed with a starry garland.
- Spray-paint old TV remotes to use as decorative touches.
- Recycle small portable television sets to use for serving.

GRAMMY AWARDS

Music is in the air, and on this night the stars who have been making the music will be rewarded for their incredible talents. Organize a bill of fare that would get a "#1 with a bullet" rating in *Billboard Magazine*—the bible of the recording industry.

Party Menu

Snacks
*Spin-the-Taco Dip Platter
*Rappin' Rumaki Roll-Ups
Chart Buster Cheese Ball

Beverages
Soft Drinks/Mineral Waters
*Tequila Sunrise Gelatin Shooters
(page 219)
Beer/Wine
Coffees/Teas

Buffet
A Billboard Buffet That's #1:
Country & Western Barbecue Ribs
Classical Clam Cakes
Salsa Slaw
Funky Fries
Jazzy Jell-O Salad
Rock 'n' Rolls

Dessert
*CD (Chocolate-Dipped) Classic
Fruit and Cheese Kabobs
Chocolate Dipping Sauce

Spin-the-Taco Dip Platter
Makes: 20 servings

1 30-ounce can refried beans	½ teaspoon salt	2 cups lettuce, chopped
1 can jalapeño bean dip	¼ teaspoon pepper	2 cups tomatoes, chopped
1 small can diced chilies	1 cup sour cream	½ cup onion, diced
3 ripe avocados	1 package taco seasoning	2 cups cheddar cheese, grated
2 tablespoons lemon juice	¼ cup mayonnaise	1 cup black olives, sliced

1. Spread refried beans onto a round cake plate or an LP covered with clear plastic wrap; then spread a can of jalapeño bean dip on top.
2. Sprinkle with diced chilies.
3. Next, mash avocados with lemon juice, salt, and pepper; spread on top of the chilies. Refrigerate for at least 1 hour.
4. Combine sour cream, taco seasoning, and mayonnaise. Spread on top of the avocado layer.
5. Top with, in order, lettuce, tomatoes, onion, grated cheese, and sliced olives.
6. Refrigerate until ready to eat.
7. Serve with tortilla chips.

Rappin' Rumaki Roll-Ups

Makes: 8 servings

¼ cup mayonnaise
¼ cup chili sauce
½ cup brown sugar
2 cans whole water chestnuts
1 pound bacon, thinly sliced (cut slab in half)

1. Preheat the oven to 375 degrees.
2. Mix mayonnaise, chili sauce, and brown sugar to make a sauce
3. Wrap a bacon strip around each individual chestnut.
4. Lay the bundles into a baking dish and pour the sauce on top
5. Bake for 45 minutes.

CD (Chocolate-Dipped) Classic

Makes: 12 3-inch squares

1 package chocolate cake mix
14 ounces caramels
½ cup margarine or butter

1 12-ounce can condensed milk (not evaporated!)
1 cup pecans, coarsely chopped

1. Preheat the oven to 350 degrees.
2. Prepare cake mix according to package directions.
3. Pour 2 cups of batter into a greased 13-by-9-inch baking pan. Bake 15 minutes.
4. In a heavy saucepan, over low heat, melt caramels and margarine or butter.
5. Remove from heat; add condensed milk. Mix well and spread over the cake.
6. Spread the remaining cake batter over the caramel layer.
7. Top with nuts.
8. Bake 30 minutes or until cake springs back when lightly touched. Cool.

Food Service and Decorative Touches

- Include Grammy Replicas, records of all sizes, and CDs in your decor.
- Set serving dishes on top of LP record album covers.
- Cover album covers with plastic wrap and use as trays for passing appetizers.
- Spray-paint 45s and LPs with gold paint.
- Cover tables with collages of sheet music and *Billboard Magazine* covers, then cover the collages with clear plastic. (See How-To's #19.)
- Arrange musical instruments—real, toy, or inflatable—on serving tables.
- Improvise a tray with a beverage holder from an LP cover. Cut a hole in the upper left- and right-hand corner about ¼ inch smaller than the circumference of the cup about 1 inch from the bottom. Your guests can then balance a plate and cup while standing, sitting, or even dancing to the award winners.
- Pull napkins through 45 records.
- For more serving and decor ideas, see page 103.

INDY 500

Arrange a little "Speedway Socializing" by gathering a gang to watch the televised event of the year for auto-race enthusiasts. Create a racy atmosphere and dish up a menu that goes the extra mile, and you'll be a certain winner.

Party Menu

Snacks
*Racetrack Reuben Ryes

Beverages
Soft Drinks/Mineral Waters
Zoom Zoom Vodka Vroom
Milk (straight out of the quart bottle—
the official winner's drink)
Beer/Wine

Buffet
Grandstand Gourmet: Hot Dogs, Burgers
*Speedy Spaghetti Pasta Salad
Corn on the Cob
Fast-Food Favorites

Dessert
*Kwik Kahlua Bars
Frozen Go-Cart Yogurt

Racetrack Reuben Ryes
Makes: 44 servings

10 slices Swiss cheese
4 tablespoons butter
1 loaf party rye bread (44 small squares)
1 cup Thousand Island dressing
½ pound smoked sausage, sliced into ¼-inch pieces
16 ounces sauerkraut, drained

1. Preheat the oven to 400 degrees.
2. Cut cheese slices into ½-by-2½-inch strips.
3. Melt butter in a small pan, then brush rye bread with butter on both sides and place all the slices on a baking sheet.
4. Bake for 5 minutes, turning bread slices after 2½ minutes of cooking time
5. Remove the pan from the oven.
6. Stack the ingredients on the bread slices to make Reubens: dressing, sausage, sauerkraut, cheese.
7. Pop into the oven for 5 more minutes to melt the cheese.

Zoom Zoom Vodka Vroom
Makes: 2 servings

1 ounce vodka
1 ounce Grand Marnier
1 ounce cherry mix*

Cracked ice
Orange juice
Cherries for garnish

1. Shake vodka, Grand Marnier, and cherry mix with ice. Strain.
2. Pour over ice into race-design glasses and fill the rest of the glass with orange juice.
3. Garnish with a cherry speared on a Grand Prix flag toothpick.

(*To make a mix, dilute cherry concentrate with ⅓ the required amount of water.)

Speedy Spaghetti Pasta Salad

Makes: 6 to 8 servings

Salad Ingredients

1 pound cooked spaghetti
2 medium tomatoes, chopped
1 bell pepper, chopped

1 cucumber, chopped
1 4-ounce can sliced mushrooms

Dressing

8 ounces Italian Dressing
Salad Supreme seasoning, to taste (found in spice section)

1. In a large bowl, combine cooked spaghetti with remaining salad ingredients.
2. In a small bowl, mix dressing ingredients. Pour the dressing over the salad and toss well. Refrigerate at least 2 hours before serving.

Kwik Kahlua Bars

Makes: 8 servings

½ cup butter
1 cup sugar
½ teaspoon salt
⅛ teaspoon vanilla
2 tablespoons coffee liqueur
3 eggs

¾ cup flour
½ cup cocoa
1 cup nuts, chopped
Coffee ice cream
Coffee liqueur
Whipped cream

1. Place butter in a glass bowl and microwave on high for 1 minute.
2. Stir in sugar, salt, vanilla, coffee liqueur, and eggs.
3. Add flour, cocoa, and nuts.
4. Spread the mixture evenly into a greased 8-inch square microwave-safe dish.
5. Microwave at 70 percent power for 4 minutes; rotate dish and microwave for 3½ to 4 minutes more. The top should be dry, but not hard, when done.
6. Cool and cut into squares.
7. Top each square with a scoop of coffee ice cream and drizzle with coffee liqueur.
8. Garnish with whipped cream.

Food Service and Decorative Touches

- Implement an all-American red, white, and blue color scheme.
- Create a backdrop for the buffet area with advertising art (available at auto supply stores).
- Include race track logos, flags, and event promotional posters.
- Cover all tables with black-and-white-checkered tablecloths, theme serving ware, and paper products.
- Make two or three stacks of automobile tires and lay wooden planks across them to create serving surfaces.
- Fill tall trophy cups with flowers and greens; accent with racing flags.
- Label a food area "Gasoline Alley" Pit Stop for concession-type foods.
- Serve food in cardboard containers in the shape of automobiles.
- Use black-and-white-checkered bandannas as napkins.
- Display toy race cars of all sizes.
- Use new, clean auto-parts packaging as snack containers or vases.

KENTUCKY DERBY

The greatest thoroughbred horses "Run for the Roses" on the first Saturday of May every year in Louisville, Kentucky. Derby fans will race over to your party to enjoy the big event with good friends and a bountiful "blue grass" buffet.

Party Menu

Snacks
*Horseradish Cheese Spread
Crackers
Pony-Pleasing Carrot Sticks
Apple Slices with Yogurt Dip

Beverages
Soft Drinks/Mineral Waters
*Kentucky Derby Mint Julep
Coffees/Teas

Buffet
Hearty Beef Stew
*Waldorf Salad (page 65)
Carrot amd Raisin Salad
Oat Bread

Dessert
*Kentucky Bourbon Bites
*Winner's Circle Cake
Strawberries and Fresh Cream

Horseradish Cheese Spread

Makes: about 2½ cups

1 pound processed cheese, cut into cubes
1 cup mayonnaise
½ cup horseradish

1. Melt cheese in the top of a double boiler or a microwave
2. Stir in mayonnaise and horseradish.
3. Pour into a small crock or ceramic bowl; chill.
4. Serve with crackers and carrot sticks.

Kentucky Derby Mint Julep

Makes: 10 servings

4 to 5 mint sprigs
1½ cups sugar
2 cups cold water
¾ cup lemon juice, fresh, if possible
Ice cubes
1½ quarts ginger ale
Mint leaves and thin lemon slices for garnish

1. Rinse mint and discard stems.
2. Place sugar, water, and lemon juice in a medium bowl; stir in mint leaves
3. Allow to stand for 30 minutes.
4. Fill a strainer with ice cubes and strain the liquid over the ice to chill.
5. Half-fill tall, chilled, and sugar-rimmed glasses with ice, then fill ⅔ with the lemon mixture. Add ginger ale.
6. Garnish with mint leaves and lemon slices.

Kentucky Bourbon Bites

Makes: 3 dozen

4 tablespoons butter	*⅓ cup bourbon*
1 pound powdered sugar	*1 cup pecans, chopped*

1. Cream butter by hand, then alternately blend in powdered sugar and bourbon by hand (not mixer).
2. Fold in pecans.
3. Drop by ⅔ teaspoonfuls onto wax-paper-lined cookie sheets.
4. Cover with wax paper and refrigerate until set.

Winner's Circle Cake

Makes: 8 to 10 servings

1 package (18½ ounces) chocolate, double chocolate, or fudge cake mix	*½ cup salad oil*
	½ cup warm water
1 box (3½ ounces) instant chocolate pudding mix	*½ cup walnuts, finely chopped*
	6 ounces semisweet chocolate morsels
½ cup sour cream	*White chocolate, melted*
4 eggs	*Rose petals and greens for garnish*

1. Preheat the oven to 350 degrees.
2. Place cake mix, pudding mix, sour cream, eggs, salad oil, and warm water in a large electric mixer bowl. Mix at low speed until ingredients are well blended. Beat at medium speed 3 minutes more.
3. Gently mix in walnuts and chocolate morsels.
4. Turn the batter into a lightly greased and floured 10-inch bundt or tube pan.
5. Bake for 45 to 55 minutes, or until an inserted toothpick comes out clean.
6. Let cake stand 5 minutes, then turn out of the pan onto a cooling rack.
7. Drizzle melted white chocolate on top of the cake.
8. Place the cake on a cake plate; decorate the base with rose petals and greens.

Tip: This cake is equally good when eaten warm or cool.

Food Service and Decorative Touches

- Use either authentic or plastic horseshoes, spray-painted gold as decorative accents wherever possible. (See Resources #2.)
- Tie a rolled-up napkin around a horseshoe and place on each dinner plate, or put them all in a large wicker basket on the buffet table.
- Arrange real, paper, plastic, or silk roses in vases on buffet and dining tables.
- Display framed photos, drawings, or paintings of horses.
- Set up the bar to look like a betting cage.
- Fill a new horse's feed bag with snacks or silverware/napkin bundles.

NBA FINALS/ NCAA FINAL FOUR

Gather the troops for a day of hoops. Whether they are huge baseball fans or not, your guests will delight in the camaraderie and excitement of watching these crucial final games. Along with the games, they'll enjoy far more than just "four" crowd-pleasing menu items.

Party Menu

Snacks
*Slim Dunk Dip
*Hot Shots Beefy Baskets
Veggie Baskets for Dipping
Cheese Ball with Crackers

Beverages
Soft Drinks/Mineral Waters
Winning Jump Shots
Coffees/Teas

Buffet
Baskets of Burgers and Hot Dogs
(with all the fixings)
*Unfried Free-Throw French Fries
*Hot Shot Slaw (page 231)

Dessert
*It's Magic Pie
Chocolate Baskets Filled with Berries
Slam Dunkin' Donuts

Slim Dunk Dip
Makes: about 3 cups

2 cups low-fat sour cream (see tip below)
¼ cup nonfat or low-fat mayonnaise
10 ounces frozen spinach, thawed, squeezed dry, and chopped
1 envelope (1.8 ounces) Knorr brand leek soup mix
¼ cup red bell pepper, minced

1. Combine all ingredients in a medium bowl; stir well.
2. Cover and refrigerate for 3 hours before serving.

Tip: Select thick sour cream (with gelatin in the ingredients); if not, the dip may be runny.

Hot Shots Beefy Baskets
Makes: 20 servings

1 pound lean ground beef or pork
½ cup mushrooms, chopped
2 tablespoons ketchup
2 tablespoons green pepper, minced

1 teaspoon onion, minced
12 biscuits, from the store or your own recipe
¾ cup sharp cheddar cheese, shredded

1. In a skillet, brown meat, then drain off the excess fat.
2. Add mushrooms, ketchup, green pepper, and onion; set aside.
3. Preheat the oven to 400 degrees.
4. Separate biscuit dough into 20 pieces; press one in each of 20 ungreased muffin cups.
5. Spoon the meat mixture into the cups and sprinkle with shredded cheddar cheese.
6. Bake for 12 minutes. Serve warm.

Unfried Free-Throw French Fries

Makes: 4 servings

5 large baking potatoes (about 2¾ pounds)
Vegetable spray

2 large egg whites
1 tablespoon Cajun spice

1. Preheat the oven to 400 degrees.
2. Slice potatoes lengthwise into ovals, then slice each oval lengthwise into matchsticks.
3. Generously coat a baking sheet with vegetable spray.
4. Combine egg whites and Cajun spice in a bowl. Add the potatoes; mix to coat.
5. Pour the coated potatoes onto the prepared baking sheet and spread them out into a single layer, leaving a little space between each piece.
6. Place the baking sheet on the bottom shelf of the oven and bake for 40 to 45 minutes, until the fries are crispy. Turn them every 6 to 8 minutes with a spatula so they brown evenly. Serve immediately.

It's Magic Pie

Makes: 8 servings

42 Oreo cookies
2 tablespoons margarine, melted
1 quart chocolate ice cream

1 pint vanilla ice cream, softened
½ cup whipped topping
Chocolate fudge sauce

1. Finely crush 22 cookies.
2. Mix 1¼ cups of the cookie crumbs with margarine; set aside the remaining crumbs.
3. Press the crumb/margarine mixture onto the bottom of a 9-inch pie plate.
4. Stand 14 cookies around edge of the pie plate, pressing lightly into the crust.
5. Scoop chocolate ice cream into balls and arrange in the prepared crust.
6. Coarsely chop remaining 6 cookies; sprinkle over the ice cream.
7. Spread softened vanilla ice cream over the cookie layer; freeze for 15 minutes.
8. Top with a layer of reserved cookie crumbs, pressing gently into the ice cream.
9. Freeze several hours or overnight.
10. Before serving, garnish with whipped topping and chocolate fudge sauce.

Food Service and Decorative Touches

- Arrange food and decorative items in any and all types of baskets.
- Spread posters, photos, and magazine pages on the table; cover with clear plastic.
- Place a new basketball on a Styrofoam base and attach flower blossoms, decorative ribbons, or streamers to the ball with double-sided tape.
- Use small Nerf-ball hoops as buffet table decor. Place them back to back and arrange fresh or artificial flowers and decorative materials inside the hoops.
- Make flowers from sports-motif pages. (See How-To's #13.)
- Collect cast-off basketball sneakers from thrift shops or garage sales. Wash and dry thoroughly, then dip in plaster of Paris. Once dried solid, paint them and use as containers for floral arrangements, or line them with plastic or foil to serve snacks.
- Attach basketball cards or toys to ponytail holders and use as napkin holders.
- Serve snacks in colorful, lacquered sports equipment packaging.
- Display balloons, pom-poms, trophies, plaques, or sports memorabilia.

SOAP OPERA AWARDS

Each year the soap opera world crowns its royalty at a gala televised awards ceremony that provides a great excuse to have a cocktail party. Along with getting deeply involved in the drama and intrigue of the awards show, your guests will also enjoy a fanfare of food and drink.

Party Menu

Snacks
*The Hot and the Spicy (Buffalo Wings)
Celery Sticks with Cream Cheese
Couch Potato Chips and Dip

Beverages
Soft Drinks/Mineral Waters
*Lazy Afternoon Soaps and Sips
Sudsy Beer/Bubbly Wine
Coffees/Teas

Buffet
Couch Potato Bar with All the Toppings:
Mashed, French-Fried, and Baked
Potatoes and Stuffed Skins
Pick A Salad

Dessert
*All My Chocolate Fudge Sundaes
To Die For (Then Come Back) Delicacies
"Evil Twin"-kies

The Hot and the Spicy (Buffalo Wings)
Makes: 10 to 12 servings

2½ pounds chicken wings
¼ cup butter
3 teaspoons hot sauce
1 teaspoon vinegar
Vegetable oil

1. Preheat the oven or broiler to broil.
2. Trim off wing tips and separate each wing into 2 sections.
3. Melt butter in a large saucepan.
4. Add hot sauce and vinegar and remove from heat.
5. Brush the wings with oil and place on the broiling rack.
6. Broil 15 to 20 minutes.
7. Toss the wings and sauce together. Serve hot.

Lazy Afternoon Soaps and Sips
Makes: 1 serving

1 ounce vodka
⅓ cup lemonade mix*
Ice

1 ounce peach schnapps
⅔ cup Sprite
Cherries and peach slices for garnish

1. Combine all ingredients except the garnish; shake well.
2. Pour over ice.
3. Garnish with a cherry and a fresh peach slice.

(*To make a mix, dilute lemonade concentrate with ⅓ the required amount of water.)

All My Chocolate Fudge Sundaes

Makes: 9 servings

1 cup flour	*1 teaspoon vanilla*
¾ cup sugar	*1 cup nuts, chopped*
2 tablespoons plus ¼ cup cocoa	*1 cup brown sugar*
2 teaspoons baking powder	*1¾ cups water (very hot)*
¼ teaspoon salt	*Ice cream (chocolate, naturally)*
½ cup milk	*Fudge sauce, heated*
2 tablespoons salad oil	

1. Preheat the oven to 350 degrees.
2. Stir together flour, sugar, 2 tablespoons cocoa, baking powder, and salt.
3. Mix in milk, oil, and vanilla with a fork until smooth.
4. Stir in nuts.
5. Spread the batter evenly in an ungreased 9-by-9-by-2-inch square pan
6. Sprinkle with brown sugar and ¼ cup cocoa.
7. Pour hot water over the batter.
8. Bake for 40 minutes. Let stand for 15 minutes.
9. Cut into 9 squares. Invert each square onto a dessert plate.
10. Top with ice cream and fudge sauce.

Food Service and Decorative Touches

- Write guests' names on individual-sized packs of facial tissue to use as seating assignments.
- Use soap detergent boxes as vases for flowers and greens. *Caution:* Do not use soap boxes or wrappers near or on food. The fragrance will not mix with aromas of foods.
- Create lavish soap opera-ish settings with crystal decanters, flower arrangements, candles, and so on.
- Glue bubble wrap around jars, boxes, and other containers used to hold flowers and snacks.
- Use Soap Opera magazine covers and pages to create napkin rings, favor wrappings, and decorative accents. (See How-To's #27.)
- Collect books that feature soap opera subjects and arrange them as part of the table decor.
- Rewrap small candy bars with wrappers designed to look like soap wrap
- Serve snacks from all sizes of tissue boxes.
- Serve beer, soda, and wine in champagne glasses.
- Have fun with food labels: The Sweet and the Gooey, The Rich and the Fattening, The Frosty and the Frigid, Search for Tamales, and so on.

SUPER BOWL

It's the biggest television viewing event of the year, drawing millions of football fans to screens of every size. Your guests will cheer your super menu of hearty sports-fan favorites—plus additions that are guaranteed to make a few extra points!

Party Menu

Snacks
*Touchdown Toasts
Pick A Meatball
Crispy Fried Pigskins
Victory Veggies
Pick A Dip

Beverages
Soft Drinks/Mineral Waters
*Pumpkin Punch Bowl
Beer/Beer/Beer
Coffees/Teas

Buffet
Chili Bowl Bar with All the Toppings
Pick A Slaw
Corn Bread and Honey Butter
Orange Bowl Gelatin Salad

Dessert
*Berry-Barb Pie in a Bowl
*50-Yard-Line Gelatin Dessert
Field Goal Fudge Bars
Locker Room Liqueurs

Touchdown Toasts
Makes: 40 servings

2 cups mushrooms, chopped
½ cup onion, chopped
Butter or margarine or oil
Rye or pumpernickel cocktail rounds
½ cup Swiss cheese, grated
½ cup cheddar cheese, grated

1. Sauté mushrooms and onions in butter until the onions are clear.
2. Drain and set aside until cool.
3. Pile a small mound of mushroom/onion mixture on each round of bread.
4. Top with grated cheeses.
5. Broil until the cheese melts, and serve immediately.

Pumpkin Punch Bowl
Makes: 36 punch-cup servings

10 cups water
6 whole cloves
2 cinnamon sticks
1 6-ounce can frozen orange juice concentrate
1 6-ounce can frozen lemonade concentrate
1 6-ounce can frozen pineapple juice concentrate

1. Combine all ingredients in a 4-quart saucepan.
2. Simmer over low heat 10 to 15 minutes.
3. Remove cloves and cinnamon.
4. Serve hot from a hollowed out pumpkin.

Tip: Provide alcohol on the side for guests to spike their punch. Brandy, tequila, and rum work well.

Berry-Barb Pie in a Bowl

Makes: 6 to 8 servings

6 cups rhubarb	Pinch of salt
1 cup raspberries	Pastry for 2 crusts
1 cup sugar	1 tablespoon sweet butter or low-fat margarine
3 tablespoons flour	Whipped topping
¼ teaspoon nutmeg	Chopped walnuts for garnish

1. Preheat the oven to 375 degrees.
2. Trim rhubarb stems and remove any tough outer strings; cut into ¼-inch pieces.
3. Mix the rhubarb pieces with raspberries, sugar, flour, nutmeg, and salt.
4. Pour everything into a pie shell and dot with butter.
5. With a knife, cut a pattern (the letters SB would be super) in the top crust for steam vents.
6. Cover the rhubarb mixture with the top crust; trim and crimp edges.
7. Sprinkle the top crust with a tablespoon of sugar, if desired.
8. Bake for 40 minutes, or until edges are bubbling.
9. Serve in small bowls with a dollop of whipped topping and a sprinkle of walnuts.

50-Yard-Line Gelatin Dessert

Makes: 12 servings

3 packages (4-serving size) brand lime-flavored Jell-O
Nondairy frozen topping, thawed

1. Prepare Jell-O according to package directions. Pour into a 13-by-9-inch glass dish.
2. When firm, use whipped topping to draw yard lines on the gelatin. Arrange toy football figures and other appropriate decorations to complete your football field.

Food Service and Decorative Touches

- Set up a concession stand to dispense gourmet game goodies.
- Cover the buffet table with Astroturf, and serve foods in football helmets or in bowls nestled in shoulder pads.
- For large crowds, have servers pass snacks from vendors' (hang-around-the-neck) trays.
- Set up a miniature goalpost at the end of the buffet table and use it to hang napkins.
- Decorate tables with sports magazines, pom-poms, streamers, or football memorabilia.
- Fashion place cards and/or seating assignments to resemble game tickets.
- Create napkins to duplicate the "penalty" flags used by referees.
- Cover chair backs with sports jerseys, using referee's striped shirts for guest(s) of honor or hosts.
- Attach football trading cards to ponytail holders for use as napkin holders.
- Use quarterback's football holder for seating charts or menus.
- Arrange bunches of fall flowers in a plastic face guard and trim with team-color ribbons, streamers, balloons, and pom-poms.

WORLD SERIES

A party to watch the final game must be impromptu, since there is no way to predict when it will be. But you can plan a World Series get-together either for a certain game night or as a theme event honoring a baseball fanatic. Either way, the fare includes grandstand goodies and fans' favorites.

Party Menu

Snacks
*Cracker Jack Caramel Corn
*Grand Slam Chili Cheese Dip
Popcorn, Pretzels, Potato Chips

Buffet
*Batter-Up Beef Pie
Pick A Slaw/Salad
Ballpark Franks

Beverages
Soda Pop/Mineral Water
*Pennant Power Punch
Beer/Wine

Dessert
*Mudsville Pie
Frozen "Yogi" Sundaes
Baby Ruth Candy Bars

Cracker Jack Caramel Corn
Makes: 32 ¼-cup servings

6 cups popped popcorn
2 cups Spanish peanuts
2 sticks margarine
2 cups brown sugar
½ cup dark corn syrup
½ teaspoon salt
½ teaspoon baking soda

1. Preheat the oven to 250 degrees.
2. Fill a large pan ¾ full of popcorn. Add peanuts.
3. In a saucepan, melt together margarine, sugar, corn syrup, and salt; boil 5 minutes.
4. Remove from heat and add baking soda. Pour over popcorn and stir.
5. Bake for 1 hour, stirring occasionally. Cool and break up into small chunks.

Grand Slam Chili Cheese Dip
Makes: 4 cups

1 pound lean ground beef
1 packet taco seasoning mix
2 teaspoons Worcestershire sauce
16 ounces cream cheese, cut into small pieces
1 can (8 to 10 ounces) green chilies and tomatoes

1. In a skillet, thoroughly brown beef and drain off grease.
2. Add all other ingredients, cover, and cook for about 1 hour, stirring frequently until the cheese melts, and occasionally after that. Serve with tortilla chips.

Pennant Power Punch
Makes: 16 punch-cup servings

1 cup vodka
1 cup peach schnapps
⅔ cup lemonade mix*
⅓ cup orange juice
Ice cubes or ice ring
2 cups champagne

1. In a punch bowl, combine everything except champagne.
2. Before serving, add champagne for a home run!

(*To make a mix, dilute lemonade concentrate with ⅛ the required amount of water.)

Batter-Up Beef Pie
Makes: 6 servings

2 cups cooked beef, cut into ½-inch pieces
½ cup onion, chopped and sautéed in butter
1 cup cooked carrots, cut into chunks
1 cup potatoes, peeled, cooked, and
   cut into chunks
1 cup beef gravy
¼ cup butter

1½ cups flour
1 cup cheddar cheese, grated
1 tablespoon sugar
1 tablespoon dried minced onion
2 teaspoons baking powder
1 teaspoon salt
1½ cups milk

1. Preheat the oven to 350 degrees.
2. Combine beef, onion, carrots, potatoes, and gravy. Set aside.
3. Put butter into a 8-inch square baking dish, and place in the oven to melt.
4. Combine the remaining ingredients in a mixing bowl and stir until thoroughly blended; pour into the baking dish with the melted butter.
5. Without stirring, pour beef mixture over the batter. Bake for 30 to 35 minutes

Mudsville Pie
Makes: 8 to 10 servings

Crust
1½ cups crushed chocolate cookies
   (use a food processor or rolling pin)

2 tablespoons confectioners' sugar
6 tablespoons unsalted butter, melted

Filling
6 cups or 3 pints chocolate ice cream
1 cup ready-made fudge topping
4 cups whipped cream

¾ cup crushed chocolate cookies or
   chocolate graham crackers

1. Preheat the oven to 350 degrees.
2. Mix cookie crumbs, sugar, and butter in a bowl until thoroughly combined.
3. Spread the mixture evenly in a pie pan, pressing it against the bottom and sides.
4. Bake for 10 minutes and let cool.
5. Spoon half of the chocolate ice cream into the shell and freeze for 30 minutes
6. Spread fudge over the ice cream and freeze for another 15 minutes.
7. Top with remaining filling ingredients; freeze for at least 3 hours.

Food Service and Decorative Touches
- Display finalist-team promotional items, balloons, streamers, and baseball gear.
- Serve snacks and create flower arrangements in inverted baseball hats.
- Inflate balloons, anchor them in the middle of the table, and attach a baseball hat on top of each one. Use a marker to draw faces on the balloons.
- Attach customized baseball cards to ponytail holders for napkin rings.
- Spread sports-related printed material on the buffet table; cover with clear plastic.
- Serve snacks in baseball-glove-shaped bowls. Nestle dip bowls in baseball mitts.
- Have servers hawk food from trays hanging around their necks.

Part Three
PICK A
FAVORITE
Basic Tried-and-True Recipes to
Be Used for Any and All Occasions

Many of the menus in this book direct you to "pick" an item from a food or drink category such as dips, sloppy joes, salads, or specialty beverages. This section is divided into groups of frequently served party fare. You can mix and match these recipes freely to build your custom party menu.

Although the book already offers dozens of drink recipes, the additional ideas in the Pick A Beverage section are meant to appeal to your adventurous "spirits." This section introduces the wildly popular gelatin shooters—party treats made by adding liquor to your favorite Jell-O flavors. This style of drinking is not only delicious but also fun in its novelty. In addition, since most festive gatherings include the traditional bowl of punch—with or without alcohol—this section includes a variety of punches: hot, cold, creamy, or sparkling. All the punches can be served without alcohol; simply provide alcohol on the side for guests to help themselves.

To get to the "meat" of your party menu, you can Pick A Sloppy Joe or Meatball to supplement both the snack and the buffet areas of your menu. *Pick-A-Party Cookbook* proudly presents the international versions of these traditional favorites.

Along with the basic recipes listed in the Pick A Slaw or Salad sections, you will find some exciting and exotic blends of ingredients to please the palates and satisfy the stomachs of your party guests. These "try 'em you might like 'em" offerings are guaranteed to spice up your party menus.

The last section offers the recipes that could start or finish the party—the dips. You will find some wonderful dips to serve with chips, vegetables, or fruit. Dip in and enjoy!

PICK A BEVERAGE

Gelatin Shooters

Gelatin shooters substitute alcohol for a water portion of a flavored-gelatin recipe. The shooters, served in small plastic or paper cups or glass shot glasses, are swizzled with a toothpick or another stirrer to liquefy them a bit before drinking.

Suggested proportions for gelatin shooters

Large box of Jell-O: 2 cups hot water, 1½ cups cold water, ½ cup alcohol. (Vary alcohol amounts: ½ cup for 40-proof alcohol, ¼ cup for 80-proof.)

Suggested preparation for gelatin shooters

1. Place 3-ounce paper cups, plastic pill cups, or small glasses with stems in a cake pan.
2. Prepare gelatin according to recipe, substituting alcohol as recommended above.
3. Let the gelatin/alcohol liquid cool to room temperature, then pour about 2 ounces into each cup/glass, filling them about ⅔ full (makes about 6 to 8 servings).
4. Refrigerate the pan of shooters until they set.

Tip: Sugar-free gelatins work well because they dissolve easier.

Popular Combinations

Some gelatin flavors go better with some liquors. The fun is in experimenting. The following combinations and recipes are excellent:

1. Apple gelatin: champagne, white wine, apple brandy, aquavit
2. Blueberry gelatin: raspberry schnapps, cherry brandy
3. Cherry gelatin: cherry brandy, brandy
4. Lemon gelatin: vodka, Kentucky whiskey
5. Lime gelatin: tequila
6. Orange gelatin: brandy, Grand Marnier, peach schnapps, vodka
7. Peach gelatin: bourbon
8. Raspberry gelatin: raspberry schnapps
9. Strawberry gelatin: light rum, strawberry liqueur
10. Tropical fruit: Mohala mango liqueur, dark rum
11. Watermelon gelatin: Midori melon liqueur
12. Sparkling white wine gelatin: champagne, white wine, vodka, white rum, flavored schnapps

Go Ga Ga with Gelatin

Fuzzy Navel: orange Jell-O + 1⅓ cups peach schnapps
Stirrer: maraschino cherry on a toothpick

Mai Tai: mixed fruit Jell-O or tropical punch Jell-O + ½ cup dark rum
Stirrer: pineapple chunk on a toothpick

Beri-Beri: blueberry Jell-O + 1 cup strawberry schnapps
Stirrer: brandied cherry on a toothpick

Melancholy Baby: watermelon Jell-O + 1 cup melon liqueur
Stirrer: small cantaloupe piece on a toothpick

Bouncy Beer Belts: strawberry Jell-O + 2 cups malt liquor
Stirrer: pretzel stick

Apricot Sours: lemon Jell-O + ½ cup apricot brandy
Stirrer: orange piece on toothpick

Strawberry Daiquiri: strawberry Jell-O + ⅛ cup light rum + ⅙ cup raspberry liqueur
Stirrer: blueberry on a toothpick

Tequila Sunrise: orange Jell-O + 2 cups tequila + touch of grenadine
Stirrer: small piece of lime, rolled in salt, on toothpick

Whisky Sour: lemon Jell-O + ½ cup whiskey
Stirrer: orange piece on a toothpick

Island Pineapple Rum: pineapple-orange Jell-O + ½ cup dark rum
Stirrer: pineapple chunk on a toothpick

The Czar: lemon Jell-O + 1 cup consommé (bring to a boil, cool, and chill) + 1 cup vodka; top with a dollop of sour cream and a spot of caviar.
Stirrer: cocktail onion on a toothpick

The Factory Whistle: blueberry Jell-O + ½ cup vodka + ½ cup blueberry schnapps
Stirrer: swizzle with a whistle on top

M*A*S*H Mess: lime Jell-O + ½ cup dark rum + ½ cup blackberry brandy
Stirrer: martini olive on a Popsicle (tongue depressor-type) stick

Shamrock Shots: lime Jell-O + ½ cup crème de menthe + ½ cup ginger ale
Stirrer: Irish flags on toothpicks

Bahama Mamas for a Bunch
Makes: 72 2-ounce servings

1 6-ounce can frozen orange juice, undiluted
10 ounces frozen strawberries in sugar
3 packages (2-cups size) orange Jell-O
3 packages (2-cups size) strawberry Jell-O
3 packages (2-cups size) pineapple sugar-free Jell-O
2 cups boiling water
4 cups dark rum
2 cups coconut rum

1. Blend orange juice with strawberries.
2. Dissolve gelatins in boiling water.
3. Combine all ingredients and pour into shooter containers.
4. Let set and serve with kabobs of pineapple, cherry, and strawberry chunks

Grape Greatness for a Group
Makes: 72 2-ounce servings

1 6-ounce can frozen grape juice, undiluted
1 6-ounce can frozen cranberry/raspberry juice, undiluted
3 packages (2-cups size) grape Jell-O
3 packages (2-cups size) cranberry/raspberry Jell-O
3 packages (2-cups size) strawberry Jell-O
2 cups boiling water
3 cups peach schnapps
3 cups vodka

1. Blend frozen juices, then mix with other ingredients.
2. Dissolve gelatins in boiling water.
3. Combine all ingredients and pour into shooter containers.
4. Let set and serve with kabobs of seedless grapes and raspberries.

Serving Ideas for Gelatin Shooters
- Attach a gumdrop onto a toothpick, and plunge into the shooter-filled cup.
- For smaller groups, make shooters in 2-ounce shot glasses or 3-ounce stemmed glasses (as opposed to paper or plastic cups).
- For a brunch, make shooters in small plastic-egg halves and set them out in egg cartons.

The Bawdy Body Shot for Lovers
(Submitted by Deena Sachs, Minneapolis, Minnesota.)

One of the latest crazes for party drinking is to drink shots of liquor, predominantly tequila, with a lick of salt to start and a squeeze of fresh lime as a chaser. Over time, couples have invented a new way to enjoy these shots by making them a "contact sport" and calling them Body Shots. The concept, a sure-shot party hit, works as follows:

Person 1 moistens a spot on his or her neck and coats it with salt. Person 1 also holds a lime wedge in his or her mouth. Shot Drinker licks the salt from Person 1's neck, downs the shot of tequila, and kisses Person 1, removing the lime wedge. Tequila shot completed.

This great variation was invented by a nontequila drinker:

Person 1 smears a small bit of butterscotch ice cream topping on his or her neck and places a small chocolate cookie, topped with whipping cream, into his or her mouth. Shot Drinker licks the topping from Person 1's neck, downs a shot of root beer schnapps, and kisses Person 1, removing the chocolate cookie with whipped cream. Sugar shot completed.

Punches

Wedding Punch

Makes: about 6 quarts

2 12-ounce cans frozen pink (or yellow) lemonade concentrate
1 12-ounce can frozen limeade concentrate
1 46-ounce can pineapple juice
3 lemonade cans cold water
2 liters 7-Up (or your favorite carbonated beverage)

Pour all ingredients over a decorative ice ring.

Holiday Punch

Makes: 4 quarts

1 package (2 quarts) lime Kool-Aid
1 quart pineapple juice
1 quart lime sherbet
2 quarts ginger ale

1. Mix Kool-Aid in a punch bowl. Add pineapple juice.
2. Just before serving, add sherbet by spoonfuls. Add ginger ale

Tip: Match the color of Kool-Aid to the holiday.

Tea Party Punch

Makes: 16 small cups

2 teaspoons instant tea
2 cups boiling water
1 cup sugar
1 cup orange juice
½ cup fresh or frozen lemon juice
1 teaspoon orange flavoring
1 pint ginger ale
1 pint orange sherbet

1. Combine tea and boiling water; pour over sugar and stir until sugar dissolves.
2. Add juices and flavoring; chill.
3. Before serving, add ginger ale and scoops of sherbet.

Sunny Fruit Punch

Makes: 2 gallons

1 12-ounce can frozen orange juice concentrate
1 12-ounce can frozen lemonade concentrate
48 ounces apricot nectar
48 ounces pineapple juice
2 liters ginger ale

1. In a large punch bowl, dilute orange juice and lemonade according to directions.
2. Add remaining ingredients and mix well.

Sparkling Apricot Punch

Makes: enough for a crowd

2 750-ml bottles sparkling apple cider, chilled
46 ounces apricot nectar, chilled

In a large punch bowl, combine apple cider and apricot nectar.

Golden Glow Punch

Makes: 36 servings

1 gallon Tang orange drink
2 liters ginger ale

46 ounces pineapple juice
Orange slices for garnish

1. In a punch bowl, combine all ingredients except garnish.
2. Float orange slices on top.
3. Serve in small gold cups.

Hot Apple Cider Punch

Makes: 20 to 24 4-ounce servings

6 whole allspice nuggets
6 whole cloves
1 6-ounce can frozen lemonade concentrate
1 6-ounce can frozen orange juice concentrate
4 quarts apple cider

1 cup brown sugar
1 teaspoon nutmeg
3 cinnamon sticks
Rum (optional)

1. Wrap whole allspice and cloves in a piece of cheesecloth.
2. Combine all ingredients in a saucepan and heat, stirring occasionally.

Tip: The punch may be kept warm in a Crock-Pot.

Chilled Apple Punch

Makes: 40 4-ounce servings

3 apples, unpeeled, cut into 1-inch cubes
1 quart strawberries, hulled and quartered
4 mint sprigs

85 ounces apple juice, chilled
15 ounces apple cider, chilled
57 ounces lemonade, chilled

1. Combine fruit and mint with apple juice in a large punch bowl.
2. Mix well, cover, and refrigerate until serving.
3. Just before serving, add chilled apple cider and lemonade.

Banana Punch

Makes: 22 to 24 4-ounce servings

7 cups water
½ cup sugar
5 bananas, mashed
1 6-ounce can frozen orange juice
   concentrate

1 6-ounce can frozen lemonade
   concentrate
46 ounces pineapple juice
1 quart ginger ale
Vodka (optional)

1. Boil water and sugar for 5 minutes.
2. Cool and add the remaining ingredients except ginger ale and vodka. Freeze until solid.
3. Remove from freezer 2 to 3 hours before serving, so the punch has a slushy consistency.
4. Transfer the slushy mixture to a large punch bowl and add ginger ale. Float assorted fruit on top.
5. If desired, add vodka when you add the ginger ale.

Hot Cranberry Tea Punch

Makes: 12 4-ounce servings

8 tea bags (of choice)
4 cups boiling water
2 cups unsweetened cranberry juice
2 cups apple cider
½ cup brown sugar

1 cinnamon stick
½ teaspoon ginger
4 whole cloves
Orange slices for garnish

1. Pour 4 cups of boiling water over tea bags and let them brew for about 10 minutes.
2. Add cranberry juice, apple cider, brown sugar, and spices.
3. Stir until the sugar dissolves. Remove the cinnamon stick and the cloves.
4. Garnish with orange slices.
5. Ladle the punch into small tea or coffee cups.

Hot Buttered Cranberry Punch

Makes: 12 4-ounce servings

16 ounces jellied cranberry sauce
⅓ cup brown sugar
¼ teaspoon cinnamon
¼ teaspoon ground allspice
⅛ teaspoon ground cloves

⅛ teaspoon nutmeg
⅛ teaspoon salt
2 cups water
2 cups pineapple juice
Butter

1. In a medium saucepan, mash cranberry sauce with a fork; mix with sugar, spices, and salt.
2. Add water and pineapple juice; cover and simmer for 2 hours.
3. Ladle the punch into mugs, and float a small pat of butter in each serving.

Razz Ma Tazz Punch

Makes: 24 4-ounce servings

2 6-ounce cans frozen lemonade concentrate
4 liters raspberry soda
1 quart raspberry sherbet

1. Scoop frozen lemonade into a punch bowl. Add soda and stir.
2. Top with sherbet.

Strawberry Punch

Makes: 16 4-ounce servings

1 6-ounce can frozen lemonade concentrate
10 ounces frozen strawberries, thawed
1 quart ginger ale
1 pint lemon-lime sherbet

1. Prepare lemonade according package instructions; chill.
2. Combine lemonade, strawberries, and ginger ale in a punch bowl.
3. Add sherbet and mix until sherbet dissolves.
4. Keep the punch cold with a floating ice ring.

Percolator Punch

Makes: 12 4-ounce servings

1 quart apple cider
1 pint cranberry juice
1 cup orange juice
¾ cup lemon juice

1 cup sugar
3 cinnamon sticks
1 tablespoon whole allspice
1 tablespoon whole cloves

1. Pour all liquid ingredients into a large percolator.
2. In the grounds basket, add sugar and spices.
3. Serve hot in mugs or cups. For a stirrer, insert a small apple cube, orange slice, and raisin onto a long toothpick.

Easy-Breezy Apple Raspberry Punch

Makes: 24 ½-cup servings

2 12-ounce cans frozen apple raspberry juice concentrate, thawed
2 liters lemon-lime carbonated beverage, chilled

Pour both ingredients into a large punch bowl. Add an ice ring, if desired.

Hawaiian Sunset Punch

Makes: 1 serving

1 ounce vodka
½ cup cranberry juice
½ cup pineapple juice

1 ounce cherry mix*
Ice
Pineapple slices and maraschino cherries for garnish

1. Combine all ingredients except garnish; shake well. Pour into a decorative glass.
2. Garnish with pineapple slices and cherries.

(*To make a mix, dilute juice concentrate with ⅓ the required amount of water.)

Martini Madness

(The following martini recipes are served at The Hard Rock Hotel in Las Vegas.)

Hamlet's Martini

1 ounce iced vodka + 1 ounce iced gin + a splash of dry vermouth
Garnish with a cocktail onion on a sword.

The Melontini

2 ounces iced vodka + ½ ounce Midori
Garnish with a melon ball.

The Fuzzitini

2 ounces iced vodka + ½ ounce peach schnapps + a splash of Triple Sec
Garnish with a lime twist.

The Chocotini

2 ounces iced vodka + ½ oz chilled espresso + a splash of dark crème de cacao
Garnish with 3 espresso beans and rim with chocolate shavings.

Note: Always serve martinis in chilled glasses.

Stocking the Bar

Bar Supply Requirements for a 2- to 3-Hour Party

For a full bar, for every 10 guests:
1 case beer (mix light, regular, domestic, and imported)
5 bottles of wine (4 white, 1 red)
5 bottles of champagne
1 liter of premium vodka
1 half-liter of scotch
1 half-liter of rum
(For 20 or more guests, add another choice, e.g., tequila, gin.)

4 liters soda (cola and 7-Up or ginger ale—diet and regular)
4 quarts of juice (2 orange, 1 cranberry, and 1 grapefruit)
1 liter each sparkling water, seltzer, tonic
3 lemons, 3 limes, olives
35 pounds of ice
20 to 30 drink glasses and cocktail napkins

Bulk Beverage Information

Wine: 1 case yields 76 4-ounce servings
Whisky: 1 750-ml bottle yields 17 1½-ounce drinks
Punch: 1½ gallons yields 50 4-ounce servings
Soft Drinks: 1 liter bottle or 6 pack yields 10 6-ounce servings
Mineral Water: 5 16-ounce bottles yields 10 8-ounce servings
Coffee: 2 cups percolator grind coffee yields 30 6-ounce servings
Beer: 1 20-gallon keg yields 320 8-ounce servings or 160 16-ounce servings

Beverage Serving Ideas

- Write guests' names on cups or glasses so they can reuse them.
- At smaller parties, serve your guests a first drink, then let them serve themselves.
- Set out nonalcoholic punch, coffee, juices, and sodas, as well as bottles of alcohol. Guests may then add alcohol to their beverages, as they desire. This precludes the chance that someone will drink an alcoholic beverage by mistake.
- Remove alcohol from serving areas one hour before the party is scheduled to end.
- Present designated drivers with fun token gifts.
- Be adamant about not allowing guests to drive home drunk. This is a host's responsibility. If necessary, send a guest home in a taxicab.
- Freeze an inch of water in the bottom of an ice bucket to keep ice frozen longer.

Tip: This is the fastest way to chill a bottle of wine or champagne: Place the bottle in a bucket or any tall container, lay some ice around the bottom, and sprinkle the ice with a few tablespoons of salt. Continue to add salt and ice until the ice reaches the neck of the bottle. Fill the container with tepid water and let it sit for ten minutes. Bottle is chilled.

PICK A SLOPPY JOE

Basic Sloppy Joe Recipe
Makes: 12 servings

2 pounds lean ground beef, pork, or turkey (or a mixture)
½ cup onions, finely chopped

1. Brown meat in a large skillet. Add chopped onions and cook a few minutes longer.
2. Remove grease with a turkey baster.

SLOPPY JOES WITH AN INTERNATIONAL FLAVOR
Sloppy Josés

2 packets taco seasoning mix
1 4-ounce can chopped green chilies
¾ cup water

Shredded lettuce, chopped tomatoes,
and sliced black olives for topping
Soft flour tortillas

1. Follow the basic recipe above and add taco seasoning mix, chilies, and water.
2. Top with shredded lettuce, chopped tomatoes, and sliced black olives
3. Serve on soft flour tortillas.

Sloppy Guiseppes

½ cup green pepper, chopped
4 tablespoons flour
1 teaspoon dried oregano
¼ teaspoon garlic powder

2 15-ounce cans tomato sauce
4 tablespoons Parmesan cheese, grated
Italian rolls, split and toasted

1. Follow the basic recipe. As the meat cooks, add all other ingredients except rolls.
2. Serve on split, toasted Italian rolls.

Sloppy Sergeis

1 tablespoon dried dill weed
4 teaspoons paprika
2 10¾-ounce cans condensed
cream of mushroom soup

½ cup water
½ cup sour cream
Rye rolls, split and toasted

1. Follow the basic recipe. As the meat cooks, add all other ingredients except rolls
2. Serve on split, toasted rye rolls.

Sloppy Jacques

4 tablespoons flour
½ teaspoon pepper
½ teaspoon dried thyme

1 10¾-ounce can condensed onion soup
¼ cup white wine
French bread slices or rolls, toasted

1. Follow the basic recipe. As the meat cooks, add all other ingredients except bread
2. Serve on toasted French bread slices or rolls.

Curried Meatballs

Makes: 36 meatballs

1½ pounds ground meat
½ cup almonds, finely chopped
1 egg, slightly beaten
¾ cup dry bread crumbs
2 cloves garlic, minced

2 8-ounce cans water chestnuts,
  drained and finely chopped
1 tablespoon soy sauce
Cornstarch
Oil for frying (optional)

1. Mix all ingredients except cornstarch.
2. Shape the mixture into 1-inch balls.
3. Roll the meatballs in cornstarch and refrigerate for several hours
4. Fry the meatballs in oil until well done (or oven-fry).

Curry Sauce

2 tablespoons cornstarch
½ cup water
¾ cup sugar
¼ cup soy sauce

½ cup white wine vinegar
½ teaspoon ginger
2 teaspoons curry powder
1 14-ounce can pineapple chunks,
  drained (reserve liquid)

1. Dissolve cornstarch in water.
2. Mix all ingredients, except pineapple, in a sauce pan.
3. Add pineapple juice, to taste.
4. Bring the sauce to a boil and cook, stirring constantly, for 2 to 3 minutes
5. Add pineapple chunks and pour the sauce over cooked meatballs.
6. Serve hot in a chafing dish; provide toothpicks.

Creamed Swedish Meatballs

Makes: 30 meatballs

1 cup fine bread crumbs
2½ cups milk
2 pounds ground meat
1 cup onions, finely chopped
2 eggs, slightly beaten
1½ teaspoons salt
¼ teaspoon black pepper

1 teaspoon nutmeg
½ cup butter or margarine
¼ cup flour
3 beef bouillon cubes
3 cups hot water
1½ cups light cream

1. In a large bowl, soften bread crumbs in 1 cup of milk.
2. Add ground meat, onions, eggs, and seasonings; mix thoroughly.
3. Shape the mixture into 1-inch balls.
4. Heat butter in a skillet.
5. Add meatballs; brown on all sides and remove from the skillet.
6. Stir flour into the skillet drippings; blend well.
7. Dissolve bouillon cubes in hot water; add to flour mixture gradually, stirring constantly, until smooth.
8. Add remaining milk and cream; cook over low heat, stirring constantly, for 3 minutes.
9. Add meatballs; simmer for 10 to 15 minutes longer, stirring occasionally.
10. Serve in a chafing dish; provide toothpicks.

Hawaiian Meatballs

Makes: 30 meatballs

1 pound lean ground meat
1 cup fresh bread crumbs
½ cup onion, chopped
½ cup green bell pepper, chopped
1 egg, beaten

1 4-pound can crushed pineapple,
    drained (reserve juice)
⅛ teaspoon cloves
2 tablespoons pineapple syrup

1. In a large bowl, combine all ingredients; mix well.
2. Shape the mixture into 1-inch balls and oven-fry.

Hawaiian Sauce

⅓ cup pineapple syrup/juice
½ cup ketchup
⅓ cup brown sugar

1. Combine all sauce ingredients in a saucepan and heat sauce until it begins to boil.
2. Remove from heat and pour the sauce into a chafing dish.
3. Place the meatballs in the sauce. Skewer a pineapple chunk into each meatball with a toothpick.

Cranberry Meatball Sauce

Makes: enough for 30 meatballs

8-ounce can tomato sauce
1-pound can cranberry sauce

1. Prepare the meatballs following the basic recipe on page 228.
2. In a saucepan, heat together tomato and cranberry sauces until thoroughly heated and combined.
3. Place the meatballs into a chafing dish and pour the sauce on top.

UNIQUE POTATO SALAD RECIPES

Warm Potato Salad Julienne

Makes: 6 to 8 servings

2 pounds medium Russet potatoes,
    peeled and cut into julienne strips
Vegetable cooking spray
1 cup red bell pepper, chopped
½ cup green onions, finely chopped

½ cup celery, finely chopped
2 tablespoons rice wine vinegar
4 teaspoons hoisin sauce
2 teaspoons sesame seeds, toasted

1. Soak potatoes in cold water for 15 minutes; drain. Blot dry with paper towels.
2. Preheat the oven to 450 degrees.
3. Arrange potatoes in a single layer in a large shallow pan coated with vegetable cooking spray. Bake for 30 minutes, stirring every 10 minutes.
4. Combine potatoes, bell pepper, onions, and celery in a serving bowl.
5. In a separate bowl, combine vinegar and hoisin sauce. Pour over potato mixture, tossing gently. Sprinkle the salad with sesame seeds and serve immediately.

German Potato Salad

Makes: 8 servings

6 slices bacon
¾ cup sugar
2 tablespoons flour
¼ cup cider vinegar

¼ cup water
8 medium potatoes, boiled, peeled, and sliced
2 tablespoons onions, finely chopped
3 tablespoons parsley, chopped

1. Cut bacon into small pieces and fry; reserve ¼ cup bacon grease.
2. Add sugar to the bacon grease in the pan; stir in flour, then vinegar and water
3. Simmer until the liquid is clear, then pour over warm potatoes.
4. Top with crumbled bacon, onions, and parsley; mix well.

Potato Salad and Ham Ring

Makes: 8 servings

1½ cups cooked ham, diced
2 tablespoons onion, minced
½ cup mayonnaise
½ cup chili sauce
1 teaspoon horseradish

2 teaspoons prepared mustard
¼ teaspoon hot sauce
1 envelope unflavored gelatin
½ cup water
Salad greens and tomato wedges for garnish

1. In a large bowl, combine all ingredients except gelatin, water, and garnish.
2. In a small saucepan, soften gelatin in water; dissolve over low heat, then remove from heat, blend into ham mixture, and turn into a 6-cup ring mold. Chill well.
3. Top with a potato salad layer (see below), and chill until the potato layer is firm.
4. Turn out rings onto a serving plate; garnish with salad greens and tomato wedges.

Potato Salad Layer

3 cups basic potato salad
1 envelope unflavored gelatin

½ cup water

1. In a small saucepan, soften gelatin in water; dissolve over low heat
2. Remove from heat; blend into potato salad.

PICK A PASTA SALAD

General Directions for Pasta Salad:

1. Cook pasta according to package directions. Drain, cool, and put into a large bowl.
2. Add remaining salad ingredients, an indicated in the recipe.
3. In a small bowl, mix dressing ingredients, as indicated in the recipe. Pour the dressing over the salad and toss well to evenly coat all ingredients.
4. Refrigerate at least 2 hours before serving.
5. Garnish as suggested immidiately before serving, to prevent the garnish from wilting. This especially applies for parsley and other greens.

Pasta Nicoise

Makes: 4 to 6 servings

Salad Ingredients
1 cup uncooked shell macaroni
6-ounce can water-packed tuna, drained and flaked
5 medium green pitted olives with pimento
1 stalk green onion, finely chopped (1 to 2 tablespoons)
1 small clove garlic, minced (about ½ teaspoon)
1 cup cooked red potato, unpeeled, cut into 1-inch cubes

Dressing
1 tablespoon olive oil
1 tablespoon white wine vinegar
1 tablespoon lemon juice
⅛ teaspoon ground oregano
Black pepper, to taste

Garnish
2 anchovy strips, cut into pieces
2 hard-boiled eggs, sliced or sectioned

Bleu Cheese Pasta Salad

Makes: 6 servings

Salad Ingredients
8 ounces uncooked pasta, your choice
4 ounces blue cheese, crumbled
2 cups walnuts, toasted and chopped
1 cup celery, chopped

Dressing
4 tablespoons mayonnaise
⅛ teaspoon salt
⅛ teaspoon white pepper

Garnish
3 tablespoons parsley, minced

Tuna Vegetable Pasta Salad

Makes: 6 to 8 servings

Salad Ingredients

½ pound uncooked rotini
12½-ounce can water-packed tuna,
    drained and flaked
2 cups cucumbers, thinly sliced

1 medium tomato, chopped
½ cup celery, chopped
¼ cup green pepper, chopped
¼ cup green onions, sliced

Dressing

1 cup Italian dressing
¼ cup mayonnaise
1 tablespoon prepared mustard

1 teaspoon dill weed
Salt and pepper, to taste

Garnish

Cherry tomatoes
Fresh parsley

Bangkok Pasta Salad

Makes: 4 to 6 servings

Salad Ingredients

4 ounces uncooked cappellini or other thin pasta
4 green onion, whites only, thinly sliced
½ cup carrots, thinly sliced or julienned
½ cup cucumber, cut into thin, 2- to 3-inch long strips
1 cup cooked chicken, cut into thin, 2- to 3-inch long strips

Dressing

¼ cup peanut butter, chunky style
2 tablespoons soy sauce
1 teaspoon Dijon mustard

¼ teaspoon red pepper flakes
2 tablespoons rice wine vinegar
2 teaspoons sesame oil

Garnish

½ cup cilantro, chopped
Peanuts, chopped

Fruity Chicken Pasta Salad

Makes: 6 servings

Salad Ingredients

1 cup uncooked ring macaroni
6 ounces dried, mixed fruit, diced
1 cup jicama, cubed

¾ pound cooked chicken breast,
    cut into bite-sized pieces
2 green onions with tops, sliced

Dressing

1 teaspoon red chilies, ground
¼ teaspoon salt

½ cup mayonnaise or salad dressing
2 tablespoons sour cream or plain yogurt

Note: Cook dried fruit together with the macaroni.

Veggie-Mac Pasta Salad

Makes: 4 to 6 servings

Salad Ingredients

1½ boxes uncooked macaroni
Equal amounts of the following chopped vegetables: celery, carrots, cucumbers, green peppers, radishes, tomatoes
1 medium onion, chopped

Dressing

Miracle Whip salad dressing, to taste
Sweet pickle relish, to taste

Rainbow Garden Pasta Salad

Makes: 6 to 8 servings

Salad Ingredients

16 ounces uncooked pasta (shells or rotini)
½ cup red onion, chopped
1 cucumber, seeded and sliced
½ cup frozen peas
1 small can sliced olives (green or black)

1 to 2 cups chopped fresh vegetables, your choice: cauliflower, broccoli, carrots, green beans, asparagus, celery, multicolored bell peppers
1 cup mozzarella cheese, cubed (optional)

Dressing

Favorite Italian dressing, to taste

Wagon Trail Pasta Salad

Makes: 6 servings

Salad Ingredients

6 ounces uncooked wagon wheel pasta
5 all-beef hot dogs, boiled and sliced into rounds
¼ cup red or green pepper, finely chopped
⅓ cup sweet pickles, thinly sliced
2 green onions, thinly sliced

Dressing

½ cup mayonnaise
1 tablespoon prepared mustard
2 teaspoons cider vinegar
Salt and pepper, to taste

Garnish

Fresh parsley

Linguine Tuna Salad

Makes: 4 to 6 servings

Salad Ingredients

7 ounces uncooked linguine, broken in half
12½-ounce can water-packed tuna, drained
10 ounces frozen peas, thawed
2 medium tomatoes, chopped

Dressing

¼ cup lemon juice
¼ cup vegetable oil
¼ cup green onions, chopped

2 teaspoons sugar
1 teaspoon seasoned salt
1 teaspoon Italian seasoning

Note: Add hot linguine to the dressing.

Chinese Chicken Pasta Salad

Makes: 4 servings

Salad Ingredients

2 cups cooked thin spaghetti, drained
8 ounces cooked chicken, diced
1 ounce dry-roasted peanuts

1 cup bean sprouts
½ cup scallions, sliced
½ cup red bell pepper, diced

Dressing

1 teaspoon peanut oil
1 garlic clove, minced
2 tablespoons water
2 tablespoons soy sauce

½ teaspoon pared ginger root, minced
½ teaspoon Chinese sesame oil
2 tablespoons creamy peanut butter
Dash of ground red pepper

Garnish

Mandarin orange slices

Note: Place all the dressing ingredients in a blender and mix until smooth.

Southwestern Pasta Salad

Makes: 4 to 6 servings

Salad Ingredients

4 ounces uncooked pasta shells or other small pasta
15-ounce can red kidney beans, rinsed and drained
12-ounce can corn, drained
4 to 5 green onions, finely chopped
4 to 5 canned green chilies, finely chopped

Dressing

½ teaspoon ground cumin
1 teaspoon dried oregano
2 tablespoons lemon juice

½ cup mayonnaise
½ teaspoon salt
¼ teaspoon freshly ground pepper

Island Pasta Salad

Makes: 6 to 8 servings

Salad Ingredients

1 pound 3- or 5-color rotini
1 can hearts of palm, sliced, and/or
1 can water-packed artichoke hearts, quartered

For the following ingredients, choose amounts to suit your taste:
Black olives, pitted and halved
Fresh mushrooms, cut into chunks
Red and yellow tomatoes, cut into chunks
Red, yellow, and green peppers, cut into strips
Mozzarella cheese, cubed

Dressing

Balsamic vinegar dressing, to taste

Turkey/Grape Pasta Salad

Makes: 4 to 6 servings

Salad Ingredients

1 pound uncooked small-circles pasta
1 cup cooked turkey breast, cubed
½ cup red onion, chopped

1 cup fresh green grapes
1 handful fresh cilantro
1 cup Monterey jack cheese, cubed

Dressing

½ cup mayonnaise
¼ cup honey
¼ cup sour cream
Salt and pepper, to taste

Wheel of Fortune Pasta Salad

Makes: 6 servings

Salad Ingredients

4 cups cooked pasta wheels
  drained and cooled
1 raw carrot, sliced into thin matchsticks
1 medium onion, chopped
1 rib celery, thinly sliced

½ green pepper, chopped
5 radishes, thinly sliced
6-ounce can water-packed tuna,
  drained and flaked

Dressing

¼ cup extra-virgin olive oil
½ teaspoon honey
¼ cup brown rice vinegar
¼ teaspoon salt

½ garlic clove, mashed
Freshly ground black or cayenne
  pepper, to taste (optional)

PICK A DIP

Hummus Dip
Makes: 2 cups dip

1 cup cooked garbanzo beans, drained
3 tablespoons tahini (crushed sesame seeds)
½ cup lemon juice
1 clove garlic
½ teaspoon cumin

½ teaspoon salt
Water
Olive oil
Fresh parsley, chopped, for garnish
Pita bread

1. Place drained beans in a blender.
2. Add tahini, lemon juice, garlic, cumin, salt, and enough water to almost cover beans. Blend until smooth.
3. Pour the dip into a serving dish.
4. Pour a very thin layer of olive oil on top the dip and sprinkle with chopped parsley.
5. Serve with pita bread.

Olive Dip
Makes: 2½ cups dip

1 cup cream cheese, softened
1 cup sour cream
¼ cup black olives, chopped
½ teaspoon garlic powder

1 teaspoon dried parsley, crushed
2 tablespoons Worcestershire sauce
1 tablespoon paprika
1 tablespoon fresh parsley, chopped

1. Beat cream cheese to a smooth consistency.
2. Blend in sour cream, then add the remaining ingredients and blend well.
3. Cover and chill until serving.

Mexican Bean Dip
Makes: about 4 cups

31-ounce can pork and beans
   in tomato sauce
4 slices crisp bacon, broken into
   small pieces (save drippings)
½ cup sharp cheddar cheese, shredded
1 teaspoon garlic salt

1 teaspoon chili powder
½ teaspoon salt
2 teaspoons vinegar
2 teaspoons Worcestershire sauce
Cayenne pepper, to taste

1. In a blender, blend beans until smooth.
2. Pour bacon drippings into a microwave-safe bowl and add the blended beans
3. Stir in remaining ingredients except bacon.
4. Cover the bowl with plastic wrap or a glass lid.
5. Microwave for 7 to 8 minutes or until mixture is hot in the center.
6. Scoop the dip into a serving bowl and sprinkle with bacon pieces

Mexican Cheese Dip

Makes: 2 cups

2 tablespoons butter
1 small onion, chopped
1 garlic clove, minced
2 tablespoons jalapeño or chili pepper

2 tablespoons all-purpose flour
1 cup milk
1 medium tomato, chopped
1 cup cheddar cheese, shredded

1. Combine butter, onion, garlic, and pepper in a 4-cup microwave-safe casserole.
2. Microwave uncovered on high for 2 to 3 minutes or until the butter melts and the vegetables soften.
3. Blend in flour, then microwave on high for 30 seconds.
4. Gradually whisk in milk until smooth.
5. Add tomato; microwave covered for 3 to 5 minutes or until mixture comes to a boil and thickens, whisking once.
6. Stir in cheese until it melts.
7. Serve the dip warm with tortilla chips or veggies.

Curry Dip

Makes: 2 cups

1½ cups Miracle Whip or mayonnaise
¼ cup milk
2 teaspoons curry powder
1 tablespoon onion, grated

½ teaspoon dry mustard
½ teaspoon salt
Dash of pepper
Dash of Tabasco sauce

1. Combine all ingredients in a medium bowl and mix well.
2. Refrigerate the dip for 4 hours to set.

Swiss Chalet Dip

Makes: 3 cups

1 cup dry white wine
2 cups Swiss cheese, shredded
1 tablespoon unbleached flour
1 tablespoon brandy
1 garlic clove, crushed

1 tablespoon white onion, finely diced
¼ cup smoked ham, finely diced
Black pepper, to taste
Nutmeg, to taste

1. Place wine in a saucepan over medium-high heat.
2. Mix together Swiss cheese and flour and gradually add to the wine, stirring constantly, until all the cheese melts and mixture is smooth.
3. Remove the saucepan from heat and add the remaining ingredients; mix well.

Part Four

PARTY PLANNING HELPERS

As a finale to this book of menus, recipes, food presentation, and table decor, here are even more creative serving tips, how-to directions, and valuable resources to aid you in your party planning. Some of the information has been handed down from generation to generation, proving successful year after year.

Throughout the book you have been directed to this section for further explanation and direction. The How-To's section provides simple do-it-yourself instructions to help you create decorative and functional items from supplies you can easily obtain, if you don't already have them on hand.

The Resources section will help you find customizable and specialty food items, serving equipment, or decorative supplies. For readers who are familiar with (or in love with) the Internet, the food and beverage Web sites included in the Resource section will offer a wealth of recipes and general party planning information.

As a special *Pick-A-Party Cookbook* feature, selected party menus feature recipes submitted by some of the countries top party/event professionals and cookbook authors. The individuals or companies that have generously shared their favorite or prize-winning recipes with us have been credited in this section of the book.

The recipe index lists every recipe found in this book, including those provided in the Pick A Favorite section. They are organized to follow the party menus—Appetizers, Beverages, Buffet Items, and Dessert—with a number of subcategories within each section.

And finally, use the helpful party planning sheet to make your party adventure more efficient and organized. Simply make copies of the sheet, enlarging it if you like, and fill in the blanks for spectacular party success. Be sure to save the final planning sheets for future reference—to avoid duplicating menu items in future entertaining.

Take a little time to read this section and you will glean a variety of bright ideas guaranteed to make your guests smile.

HOW-TO'S

Seating Assignments/Place Cards

1. Musical Poster with Notes

Supplies
Black construction paper
White, silver, or gold ink
White poster board
Rubber cement

Directions
1. Cut 3-inch music notes from black construction paper.
2. Using white, silver, or gold ink, write guests' names and table assignments on the notes.
3. On a sheet of white poster board, draw a staff and a music graph.
4. Place the music notes, in alphabetical order, onto the staff. Attach the notes with a drop of rubber cement.

2. Instant-Photo Place Cards

(This idea works well for relatively small groups, and these place cards make dandy take-home favors. The more people you have, the more time-consuming and, possibly, expensive, this will be.)

Supplies
Instant camera and film
Inexpensive frames, 1 for each guest or couple (hand-trimmed cardboard works great)

Directions
1. Take an instant photo of each guest or couple as they arrive.
2. Place each photo in an inexpensive frame.
3. Arrange the photos around the tables, to indicate where you want guests to sit.

3. Chocolate Squares Place Cards

Supplies
Large dark chocolate bars or small dark chocolate candy bars
Edible gold paint (found in the cake decorating section)
Sugar cubes

Directions
1. Break chocolate bars into 3- or 4-inch squares, or use small chocolate candy bars.
2. Write guests' names with edible gold paint on the smooth side of the chocolate.
3. Use sugar cubes to prop up the chocolate place cards at place settings.

244

4. Lollipots Place Cards

Supplies

Small colorful flower pots, 1 for each guest
Oasis (green florists' foam)
Lollipops
Gumdrops
Popsicle sticks
Easter-basket grass
Colored construction paper, cut into strips
Glue

Directions

1. Fill small colorful flower pots with oasis.
2. Poke lollipops and gumdrops onto the ends of Popsicle sticks.
3. Write guests' names on strips of colored construction paper and glue the paper strips onto Popsicle sticks, flag style.
4. Poke sticks into oasis, making a decorative arrangement
5. Cover all visible oasis with Easter-basket grass.

5. Magic Slate Place Cards

Supplies

Magic slates

Directions

1. Purchase "magic slates" in your selected theme. (These are little slates on which you can write, then lift the translucent sheet to make the writing disappear. They come in various themes and designs.)
2. Write guests' names on the slates and put a slate next to each place setting.

Tip: For Thanksgiving, have guests use their slates to make a "What I am thankful for" list, and have them read their lists aloud as a dinner activity.

6. Cookie Cutout Place Cards

Supplies

Favorite sugar cookie dough
Theme-appropriate cookie cutters
Favorite frosting
Frosting tubes
Doily (optional)

Directions

1. Shape cookie dough with theme-appropriate cookie cutters and bake the cookies according to recipe instructions.
2. Glaze or frost cookies with your favorite frosting.
3. Use frosting tubes to write each guest's name on a cookie.
4. Place each cookie on doily-lined plate, or prop up the cookies against a cup or glass at each place setting.

7. British Party Crackers

Supplies (for 1 cracker)
Cardboard tube from wrapping paper, paper towels, or bathroom tissue
Theme-related wrapping paper
Ribbon

Directions
1. Cut a 4- to 5-inch length of cardboard tube.
2. Wrap decorative theme-related paper completely around the tube, leaving 3 inches of excess paper on each end.
3. Tie ribbon around excess paper to close one end of the tube.
4. Tuck small gifts, candy, balloons, and trinkets through the open end.
5. Tie ribbon around the open end to close.
6. Write guest's name on a sticker or tag and attach the tag to the tube.
7. Place the tube next to guests' plates.

Table Top Decorations

8. Fancy Fan Place Cards

Supplies
Variety of sturdy papers, such as newspaper, magazine art, craft paper, wallpaper, music paper, maps, paper doilies, wrapping papers
Hole punch
Ribbon
Small cards

Directions
1. Fold tiny fans out of a variety of papers.
2. Punch a hole through one end and string a ribbon through the hole; leave the ribbon untied.
3. Write your guests' names on small cards and punch a hole in one corner of each card. Thread a card onto the ribbon of each fan; tie the ribbon to hold the card in place.

9. Gift Package with Twinkle-Light Bow Centerpiece

Supplies (for 1 package)
Empty box (approximately the size of a large facial tissue box)
Elegant or whimsical wrapping paper
Small string of battery-operated twinkle lights
Mylar or iridescent star garlands or other special decorations
Mirror tile, round or square

Directions
1. Wrap an empty box with elegant or whimsical wrapping paper.
2. Wrap a small string of battery-operated twinkle lights around the package and make a bow of lights.
3. Trim the package with with Mylar or iridescent star garlands or other special decorations.
4. Place the package on a round or square mirror tile for a dramatic effect.

Tip: You don't have to make all the packages the same size—varying shapes and sizes may add more interest. Also, you can use the same wrapping paper for all the packages, or choose a variety of coordinating designs.

10. Tin Can Containers
Supplies
Decorative tin cans or boxes with interesting or colorful labels (tomato sauce, fruit, vegetables, or grains)
Stones or other small heavy items
Ribbons
Flowers, herbs, bread, or vegetable sticks

Directions
1. Thoroughly clean empty decorative tin cans or boxes.
2. Line the bottom with stones or other small heavy items to prevent the containers from tipping.
3. Decorate the containers with ribbons.
4. Arrange bunches of flowers, herbs, bread sticks, or vegetable sticks in the containers; display them on party tables.

11. Faux Sand Castles
Supplies
Milk and juice cartons of various sizes (or blocks of Styrofoam)
Glue
Sand
Shallow trays
Miniature pails and shovels

Directions
1. Spread a thin layer of glue over milk and juice cartons of various sizes, then coat the cartons entirely with sand.
2. Create your castles on shallow trays filled with sand, and surround with miniature pails and shovels.

12. Miniature Hay Bales
(A great decorative item for a western-theme party.)
Supplies
Large tissue boxes
Craft glue
Straw

Directions
1. Cover large tissue boxes with craft glue, then cover with straw.
2. After the glue dries, use bales on buffet tables as bases for serving containers or on dining tables as bases for centerpieces.
3. Leave tissue box opening uncovered and arrange flowers or other decorative items in it for centerpieces.

Tip: If you make larger bales, weigh the boxes down with rocks or gravel, and tie string or wire around the boxes—to look authentic and to keep the straw in place.

13. Fabulous Famous Paper Flowers
(These flowers add a festive touch to the table decor, serve as fun party favors, and can even be done as a party activity.)

Supplies
2 20-by-30-inch sheets of tissue paper (size will vary according to planned use)
Pair of scissors
24-inch length of florist's wire or 1 paper-covered stem (available at craft stores)
Green florist's tape

Directions
1. Layer tissue-paper sheets with edges aligned. Fold the layered sheets in half lengthwise.
2. Cut along the fold line. You will now have 4 10-by-30-inch pieces.
3. Layer all 4 pieces with edges aligned. Beginning at the shorter end, make 1-inch-wide fan folds along the entire length of layered pieces, keeping folds and edges even. *Tip: Hold pieces in alignment with a staple at the center of each 10-inch end.*
4. Bend florist's wire in half, and slip wire over center of folded tissue paper; twist wire tightly. (See Diagram 1.) Use longer wire for longer stems. Cover the stems with florist's tape or ribbon. For a glitzy look, dip the wire in glue and then glitter.
5. Cut the ends of the folded tissue paper to make rounded or pointed petals. (See Diagram 2.) Trim with novelty edge scissors for a nice effect.
6. To separate and fluff flower petals, begin at the center of the lower layer and pull up 1 layer of tissue paper at a time toward the center of the flower.

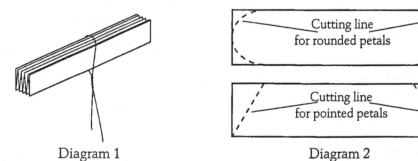

Diagram 1   Diagram 2

Variations
- Make smaller flowers by using 3 6-by-20-inch pieces of tissue paper. (For larger flowers, expand the fold size, and use only 3 pieces of paper. You can experiment with these sizes.)
- Make multicolored flowers by using 2, 3, or 4 colors of tissue paper. For example, use 3 pieces of hot pink and 1 piece of yellow.

- Use printed, metallic, or iridescent tissue papers: they work wonderfully.
- Mix in 1 or 2 layers of tulle, especially for weddings.
- Use black, white, and silver paper to make a dramatic statement.
- Make gold-and-white flowers for anniversaries.
- Put a few spots of glue on each flower, then sprinkle with glitter for a festive touch. Or use spray glue and shake glitter onto the entire flower.
- Use colored pipe cleaners for the stems, then wrap the flowers around napkins for a gala table decoration.
- Use the flowers as bows on gifts.
- Instead of making a stem, tie the flowers with ribbons to be worn in the hair or as a corsage (these make great favors).
- Use other materials: cellophane, Mylar, plastic.

14. Clay Pot of Roses

Supplies
Clay pot
Oasis (green florists' foam core)
Fresh or silk roses and greens
Moss or excelsior straw
Decorative paper or raffia ribbon and bow

Directions
1. Cut a chunk of oasis to fit the clay pot, insert the oasis into the pot, and arrange silk roses and greens in it. (If you use fresh flowers, soak the oasis in water for about ten minutes before inserting the flowers.)
2. Cover the oasis with moss or excelsior straw.
3. Trim the pot with decorative paper or raffia ribbon and bow.

Tip: Use full-sized pots for centerpieces, or miniature pots for each setting.

15. M*A*S*H Road Signs

Supplies
Cardboard or thin plywood
Paint or markers
Tall piece of wood for the post
Nails
Wood planks for the base
Turf or dirt

Directions
1. Cut long rectangles out of cardboard or thin plywood. Crudely paint or write a destination, with "miles to" on each one.
2. Nail the signs to a tall piece of wood, each sign pointing in the appropriate direction.
3. Make a base of wood, like a tree stand, and cover it with turf or dirt.

Tip: Make miniature road signs to use as tabletop decorations or table numbers.

Buffet Table Backdrops

16. Brown Paper Bag Place Mats

Supplies

Brown grocery bags
Scissors
Wood-stain lacquer
Glue
Twine or string

Directions

1. Cut grocery bags into place mat-sized pieces.
2. Crumple the paper into tight balls.
3. Spread the papers out and flatten with heavy books or weights for 24 hours.
4. Spray or brush wood-stain lacquer onto the paper. Let dry.
5. Trim the corners of each mat so they are rounded.
6. Glue twine or string around place-mat edges (before or after painting).

Tip: You can make matching napkin rings and trim them with a knot of twine

17. Carol Burnett's Green Drapes

Supplies

Large piece of green velvet (the gaudier, the better)
Gold cord and fringe
Long curtain rod

Directions

1. Fashion a drape from green velvet, and trim with gold cord and fringe.
2. Hang the dramatic dispaly on a long curtain rod behind the buffet table.

18. Paper Folding Screens

Supplies

Cardboard or foam core
Cloth, paper, or paint
Decorative tape

Directions

1. Cut cardboard or foam core into three equal rectangular pieces according to your needs—5 inches to 5 feet high.
2. Decorate each rectangle with cloth, paper, or paint.
3. Tape the three pieces together with decorative tape.
4. Use larger screens behind the buffet table; use smaller screens as decorative touches.

Tip: These screens may also be covered with photos and memorabilia to match the theme, portray the life of the guest of honor, or define a company or event purpose

19. Collage Table Covering

Supplies

Photos, magazine pages, sheet music, maps, brochures, posters, and cloth or paper
cutouts related to your theme

Paper or cloth table cover

Sheet of clear plastic

Directions

1. Select photos, magazine pages, sheet music, maps, brochures, posters, flat cloth
    items or paper cutouts related to your theme.
2. Arrange the items artfully on top of a paper or cloth table cover, overlapping the
    items to make a collage.
3. Cover the collage with a sheet of clear plastic. You can either secure the plastic
    under the table edge, so it doesn't move around, or allow it to hang.

Candles and Lighting

20. Low Container with Fat Candles

Supplies

Low basket, box, or bowl

Sand or marbles

Fat candles, variously shaped

Fresh flowers, shells, greens, or other theme-appropriate items

Directions

1. Line the bottom of a low basket, box, or bowl with sand or marbles.
2. Settle fat candles into the sand or marbles.
3. Surround the candles' base with fresh flowers, shells, greens, or other items to
    match your theme and decor.
4. Place one or more of these containers on your buffet table, at different heights

21. Frozen Luminaria Lights

(Great for outdoor winter illumination.)

Supplies

Paint buckets

Water

Large fat candles

Directions

1. Fill paint buckets with water and freeze until the water is slushy, almost frozen.
2. Push a large fat candle down into the center of each bucket, leaving at least half
    the candle above the water.
3. When the water is frozen solid and the candle is firmly in place, remove the
    frozen water chunks from the buckets, set on winter walkways, and light the
    candles. (Be sure the candles are not standing next to anything flammable—dry
    bushes, trees, and so on.)

22. Floating Candles in Clear Glass Bowl

Supplies
Stones, marbles, toys, or other small items
Bowl or glass (fish bowls, large brandy snifters, rose bowls)
Water
Small floatable candles, in shapes to match your theme
Mirror tiles, round or square

Directions
1. Place stones, marbles, toys or small items on the bottom of a bowl or glass.
2. Fill the containers half-full of water (Caution: Do not fill lipped bowls, such as fish bowls, more than half full, or the heat may crack your glass.)
3. Float small candles in the water.
4. Set the containers on mirror tiles for a dramatic and elegant look.

23. Flower Blossom Candle Holder

Supplies
Large silk flower blooms
Votive candles in glass holders

Directions
Remove a few petals from the centers of large silk flower blooms and replace with votive candles in glass holders. (Place the candles carefully, so as not to catch fire.)

24. Apple Candleholders

Supplies
Apples
Knife
Tall taper candles

Directions
1. Cut a small section out of each apple—deep and wide enough to securely hold a tall taper candle.
2. Place the apple candleholders down the center of the table or around a centerpiece of greens.

Special Seating Ideas

25. Guest of Honor Director's Chair

Supplies
Canvas director's chair
Fabric markers

Directions
1. With a fabric marker, divide the canvas back and seat of a director's chair into squares—one square for each guest, if possible.
2. Let your guests choose a square and personalize it with art or writing

26. Stuffed Shirts Chair Covers

Supplies
Men's shirts, starched and freshly pressed
Bow ties made of festive ribbon or fabric

Directions
1. Hang a starched, freshly pressed man's shirt on a chair back, with the collar facing the room, not the table. Tie the sleeves into neat knots.
2. Add festive bow ties.

Napkin Rings

27. Easy Napkin Rings from Novelty Papers

Supplies
Magazine pages, wallpaper, book covers, brown bags, blueprints, legal pads, maps, and comics
Scissors
Tape, glue, or stapler

Directions
1. Using any of the papers listed in the Supplies, cut strips 6 inches wide and 8 inches long.
2. Fold the strips into thirds, lengthwise, to make long, 2-inch wide strips.
3. Overlap the two edges lightly to form a 3-inch ring; secure the ring with tape, glue, or a stapler.
4. Pull napkins through the rings.

28. Napkin Folding
(This design works especially well with napkin rings.)

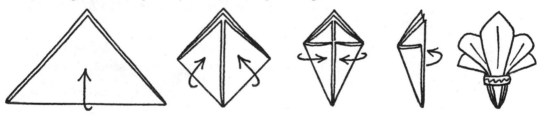

29. Innovative Napkin Treatments
- Pulled through fresh bagels
- Clamped between fake false teeth
- Threaded through gag glasses with nose
- Tied around wine-glass stems
- Tied around mug handles
- Threaded through large pretzels
- Pulled through plastic or metal cookie cutters
- Pulled through decorative shower rings

Food Preparation and Serving Ideas

30. Fancy Butter Pats

Ingredients/Supplies
Butter
Baking sheet
Decorative rubber stamps
Doily-lined plates

Directions
1. Place individual servings of butter dollops on a baking sheet and leave out until the butter begins to soften.
2. Press rubber stamps into the pats of butter to create decorative designs.
3. Refrigerate the butter until serving time, then place on doily-lined plates.

31. Pastry Bag

Supplies
Small plastic bag
Frosting
Scissors

Directions
1. Fill a small plastic bag with frosting.
2. Snip a small piece from one corner of the bag.
3. Squeeze the frosting through the hole to write on or otherwise decorate a cake.

32. Edible Flowers

Edible flowers make beautiful garnish and dessert decorations, and are also tasty and unusual additions to salads and other dishes. Crystallized rose petals, pansies, spicy pinks, and violets are particularly appropriate to decorate desserts. The following flowers may also be eaten, either fresh or cooked:

roses (red and purple are sweeter), pansies, nasturtium, sweet violets, day lilies, English daisies, and squash blossoms (which can also be sautéed). Don't forget the big one—dandelions!

Ingredients
1 egg white
1 teaspoon water
Flower petals
Granulated sugar

Directions
1. Beat an egg white until almost stiff; mix in 1 teaspoon water.
2. Dip petals into a small bowl of water to rinse; shake off the water.
3. Dip petals into the egg foam and shake off excess egg.
4. Coat the petals with granulated sugar and lay them out to dry on wax paper until the petals are dry to the touch. Crystallized petals will keep in a tin box for months.

Variation: Place crystallized mint leaves on saucers for afternoon tea.

33. Kite-Shaped Cake

Cut cakes as shown, place on platter, and frost.

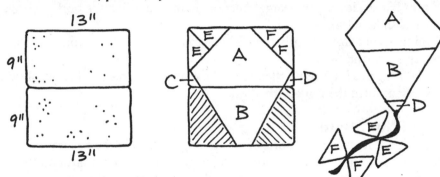

34. Chocolate Drizzle

Ingredients/Supplies
2 squares semisweet chocolate
2 teaspoons vegetable shortening
Plastic bag
Saucepan
Scissors

Directions
1. Place chocolate and vegetable shortening into a plastic bag. Seal tightly.
2. Place the bag in a saucepan half-filled with hot water (not boiling) and let it stand until the chocolate melts.
3. Remove the bag from the water and gently knead it to combine chocolate and shortening.
4. Cut a small piece from a bottom corner of the bag and squeeze chocolate glaze onto baked goods.

35. Festive Luau Pineapple

Ingredients/Supplies
Fresh pineapple
Sharp knife

Directions
1. Cut a thick slice from the top and bottom of an unpeeled pineapple.
2. Remove the pineapple center in a single cylinder, leaving ½ inch of the fruit inside the rind.
3. Cut the center cylinder in quarters lengthwise, remove core, and cut into 8 spears.
4. Replace the bottom piece, fill the shell with spears, and replace the top.

36. Kalua Pig

Ingredients/Supplies
6 pounds boneless pork
Rock salt
Ti or banana leaves
½ bottle liquid smoke
Aluminum foil, heavy duty

Directions
1. Make deep slashes in the pork and rub rock salt into cuts.
2. Spread ti or banana leaves on a large sheet of aluminum foil. Place pork on leaves and cover with liquid smoke.
3. Wrap and tie leaves around pork, then fold aluminum foil tightly around pork. Refrigerate overnight.
4. Cook at 500 degrees for 1 hour, then lower heat to 400 degrees and cook 4 hours
5. Before serving, shred the pork with a fork.

37. Cruise Ship Menu
Simply set out foods from various ports of call, arranging each in the decorative setting that depicts its originating location. Arrange these food "ports" around the room to create a cruising path. As guests "cruise the ports" around the room, they can sample the foods and beverages typical of the location.

38. Silver Spoon Service (for appetizers or sweets)
Supplies
Large silver spoons
Servings trays or platters

Directions
1. Attractively arrange bite-sized pieces of food on large silver spoons.
2. Arrange the spoons on serving trays or platters for easy serving.

Tip: Place an attractive receptacle for soiled spoons nearby.

39. Forkupine Service
Supplies
Plastic or metal forks
Blocks of oasis
Moss or excelsior or holiday basket grass
Serving trays or platters

Directions
1. Spear food piece onto plastic or metal forks.
2. Poke the forks' handles into blocks of moss-covered oasis. (You can use excelsior or holiday basket grass instead of moss.)
3. Arrange the forkupines on servings trays or platters.

Tip: Place an attractive receptacle for soiled forks nearby.

Beverage Serving Ideas
40. Floral Ice Wine Bucket
Supplies
1 large milk or juice carton
Water
Empty wine bottle
Flowers, berries, and greens

Directions

1. Fill a large milk or juice carton with water and freeze until the water is slushy.
2. Place an empty wine bottle into the ice.
3. Press flowers, berries, and greens into the surrounding ice.
4. When the water is completely frozen, peel the carton from the ice square.
5. Replace the empty bottle with a full one. Place the ice bucket into a clear glass or plastic bowl and set it on the table.

41. Fresh Pineapple Drink Containers

Supplies
Pineapples
Sharp knife
Cherries skewered on kabob sticks
Fancy drink umbrellas

Directions

1. Cut tops off pineapples about 2 inches below the leaves.
2. Cut bottoms off pineapples to create a flat surface so they can stand.
3. Hollow out the pineapples, and reserve the removed pineapple for garnish.
4. Fill the pineapples with exotic drinks. Garnish with pineapple chunks and cherries skewered on kabob sticks. Don't forget the umbrella!

Guest Comfort/Convenience

42. Food Signs and Labels

- Place neatly printed tent cards in front of exotic foods on a buffet table. Include the item's name and basic ingredients to help guests decide how much to take.
- Write a complete menu on poster board and either hang it on the wall or stand it on an easel behind the buffet table. (You can purchase decorative poster boards ideal for attractive party signs.)
- Print individual menus and decorate them to match your theme. For elegant parties, trim the menus with gold or silver cord.

43. Dress Up from the Waist Up

(This is especially fitting for crowded holiday open houses where guests will be required to sit, stand, and/or perch while eating and socializing.)

Ask guests to wear their most comfortable, casual clothing from the waist down, and their glitter-and-glitz formalwear from the waist up (including hats, hair ornaments, and jewelry). Follow through on this theme with table decorations—fill brown-bagged vases with elegant flowers and/or decorations.

RESOURCES

To request information, contact these suppliers by phone, fax, or mail. A half-page fax request sheet costs less than a postcard, and it also provides you with a record of your request. If a manufacturer sells only to the trade, they will give you the name of the retailer nearest you.

Theme Party Supplies

1. Gamblers General Store: Hundreds of items for casino-style events.
Phone: (800) 322-2447 Fax: (702) 366-0329

2. Kentucky Derby Party Kits & Equestrian Gifts: Everything for your Kentucky Derby Party.
Phone: (800) 993-3279 (Trade only. Call for a dealer nearest you.)

3. The Music Stand: Every imaginable item customized with musical motif—for ideal gifts, prizes, favors, or awards at music-theme parties.
Phone: (800) 414-4010

4. Rick's Movie Graphics: Hundreds of posters and publicity photos from the movie and recording industries—perfect for vintage or contemporary party themes.
Phone: (800) 252-0425

Personalized and Customized Products

5. Celebration Creations Theme Table Decor: Ultra-custom place cards, seating assignments, name tags, and napkin rings to match your theme.
Address: Celebration Creations, 4520 Excelsior Boulevard, Minneapolis, MN 55416

6. Jordan's Journey, Horoscope and Tarot Charts
Address: 14200 F., Centreville Square, Suite 125, Centreville, VA 20120

Food Products

7. Chocolates à la Carte: Unbelievably clever shapes, such as tools, baskets, boxes, and other unique chocolate products.
Phone: (800) 818-2462 (Call for dealer nearest you.)

8. Outrageous Fortunes, Custom Fortune Cookies: Your own message tucked inside a fortune cookie.
Address: 326 Cedar Avenue, Minneapolis, MN 55454 (Attention: Sunny Kwan)

Unique and Innovative Products

9. Holdems by Funzone: Products designed to relieve party guests of the hassle of balancing food, drinks, and personal items while trying to eat and socialize at the

same time. The trays come in brightly colored craftboard, clear plastic, and dishwasher-safe plastic.
Phone: (714) 444-4FUN (Call for nearest dealer or for quantity purchasees. Ask for Debbie.)

10. Huge Popcorn Boxes: Three-feet high boxes ideal for buffet table focal-points, centerpieces, or gift packs.
Phone: (612) 920-7297 (Ask for Shirlee Clein.)

11. Magic Mounts: The perfect way to hang posters, signs, photos, decorations, lights, balloons, or any other light items on walls, ceilings, or any delicate surface without leaving a mark or stain. Many special-event venues do not allow hanging signs or decorations of any kind. These clever hangers will solve that problem.
Phone: (800) 332-0050 (Call for dealer nearest you.)

12. NapkinWings: Delightful and vividly die-cut colored paper rings that come in a variety of designs to match most themes. You can have NapkinWings customized or use the laser sheet version to create your own.
Phone: (800) 298-5046

13. Stir Crazy Party Game: Make a party of preparing the meal. The game kit includes all directions, invitations, a chef's hat, aprons, and scorecards—you just supply the guests and the food. This game is produced by the same people who produce Mystery Party Games. In *Celebration Creations Catalog*.
For a catalog, send $3.00 (refunded on order) to: Celebration Creations Catalog, Dept PP2, 4520 Excelsior Boulevard, Minneapolis, Minnesota 55416.

14. Toga Tees: The guaranteed hit of any Toga Party, these T-shirts feature clever takeoffs on favorite Latin sayings. Great for prizes!
Phone: (888) TOGA-830

Internet Addresses/Web Sites

You can find my Web site at **http://www.geocities.com/~party expert** and reach me to ask any party-related questions at **partysachs@internetmci.com.**

Baskin Robbins **http://www.baskinrobbins.com** Ideas, called "flavorites," for kids' and adult parties. A fun site with lots of surprises.

Birthday Parties **http://www.party-creations.com** A site all about kids' birthday parties.

Drinks **http://www.mixdrinks.com** Alcoholic and nonalcoholic party refreshments, wild and wacky combinations, as well as the standard cocktails and punches.

Drinks **http://smartwine.com** *Smart Wine Magazine* gives the latest wine news and information.

Holidays **http://www.holidays.net** Loads of information on traditional holidays, with suggestions for the tried-and-true, plus some new twists.

Kraft/Jell-O **http://www.Kraftfoods.com** The site for several brands, including Jell-O recipes—hundreds of them.

Party Planning **http://www.epicurious.com** The site for the inquisitive and innovative. Top-rated site for the more adventurous party host.

Party Planning **http://www.homearts.com** Several of the top publications join together to present you with home and living features—recipes and entertaining, plus.

Party Planning **http://www.party411.com** Sheri Fox, The Party Queen, shares her expertise and bright ideas for every kind of celebration you can dream up.

Party Planning **http://www.recipecard.com** Wendy Zientek shares her fabulous recipes and party links. All major and traditional holidays are featured with recipes, decorations, traditions, and more.

Tabasco **http://www.tabasco.com** Recipes for food, drinks, snacks, and snazzy party ideas.

Vegetarian **http://www.catless.ncl.ac.uk** The vegetarian pages for party hosts who want their guests to be the only animals there.

Wedding **http://www.ultimatewedding.com** Planning tips for wedding-occasion menus—showers, rehersal dinners, receptions.

White Castle **http://www.whitecastle.com** Sliders rule! You will find prize-winning recipes and *Everything You've Always Wanted to Know about White Castles.* E-mail for recipe book: recipe@whitecastle.com.

Usenet Newsgroups

Fat-Free alt.food.fat-free Hosts can serve delicious and appealing foods that will take the guilt out of enjoying party fare.

Historic Recipes rec.food.historic Authentic recipes for your historic-era themes

Spam alt.spam What every fifties party needs—a "Spamtastic" menu.

Credits for Contributed Recipes

Books

Balanay, James. Total Authentic Luau Plan ($10 with color photos). 2208 River Run Drive #50, San Diego, California 92108 or jbalanay@pacbell.net.

Demars, John. *Caribbean Cooking* and *Caribbean Desserts* (Crossing Press). Includes recipes featuring Dutch St. Maarten in the Caribbean.

Fiock, Shari. *Family Reunions & Clan Gatherings.* Start-to-finish tool for organizing reunions, centennials, or anniversaries. Includes sample forms, strategies, publicity tips, and search techniques (Coyote Publishing). (530) 842-7279.

Parker, Eileen (Eileen Parker, Inc.). *Eat Outside the Box, an Irreverent Approach to Eating Healthy While Still Maintaining Your Sanity* (218) 724-0685.

Pfeiffer, Dianne (Strawberry Patch). *For Popcorn Lovers Only.* (404) 261-2197.

Podlesky, Janet and Greta. *Looney Spoons: Low-Fat Made Fun!* (Garnet Publishing). (800) 470-0738.

Schweiers, Bob. *Smart Drinks: Alcohol-Free Natural Beverages* (Sterling Publishing, Inc.).

Zuzu Bailey's *It's a Wonderful Life Cookbook.* Karolyn Grimes "Zuzu" and Franklin Dohanyos (Carol Publishing Group).

Products and Chefs

Aidell's Sausages. Gourmet sausage in delightfully unique taste combinations. Mail order at (800) 546-5795.

Chapman, Debra. Breton's Best at Zabars: Clinton Castle Crackers, Dare Foods, Inc., and the NY Restaurant School students. (617) 639-1808.

Creative Doily, The. From Royal Lace, dozens or recipes and instructions for crafty ways to use doilies in your table decor. (800) 669-7692.

Limoncello Restaurant. The Michelangelo Hotel, 777 Seventh Avenue, New York, New York 10019. (212) 582-7932.

Michelle from Oregon. Kwanzaa party recipes.

Murray, Marilyn. Breton's Best at Zabars: Clinton Castle Crackers, Dare Foods, Inc., and the NY Restaurant School students. (617) 639-1808.

Party Professionals

Baird, Maxine. Editor of *Balloons N FunTimes Newspaper,* quarterly. (208) 232-7160.

Celebrations Creations Catalog. Books, reports, software, and other products to inspire and assist you in planning successful and memorable special occasions and events. Send $3.00 (refundable on order) to: Celebration Creations Catalog, Dept. PP2, 4520 Excelsior Boulevard, Minneapolis, Minnesota 55416.

Gudim, Brad. The Event Suppliers Alliance, Minneapolis, Minnesota. (612) 321-0689.

Kelley, Mary. Wyoming Events, Gillette, Wyoming. (307) 682-5573.

Kring, Robin. Clearcreek Publications, Denver, Colorado. Author of several party-planning manuals and a quarterly newsletter. (303) 671-8253.

Sachs, Cathy. Culinary Concoctions, Minneapolis, Minnesota. (612) 879-4592.

Sallerson, Allys. You're Cordially Invited, Atlanta, Georgia. (770) 973-4968

APPENDIX A

Tips for Buffet-Style Service

Buffet-style service is very popular with both hosts and guests: The host saves time and effort by avoiding sit-down service, while the guests have control over the selections and amounts. This style of service is especially desirable when space for dining tables is limited and sit-down service is impossible.

The secret to pleasing party guests is to serve them uncomplicated food in an interesting and pleasing way. Efficient presentation is a top requirement of any "help-yourself" dining experience. All items should be easily accessible and attractively presented.

Tips for buffet/bar setups and arrangement:
- Invert small boxes, bowls, and containers, and cover them with cloths to create interesting heights for artistic food arrangements. At no cost at all, you can display buffet food just as professional caterers do.
- If you do not provide individual trays, place utensils wrapped in napkins at the very end of the buffet line to be picked up after all food is selected. If you have seated dining, though, the silverware can be at each place.
- For large groups (forty or more), create a flow of traffic on both sides of the table, with identical offerings on each side.
- If you are serving buffet style but have tables set for dining, allow guests to be seated, then call them by table numbers so they can avoid standing and waiting in a long, slow line. Make a general announcement to the group instructing them to wait until their table number is called.
- An alternative to calling table numbers is to call certain groups: for example, "all those with grandchildren," "all those who have traveled more than fifty miles to get here," "all who have children under five years old," and so on. This personal grouping will add a little entertainment to the buffet line wait.
- Assign someone to replenish food supplies and to clean up spills, to ensure the buffet remains as clean, plentiful, and appetizing for the last person as it was for the first.
- When you serve a variety of exotic or unusual food items, place small tent cards with the delicacies' names and key ingredients next to each dish. Also follow this rule if you label your foods with gimmicky theme-appropriate names

APPENDIX B

Quantities to Serve for Large Groups at Picnics and Other Informal Occasions

Item	25 people	50 people	100 people
Meat, Poultry and Fish			
Weiners	6½ pounds	13 pounds	25 pounds
Hamburger	9 pounds	18 pounds	35 pounds
Turkey or chicken	13 pounds	25–35 pounds	50–75 pounds
Fish, Fillets	7½ pounds	15 pounds	30 pounds
Spaghetti	1¼ gallons	2½ gallons	5 gallons
Baked beans	¾ gallon	1¼ gallons	2½ gallons
Salads			
Jell-O salad	¾ gallon	1¼ gallons	2½ gallons
Potato/pasta salad (also coleslaw)	1 gallon	1¾ gallons	3½ gallons
Ice Cream			
Brick	3¼ quarts	6½ quarts	12½ quarts
Bulk	2¼ quarts	1¼ gallons	2½ gallons
Coffee	½ pound	1 pound	2 pounds
Water	1½ gallons	3 gallons	6 gallons
Lemonade	10–15 lemons	20–30 lemons	40–60 lemons
Water	1½ gallons	3 gallons	6 gallons

RECIPE INDEX
(Arranged in the order of the party menus.)

Punches and Wines

Shooters, Gelatin and Regular
(all alcoholic)

Smoothie/Slushies/
Ice-Cream Drinks
(nonalcoholic)

Specialties

Breads/Chips/Snack Mixes

MENU/DECOR WORKSHEET

Event_____ Date _____Time _____

Theme _____ Location _____

# of Guests _____

Menu

Snacks_____ Page_____   Buffet_____ Page_____

_____   _____

_____   _____

_____   _____

_____   _____

Beverages_____   Dessert_____

_____   _____

_____   _____

_____   _____

_____   _____

Food Service/Decorative touches (resources, phone numbers, contact data, page numbers)

_____

_____

_____

_____

_____

_____

_____

_____

_____

_____

_____

_____

_____

_____

_____

Pick A Party

by Patty Sachs

Here's the new "bible" for party planners. Party expert Patty Sachs has included 160 party themes—more than any other book—to help readers turn holidays, birthdays, showers, and an evening with friends or family into special occasions.

Order #6085 $9.00

The Best Party Book

by Penny Warner

This party-planning book provides creative ideas for invitations, decorations, refreshments, games, prizes, and party favors to turn your parties into memorable celebrations. Includes ideas for seasonal parties, family events, and even special TV events.

Order #6089 $8.00

The Best Wedding Shower Book

by Courtney Cooke

Wedding showers don't have to be boring. This contemporary guide to wedding showers is packed with planning tips, decorating ideas, recipes, and activities that are fun without being juvenile.

Order #6059 $7.00

The Best Baby Shower Book

by Courtney Cooke

Who says baby showers have to be dull? This contemporary guide is packed with useful planning tips, creative decorating ideas, tasty recipes, and fun activities.

Order #1239 $7.00

Order Form

Qty.	Title	Author	Order No.	Unit Cost (U.S. $)	Total
	Age Happens	Lansky, B.	4025	$7.00	
	Are You Over the Hill?	Dodds, B.	4265	$7.00	
	Best Baby Shower Book	Cooke, C.	1239	$7.00	
	Best Baby Shower Party Game Book	Cooke, C.	6063	$3.95	
	Best Birthday Party Game Book	Lansky, B.	6064	$3.95	
	Best Bridal Shower Party Game Book	Cooke, C.	6060	$3.95	
	Best Couple's Shower Party Game Book	Cooke, C.	6061	$3.95	
	Best Party Book	Warner, P.	6089	$8.00	
	Best Wedding Shower Book	Cooke, C.	6059	$7.00	
	Dads Say the Dumbest Things!	Lansky/Jones	4220	$6.00	
	Familiarity Breeds Children	Lansky, B.	4015	$7.00	
	For Better And For Worse	Lansky, B.	4000	$7.00	
	Games People Play	Warner, P.	6093	$8.00	
	Golf: It's Just a Game!	Lansky, B.	4035	$7.00	
	Grandma Knows Best	McBride, M.	4009	$7.00	
	How to Line Up Your Fourth Putt	Rusher, B.	4075	$7.00	
	How to Survive Your 40th Birthday	Dodds, B.	4260	$6.00	
	Italian without Words	Cangelosi/Carpini	5100	$6.00	
	Joy of Sisters	Brown, K.	3508	$7.00	
	Kids' Holiday Fun	Warner, P.	6000	$12.00	
	Kids' Party Cookbook	Warner, P.	2435	$12.00	
	Kids' Party Games and Activities	Warner, P.	6095	$12.00	
	Lovesick	Lansky, B.	4045	$7.00	
	Moms Say the Funniest Things!	Lansky, B.	4280	$6.00	
	Over-the-Hill Party Game Book	Cooke, C.	6062	$3.95	
	Pick A Party	Sachs, P.	6085	$9.00	
	Pick-A-Party Cookbook	Sachs, P.	6086	$11.00	
				Subtotal	
			Shipping and Handling (see below)		
			MN residents add 6.5% sales tax		
				Total	

YES! Please send me the books indicated above. Add $2.00 shipping and handling for the first book and 50¢ for each additional book. Add $2.50 to total for books shipped to Canada. Overseas postage will be billed. Allow up to four weeks for delivery. Send check or money order payable to Meadowbrook Press. No cash or COD's please. Prices subject to change without notice. **Quantity discounts available upon request.**

Send book(s) to:

Name _____ Address _____

City _____ State _____ Zip _____

Telephone (_____)_____ P.O. number (if necessary) _____

Payment via:

☐ Check or money order payable to Meadowbrook Press (No cash or COD's please)
  Amount enclosed $ _____

☐ Visa (for orders over $10.00 only)   ☐ MasterCard (for orders over $10.00 only)

Account # _____ Signature _____ Exp. Date _____

A *FREE* Meadowbrook Press catalog is available upon request.
You can also phone us for orders of $10.00 or more at 1-800-338-2232.

Mail to: Meadowbrook Press
5451 Smetana Drive, Minnetonka, MN 55343
Toll-Free 1-800-338-2232

Phone (612) 930-1100   Fax (612) 930-1940